POPULAR DOGS' BREED SERIES

AFGHAN HOUND — *Charles Harrisson*
ALSATIAN (German Shepherd Dog) — *Joseph Schwabacher and Thelma Gray*
BASSET HOUND — *George Johnston*
BEAGLE — *Thelma Gray*
BOXER — *Elizabeth Somerfield*
CAIRN TERRIER — *J. W. H. Beynon, Alex Fisher and Peggy Wilson*
CAVALIER KING CHARLES SPANIEL — *Mary Forwood*
CHIHUAHUA — *Thelma Gray*
COCKER SPANIEL — *Veronica Lucas-Lucas*
COLLIE — *Margaret Osborne*
DACHSHUND — *E. Fitch Daglish and Amyas Biss*
DALMATIAN — *Eleanor Frankling and Betty Clay*
DOBERMANN — *Fred Curnow and Jean Faulks*
FOX TERRIER — *Elsie Williams*
GOLDEN RETRIEVER — *Joan Tudor*
GREAT DANE — *Jean Lanning*
GREYHOUND — *H. Edwards Clarke and Charles Blanning*
IRISH SETTER — *Janice Roberts*
LABRADOR RETRIEVER — *Lorna, Countess Howe and Geoffrey Waring*
OLD ENGLISH SHEEPDOG — *Ann Davis*
POODLE — *Clara Bowring and Alida Monro*
PUG — *Susan Graham Weall*
SCOTTISH TERRIER — *Dorothy Caspersz and Elizabeth Meyer*
SHETLAND SHEEPDOG — *Margaret Osborne*
SHIH TZU — *Audrey Dadds*
SPRINGER SPANIEL — *Dorothy Morland Hooper and Ian B. Hampton*
STAFFORDSHIRE BULL TERRIER — *John F. Gordon*
WELSH CORGI — *Charles Lister-Kaye and Dickie Albin*
WEST HIGHLAND WHITE TERRIER — *D. Mary Dennis*
WHIPPET — *C. H. and Kay Douglas-Todd*
YORKSHIRE TERRIER — *Ethel and Vera Munday*

THE
CHIHUAHUA

THELMA GRAY

POPULAR DOGS
London

Popular Dogs Publishing Company Ltd
3 Fitzroy Square, London W I P 6JD

An imprint of the Hutchinson Publishing Group

London Melbourne Sydney Auckland
Wellington Johannesburg and agencies
throughout the world

First published (as *The Popular Chihuahua*) 1961
Second edition, revised (as *The Chihuahua*) 1967
Third edition, revised 1968
Fourth edition, revised 1974
Fifth edition, revised 1979

© Thelma Gray, 1961, 1967, 1968, 1974 and 1979

Printed in Great Britain by litho at The Anchor Press Ltd
and bound by Wm Brendon & Son Ltd
both of Tiptree, Essex

ISBN 09 134490 5

*Affectionately dedicated to
twenty-seven enchanting little time-
absorbers, but for whom this book could
have been more easily—and certainly
more rapidly—written*

ACKNOWLEDGEMENTS

My very grateful thanks are due to Mrs D. Wells for her invaluable help in checking facts appertaining to the early history of the breed, and for her great kindness in making available to me data from her collection of Press cuttings and matters of interest in connection with Chihuahuas.

I am also grateful to the many kind people who loaned photographs; and in this and in other ways contributed to the production of this volume.

Last, and by no means least, I thank my husband for his help in correcting proofs.

The inscription on the lintel of a house in the mountain town of Taxco:

'When the dust of Mexico settles on your heart, you will find no rest in any other land.'

CONTENTS

ILLUSTRATIONS

LINE DRAWINGS IN TEXT

AUTHOR'S INTRODUCTION

*

If one feels a great affection for dogs, one loves them irrespective of the breed, but with such a great variety of dogs, all so different in size, shape, and temperament, it is inevitable that some will have a greater appeal to the individual than others.

The author plunged straight from school into the dog game, starting a kennel of Alsatians, which eventually became one of the largest in the country, and was a pioneer breeder and exhibitor of Welsh Corgis at a time when, outside Wales, they were scarcely known at all. Both these breeds are still kept in the Rozavel Kennels, though not in such numbers as they were, and many others came and went—English Setters, Greyhounds, Miniature Dachshunds, Schnauzers, Welsh Terriers, Smooth Fox Terriers, Rottweilers (Rozavel was the pioneer kennel of this breed in Britain and imported the first of them from Germany), and Toy Poodles.

The later additions to the Rozavel Kennels seem to have come to stay: the near-pocket-sized Beagles, bred from small American imported stock, and the Chihuahuas, which have probably given their owner greater pleasure than almost any other breed of dog. The story of how this last-named and most fascinating breed came to be added to the Kennel, which had usually contained working dogs of various kinds, is told in the chapter on the start of the breed in Britain.

Undoubtedly Chihuahuas are a 'different' breed; there is something special about them, hard to define, but easily recognized as one grows to know them, with their uncanny intelligence, perception, great courage, and—something often lacking in other breeds—decided sense of humour.

If you, reader, appreciate these qualities in a dog; admire an exquisite little creature with something of the nature of fine porcelain about it; and love to have a pocket-sized companion with a king-sized heart—it is Chihuahuas for you, all the days of your life.

The breed has made many friends because of its small size, distinctive expression, and exceptional intelligence and character. One of the earliest notabilities to own a Chihuahua was the famous singer, Madame Adelina Patti. This star made a series of appearances in Mexico beginning in the autumn of 1889 and ending in January 1890. In honour of the occasion, a reception was given by the President (at that time, General Porfirio Diaz). He presented Madame Patti with a magnificent bouquet of flowers, and concealed among the blossoms was a tiny Chihuahua dog.

Madame Patti christened the little fellow Bonito, kept him for many years, and took him with her wherever she travelled.

When Bonito eventually died, Madame Adelina had become a slave to the breed, as do so many of us directly we own one, and she acquired other Chihuahuas to take his place.

The little dogs were scarcely known outside Mexico, so it can be imagined that this lady's pets created a tremendous sensation wherever they went. Undoubtedly, they were the means of introducing the breed to a large public for whom they would otherwise not have existed at all.

Very many years later, but in much the same way, the well-known band-leader, Xavier Cugat, attracted attention when he used to hold a very small Chihuahua in one hand, while he conducted his band with the other. Apart from personal appearances, he also appeared in films in like manner. As a result of this, even now, people who do not know what breed of dog a Chihuahua is, may exclaim: 'Oh! That is one of those little dogs that band-leader always had with him!'

It is hardly surprising that Chihuahuas have a great attraction for cameramen. One seldom visits the Chihuahua benches at a dog show without finding half a dozen eager men with cameras. The Chihuahuas are not fond of being photographed, perhaps because they are often required to sit in silver cups, pottery mugs and pint pots, glasses, or to pose with enormous dogs; in fact in any situation which emphasizes their minute size. Such characteristics have made them popular on television, and Chihuahuas have also appeared on the cinema screen many times.

Sometimes they have been included when variety classes have been judged for the benefit of TV viewers, and they have been featured in serial programmes devoted entirely to dogs, in quiz shows, and even in advertisements.

In 1959 Champion Rozavel Uvalda Jemima was televised, together with the eight other dogs selected by the panel of experts as the best of the 3,173 exhibits at Cruft's Show on the first day. Although even this enormous entry was afterwards exceeded, it was a record for this show, and the advance publicity ensured that the broadcast was seen by a large viewing public.

The television appearances have, even more than the pictures that have appeared in daily and evening newspapers, been the greatest means of making the general public familiar with the Chihuahua as a breed. One is constantly meeting a person who says: 'That is one of those little dogs I saw on TV the other day!' but they may not be able to twist the tongue round the name. The pronunciation seems to defeat a lot of people and the permutations are endless. But enlightenment is coming and we hear people say 'There goes a "Chee-wah-wah"' and not a 'Chee-hewer-hewer', or even a 'Hula-hula' or a 'Minnehahah' as visitors to one dog show were heard to call them.

One of the current personalities who has very properly fallen for the breed is that 'great' stage and screen star, Fred Emney. He has a pet Chihuahua which makes an amusing contrast to his own giant statistics.

Talking of vital statistics is bound to remind us of the glamorous Miss Jayne Mansfield, the lovely film star who was a devoted Chihuahua lover, and who made a surprise visit to the judging ring at one of the Ladies Kennel Association shows at Olympia, London, and delighted the exhibitors by her interest in the midgets.

Older readers will remember Miss Lupe Velez, a Mexican film actress of an earlier era, who also kept and loved Chihuahuas. Hutchinson's *Dog Encyclopaedia* includes a picture of her feeding one of her pets.

Almost everyone is familiar with the brief and tragic history of the Emperor Maximilian, the Austrian Archduke who was offered the crown of Mexico in the year 1864. He married a Belgian Princess, but one misfortune after another dogged his earnest efforts to rule his country, and eventually he was murdered, and his Empress, who had fled to Europe to try to enlist some support for her husband, lost her reason. In the short space of time which this unhappy couple spent in Mexico, however, we are told they kept large numbers of Chihuahua dogs which ran about the Palace, and which were the much-loved pets of the Empress Carlotta.

In modern times Chihuahuas have attracted attention. One such incident, relating to a dog that had been sold to a client in Sweden, records that the dog is regarded as a hero by his owners because he put a burglar to flight.

One breeder, who lives on a farm, took part in a small shoot, which was not a success because the hedgerows were dense and thick with brambles and the gundogs put up a poor show. Someone suggested fetching the Chihuahuas, all of which were known to be keen hunters, and to the amazement of the guns the tiny little things flushed every pheasant or rabbit in the hedges and enjoyed every minute of it. One of them was a little bit gun-shy to begin with, but soon got caught up in the general enthusiasm and joined in with the rest.

A Chihuahua is believed to be the only dog to dine in the House of Commons, since dogs are not allowed in the Palace of Westminster. The occasion was a dinner held by the British Mexican Society, and the guest of honour was his Excellency the Mexican Ambassador. The little Chihuahua, cuddled up in his owner's fox fur, sailed past the keen eyes of doormen and policemen and was soon happily established in the dining-room. He sat on the palm of the Ambassador's hand, and later, on a tour of the House, for a brief moment in the Speaker's Chair.

The following day there were large headlines in the Press: 'Dog dines in the House of Commons', and a description of the incident, with special reference to Miguel's 'diamond' collar, and to the fact that his visit would probably lead to questions being asked in the House. The next time the invitations went

out they stated: 'Dogs are not allowed in the Palace of Westminster.' In effect, it said: 'No dogs—not even Chihuahuas.'

Who was the writer who said, with such truth, that love of
animals brings suffering? Indeed, this has to be so because their
life-span is so short compared to our own. It was this same
writer who said that he thought that animals did not stay so
long on earth because they deserve heaven more than we do.
While we are privileged to have them with us, the happi-
ness our dogs bring us cannot be measured in words. It is
because I have had this richness in such measure that I hope
this book may enable others to enjoy it too, and those who
already know and love the breed may possibly find something
within its pages which may add to their pleasure, and to the
well-being of their lovely little Chihuahuas.
1961

It is only five years since the book was published, and yet
much has happened to the Chihuahua. Most notable is the
separation of the varieties, now known as Chihuahuas (smooth-
coat) and Chihuahuas (long-coat), and at certain Championship shows the Challenge Certificates are offered for each
variety. At the time of writing, the smooths still outnumber the
long-coats and consequently their higher registration totals entitle
them to more sets of Certificates. The long-coats are rapidly
increasing in popularity and one can foresee that in a few
years they will overtake the smooths. Opinions are still very
much divided as to which are the most attractive, but clearly
both coats have great appeal, and the breed as a whole
continues to attract new adherents to its ranks. The writer has
been privileged to make a series of extensive overseas judging
tours, stretching one and a half times round the world, and it
has been most interesting to compare the quality of the
Chihuahuas in other countries with those being currently
exhibited in Britain. The conclusion is that we have a cross
section of the finest Chihuahuas in the world, and that many
of our best dogs and bitches would be difficult to defeat anywhere and in any company. We do not fall into the mistake of

being complacent, however, for we also see far too many mediocre specimens at shows, and one sometimes wonders if breeders have really schooled themselves to view their stock objectively. It is easy to admire the good points that one's animals possess, and harder to keep the faults before one's eyes, but in no other way can we raise the overall level of the breed.

In addition to new breeders, many new Chihuahua owners join our ranks daily, a number of whom keep their little dogs purely as pets and for the pleasure they give. It is a joy to the writer that friends from both sections of this Chihuahua-lover fraternity say that they find this book useful. It was meant to be so, to help others to enjoy their Chihuahuas, and to keep them well and happy. We hope it will continue to do so.
1966

It is gratifying that, so hard on the heels of the second, a third edition of *The Chihuahua* is called for. This time I have made no revisions to the text or illustrations, but Appendices A and C have again been brought up to date.
1968

Appendices A and C have once more been extended in this fourth edition. I have also replaced three photographs and made a few minor revisions to the text. The reader's attention is drawn to the new addendum which *précis* the exhaustive research which Mrs Eileen Goodchild has recently done into the origins of the breed.
1974

For the fifth edition I have made a few more small revisions to the text and again brought the appendices up-to-date. One of the photographs has been replaced and two added.

It would be impossible to complete this introduction without special reference to the dog described in his obituary as 'Britain's most successful Chihuahua sire of all time.'

Following Ch. Rozavel Chief Scout's death at the age of twelve years, Brian Mitchell wrote: 'A show career highlighted by seven C.C. wins (one at Crufts) was followed by an extraordinary dominance at stud. He sired upwards of fourteen British Champions, the first in his first litter, and many overseas title winners. Most Rozavel Champions have been from uncle/niece or nephew/aunt matings—Chief Scout, and his sire and dam, among them. His long-coat sire, Ch. Rozavel Wolf Cub, was a grandson of Ch. Rozavel Humo, sire of the mainly American-bred smooth dam of Ch. Rozavel Chief Scout, Rozavel Star Sapphire. This remarkable dog's influence for balance and superb fronts—his own front was considered a breakthrough—has continued over many generations in both coats. Among his grandprogeny are the smooth-coat record holder and the long-coat dog record holder for C.C.'s.'

In quoting the above extract, which appeared in the British canine weekly publication *Dog World*, one ponders on the outcome of the controversy, current as this book is reprinted, concerning the possible separation of the two varieties. The Kennel Club has the matter under consideration and are debating whether or not to prohibit the cross-mating of the two coats. That this rule should be implemented eventually is generally agreed, and while there are those who maintain that the time has come, a large majority feel that it is rather too soon.

Certainly, if long-coat had never been mated to smooth, we would never have had Chief Scout. If he had not been born, his wonderful progeny, both long-coat and smooth-coat, would never have been available to give the Chihuahua breed the many priceless characteristics that are his legacy and which have uplifted the quality of the breed to a level which many International judges agree is the highest in the world.

1979   T.G.

ONE

THE ORIGIN OF THE BREED

A LONG-ESTABLISHED governing body called the **Kennel Club** controls the breeding and exhibiting of Britain's vast and ever-increasing population of pedigree dogs.

Statistics suggest that one family in every five keeps a dog, though, of course, a considerable proportion of them are not thoroughbred.

The Kennel Club recognizes over one hundred different varieties, and apart from the breeds tabulated under separate classifications there are a few less well-known, numerically smaller types of canine officially recorded under the heading 'Any Other Variety'.

Until a few years ago the Chihuahua was included among these minorities, and largely because of the many difficulties entailed when importing was undertaken, the little dogs had always been rare in this country. It was a long time before the breed became at all widely known, but its popularity has gradually increased in recent years so that in spite of setbacks the number of registrations at the Kennel Club reached a total which enabled the Committee to recognize it as a separate Toy breed.

Frequently described as 'the smallest breed of dogs in the world', an accurate survey of the average sizes and weights of the modern Chihuahuas would support this claim. There are several other breeds of dogs within the Toy group which produce some very tiny animals, but in those breeds the majority are rather larger.

How did the Chihuahua get its name? From the famous State of Chihuahua, in Mexico. Travellers from the United States of America seem to have picked up tiny dogs to take home with them from Chihuahua, and the name attached itself to the breed when it first began to become known to a public outside its native land. This was not, so far as we can tell, because the little dogs necessarily originated in that part of Mexico, or because the State had any other special claim to them. They probably have a close connection with the Allende Valley.

When we try to delve into Mexican history in an attempt to trace the beginnings of the Chihuahua dog we are at once reminded of the man who found himself knowing more and more about less and less. Few breeds have had more romantic and fanciful theories expounded about them, and while some of these may be basically sound, and certainly merit more consideration than others, real historical facts are scarce. Records of all kinds are hard to substantiate, vague, and altogether obscure. It is because so much mystery surrounds its origin that we are certain that the breed is an ancient one. Quite a lot is known about breeds of more recent creation, and the various types of dogs that have participated in their evolution are tabulated and acknowledged. It is when a breed or variety has its beginning in the mists of time that it is almost impossible to know whence it has come to us over the years.

Before we start to examine the possible origin let us consider the country itself, for at least we are certain that this extraordinary, diminutive canine developed into something resembling its present form, in Mexico, whether it actually started there or was introduced at some period.

Mexico is a land with a colourful but turbulent history. Its terrain includes some of the world's grandest and most picturesque scenery, with a wide variation of soil and climate. There are parched and sandy plains—and much of the State of Chihuahua is desert—but there are also areas of profuse fertility, rendered almost impenetrable by the masses of aromatic shrubs and flowers which flourish in the midst of forests. These forests are often composed of trees of a size and type found only in the tropics. There are, even now, small, primitive, and insanitary villages beside roads that eventually take the traveller into large modern cities with sumptuous buildings which compare with those found anywhere else in the world.

Lakes, deserts, jungle-like forests, mountains, plains: Mexico has them all.

As can easily be imagined from all this, the climate ranges from burning heat to icy cold, from an atmosphere of humidity to bitter winds which, in the winter seasons, freshen into tempests. The varying weather conditions have not changed, and even the countryside has altered little, so it is not really difficult to build up a picture of Mexico at the time of its 'discovery' and the famous Conquest. Although there were the great areas of barren soil, there were also enormous areas of fertile, volcanic land; hundreds of years ago this was thickly covered with vegetation of all kinds. The plateaus were wooded, mainly larch, oak, cypress, etc., and some pine forests.

What do we know of the early inhabitants of this fairyland? Some of the first known were the Mayan Indians. They kept a small dog known as the Techichi, an ancient Nahuatl name —and although this must have been a rather larger animal, it is more than possible that it was the ancestor of the Chihuahua breed as we know it today. Historians say it was 'small and fat' but no more. There exists in Mexico a hairless dog, smaller than Xoloizcuintli, which is called Tepeizcuintle, but which some owners refer to as Techichi.

Following the Mayas, the most renowned peoples were the Toltecs, who constructed the pyramids of Cholula, upon which have been found carvings which much resemble Chihuahua dogs.

The Toltecs cultivated the territory known as Anahuac (a name meaning 'near the water'), which is thought to have applied to the lakeside country in the Mexican valley, or to the land that lay between the Atlantic and the Pacific.

On the whole, remarkably little is known of these people, who probably settled there before the close of the seventh century. Most of the information that has come to us has been in the form of legends rather than actual records, but we know that the Toltecs were highly skilled in agriculture, and some of the ruins discovered at Tula (said to have been their capital city) are attributed to them. They are said to have been the true foundation of the civilization which distinguished their part of the Continent in later years, yet, after a period of four centuries these people mysteriously vanished. Perhaps they were decimated by famines, plagues, and unsuccessful wars. Nobody really knows what happened to them. They did not even leave very much for posterity, though archaeologists think that the splendid ruins of Mitla and Palenque were the labours of their race.

About a hundred years elapsed before a numerous, tough, and aggressive tribe called the Chichimecs entered the deserted country. They were speedily followed by others of a much higher civilization, and the most famous of these were the Aztecs or Mexicans.

These people came from the north and reached the borders of Anahuac towards the beginning of the thirteenth century. Instead of making a permanent settlement, they adopted a nomadic life, travelling around the various parts of this Mexican valley.

Throughout their wanderings they suffered appalling hardships and casualties of a kind that were bound to beset explorers in such a wild and inhospitable land. The Aztecs were governed by a superstition that an oracle had spoken, telling them to settle only when they found a place by a lake, and they would know it by a sign. At some stage in their travels they halted on the shores of the largest lake. There they beheld a large cactus of the type known as the prickly pear, and perched upon it was a mighty eagle with its wings outspread, and in its talons it grasped a serpent. This, they felt sure, was the sign which the oracle had predicted. The sight was hailed as a good omen, and the people decided that fortune would favour a city built upon that very spot. On that summer day Mexico came into being. They built their city, and they called the place Tenochtitlan in token of its miraculous origin. Eventually it also became known by its other name—Mexico.

This took place in the year 1325, and the legend has been perpetuated until the present day, for the device of eagle, cactus, and snake is superimposed upon the green, white, and red flag of the Mexican republic, and a very beautiful and decorative banner it is.

The Aztecs' troubles were by no means over, however, and

their empire was still to endure terrible sufferings and hardships. They were a courageous people who rose above their setbacks, and they gradually extended their hóld over the country stretching into Guatemala and Nicaragua, until, by the beginning of the sixteenth century, they were very widely established indeed.

We learn much of the artistic accomplishments of this somewhat warlike people. How their warriors were gorgeously turned out in coats of mail made of gold and silver; of their helmets of wood, carved like the heads of wild animals; of vestments made of featherwork, gorgeous relics of a now lost art in which they excelled; and of their exquisite ornaments, including collars, earrings, and bracelets set with precious stones.

The degree of civilization reached has been compared with that enjoyed by our own Saxon ancestors at the time of King Alfred, yet, on the other hand, the Aztecs indulged in primitive and revolting customs which placed them on an animal plane far removed from the Saxons. The complex Aztec religions demanded human and animal sacrifices, and their altars ran with blood and reeked of slaughter. Their selected victims were often their enemies, or disobedient slaves, but sometimes innocent men and women who underwent unspeakable tortures before finding oblivion in death. Even cannibalism was a regular practice.

It was in the year 1519 that the Spanish expedition, under Hernando Cortez, set out to conquer Mexico. The years that followed were a long succession of bloody battles, bitter, drawn-out struggles, of trickery and deceit. The Spaniards pursued commendable missionary efforts in the hope of converting the Indians to Christianity, and they tried hard to wean them away from their heathen rituals.

A letter is said to be in existence in which Christopher Columbus informs the King of Spain that he found, on landing in Cuba, 'a small kind of dogs which were mute and did not bark as usual, but were domesticated'. Cuba is not far from Mexico, so perhaps the dogs referred to could have been Chihuahuas or Techichi, though lack of voice hardly fits the modern Chi dog.

In so far as is known there exists today only one breed of

dog that is barkless. This is the Basenji, a native hunting dog from the Congo. The Basenji is not dumb, but it does not bark as do other dogs. It can make odd noises, successively referred to as 'yodel', 'crow', or 'howl'. When inter-bred with other breeds, the Basenji develops a normal bark, though, pure-bred, it does not learn to bark when kept with dogs with normal voices.

Could the Chihuahuas have been mute or barkless as the Basenji? And has some other blood been introduced at some stage or other to produce the shrill little noises we associate with the present-day Chi's? This possibility cannot be lightly cast aside. It is worthy of some consideration, especially in the light of some of the suggestions that have been made in attempts to explain the genetic make-up of the Chihuahua breed, a subject which we shall examine in another chapter.

If the first discoverers of the New World did, in fact, find a Chihuahua-like dog there, or any other kind for that matter, it is reasonable to assume that they returned to Europe with some specimens.

Mrs Wells had her attention drawn to a painting by Botticelli, 'Moses Leaving Egypt', in which there is a small dog remarkably like a modern Chihuahua. The head is clearly portrayed and, incidentally, not like that of an Italian Greyhound. It is white or a light colour, and apparently smooth, not long-coated.

It is interesting to note that Amerigo Vespucci (1451–1512), after whom America is named, was a contemporary of Botticelli (1444–1510). Botticelli lived in Florence, near to the Vespucci family, and was on very good terms with them. (They introduced him to the Medici and he painted 'Mars and Venus' for them.) Amerigo Vespucci made several journeys to the New World, and visited Espanola and San Domingo between 1492 and 1503 (prior to the Spanish Conquest of Mexico). He was known to have been interested in the native peoples and their habits and customs. A reproduction of the painting of 'Moses Leaving Egypt' can be found in Berenson's *Italian Painters of the Renaissance*, No. 208 (Phaidon), but in spite of the picture I do not think we should go so far as to claim that Moses had a Chihuahua! But if indeed the Italians had them as well as, and possibly before, the Spaniards, this might explain the existence of Chihuahuas in Malta. It is a fact that the breed has been kept on that island for a considerable time and is popular with the natives there today. The comparative isolation of the little island has no doubt contributed to the preservation of the breed there.

Many of the archaeological excavations in Maya territory, and including some at Chichen Itza, in the Mexican State of Yucatan, have established the fact that a small dog was commonly kept, at least before the seventh century. It is described as being of the greyhound type.

There seems, too, to be a good deal of evidence that the Aztecs kept several types of dog. In the middle of the sixteenth century the Spanish friar, Bernardino de Sahagun, made and set on record a famous study of the Aztecs. He gives seven different names of native dogs, one Tlalchichi 'short of stature and fat, which are excellent to eat'. Other references to dogs from other authors of standing are:

'The dog . . . was almost universally domesticated. In the North [America] it was a beast of burden; in Mexico an article of diet.'

'The Aztecs were poor in domestic animals. They had several varieties of dogs, one of which was bred for food.' *One* bred for food, you notice.

'Wool was almost never made into cloth, since dog-hair was all they had.' So all their dogs were not hairless!

Spence says in *The Gods of Mexico*, writing of the dead:

'Then he reached a broad river which he crossed on the back of a *little red* dog, sometimes included in the grave-furniture for the purpose.' This seems to discount the theory that the original dog of the tombs and the legends was a large grey hairless dog like the modern Xoloizcuintli.

Among the wealth of material that has come down to us from the early Indians, and is to be found in museums in various parts of the world, there are Aztec carvings, pottery, statues, coloured drawings, and hieroglyphics.

Many of these point to the existence of a dog of Chihuahua type during their times. Especially from Colima, whence so many exciting discoveries have been reported, have come statues which are surely and unmistakably Chihuahuas. Relics of the Huasteca tribe, too, include clay figures of dogs which appear to be Chi's, even if judged by modern standards.

We have a photograph of one of the pottery dogs from Colima facing page 36. The model is kept in the North-West Mexico Anthropological Museum, where it is described as 'an over-fed dog to be eaten by humans'. We know that small dogs were a delicacy in those unenlightened years, but to most of us the statue looks an accurate conception of a Chihuahua bitch in whelp.

Let us study the picture. Note the curiously flat, sickle-like curved tail. A flat tail is a most unusual feature in a dog of any breed excepting a pure-bred Chihuahua. This Colima dog also has the true domed skull and the large, flaring ears. Note the big, but not protruding eyes, and the very slightly truncated foreface. In fact this is a recognizable and faithful model of a Chihuahua; it really does not look like a dog of any other breed.

Similar pottery figurines were shown at the Tate Gallery, London, on the occasion of the Exhibition of Mexican Art held in 1953. Priceless relics and treasures drawn from museums and private collections all over the world were gathered together there and beautifully displayed. Breeders and judges of Chihuahuas who visited this exhibition noted the remarkable likeness to their breed in some of the pottery figures.

We have been supplied with some interesting information about these pottery dogs by Mrs Konietzko, a member of the Royal Anthropological Institute of Great Britain and Ireland and of other international institutions. Also from Dr Disselhoff, Director of the Museum of Ethnology in Berlin, and, finally, from Dr Walther Christen, of Hamburg, Germany, who owns one of these models, which is in all respects a typical representation of a Chihuahua. This model has been certified as a genuine antique by Dr Disselhoff, who tells us that almost all of these models have been found in the Colima district in Western Mexico, though the breed of Chihuahua dogs were most likely spread all over Mexico during Aztec times. It is almost certain that the model is a very old one, at least 500 years and possibly as much as 2,000 years old. Most of the Chihuahua models, including dogs in standing, sitting, and recumbent positions, have been stolen from the temples and tombs and sold to foreign buyers, so it is very difficult if not impossible to find any more around Colima. Nevertheless, at the time of writing, Dr Disselhoff is endeavouring to get permission to take a team of scientists to Mexico to excavate in that district, so it is possible that, if he is successful, he may be able to throw some light on the scant history of the Chihuahua breed.

It is known that the pre-Conquest Indians kept dogs in Mexico, because of the skeletons that have been found, though it is said that these were larger than the under 6-lb dogs of today. The discovery of these canine bones probably provides the basis for the particular school of thought which believes that the original Chi was a considerably larger dog than its modern version.

It is also an established fact that some small dogs were bred and specially fattened for food purposes in early Mexico. From what we know of the desert and the more barren parts of the country it must have been hard to sustain human life, so it is not difficult to perceive that, consequent on these rugged conditions, meat from specially fattened dogs was an important item in the diet of the people. In any event, it would not be an isolated instance of a people using dogs for food. The Chow Chow is the edible dog of China and was still so used until comparatively recently. A lady who had lived in China told me that when she wanted to buy a Chow Chow puppy for a pet she would go to the market and ask for one for roasting. She would then be offered a young dog, otherwise she would probably be shown the older dogs, sold for boiling, a revolting idea to dog lovers today.

In direct contrast to this brutal fact is the well-established story that the Mexicans kept their tiny dogs because they believed that they would guide the souls of the dead to a state of everlasting bliss. Most of the records emphasize, as we have mentioned before, that a reddish-brown dog was sacrificed on funeral occasions. Special significance was also attached to the blue- or clay-coloured dogs (note the colours—both popular in the show ring today) which were interred or cremated with the body of the deceased. So long as can be remembered there has been a superstition in Mexico—a country where necromancy and witchcraft flourishes even today—that sickness can be cured by transferring it from the suffering person to a dog.

In her book *An Artist Goes to the Dogs*, Vere Temple has some intriguing little items about Chihuahuas. She writes of the Chihuahua:

> It was also used as a kind of scapegoat; a red-skinned dog was buried over the grave of the deceased, whose sins then passed into the soul of the dog. Red was considered to be the colour of sin and the devil, just as blue was considered to be symbolic of the West, the Earth, and the fertility goddesses; so that blue or blue-grey Chihuahuas were greatly revered.
>
> It was believed also that the Chihuahuas could remove sickness by transferring it to another person. In cases of fever, images of dogs were placed on an aloe leaf in the pathway, and the first passer-by was supposed to take the sickness away with him in his heel bones.
>
> The dogs had second-sight, too, and could predict the future.
>
> On one occasion, Montezuma's pet Chihuahua foretold that a flood would devastate the earth, so the king built himself an ark, but forgot to invite his pet—who too, with great presence of mind, built himself a little ark made of bamboo, in which he safely weathered the floods; and when the water subsided, he jumped into the lap of the king who was delighted to see him again.
>
> Oddest of all was the power over the human body ascribed to animals by the Aztecs; under this system, the Chihuahua was supposed to rule over the nose.
>
> The natives of Chihuahua (a district which gives its name to the dog) claim that buried treasure lies there, left by some ancient Aztec king—they say that the little dogs are there to guard it, and under no conditions will they harm the dogs or interfere with them. So the Chihuahuas still run wild in Mexico, preying upon other small animals.

Some of this information is rather fanciful, albeit colourful and endearing, the really interesting item being the reference to the Aztec superstition that the Chihuahua is 'supposed to rule over the nose'. We know that there has always been an idea that the Chihuahua has a beneficial effect on certain human ailments, notably rheumatism and its kindred aches

Ch. Rozavel Francisco

Ch. Rozavel Uvalda Jemima

J. Konietzko, Hamburg

Clay dog, from Colima District, not less than 500 years old,
but more probably 2,000 years old

Mexican dog, 'overfed to be eaten'. A statuette in the
Anthropological Museum, Mexico

Madame Adelina Patti and
her Chihuahua—a photograph
taken about sixty years ago

A Mexican Hairless
Alacran de Chontallan

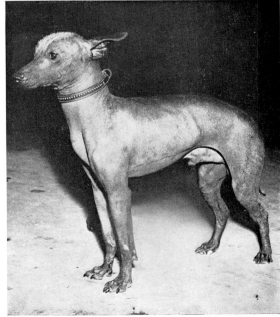

Sport and General

Tolteca

Derek Lambourn, Cardiff

Mixcoac

R. L. Nowak

Bowerhinton Chico of Belamie and Jofos Ferronita

and pains, and asthma. Could the Aztec connection of the human nose and the Chihuahua have started this belief? Or is it possible that the breed really does help sufferers from this latter distressing affliction?

Only recently there was much publicity in the Press when a Chihuahua dog was lost, its owner being a small girl who was a martyr to asthma. Her parents had bought the dog because they had been told that it could alleviate the symptoms, and the child's health was visibly improved directly she had the dog. When it strayed, her asthma returned and she was very ill until the dog was recovered, and then she was well again, with her pet safely home. Sceptics will feel that the nervous upset caused by the loss of her dog could bring on an attack, and that the delight in having it back home could cause her to forget her symptoms. But, discussing this particular case, a doctor declined to say that it was impossible for the dog to have some kind of beneficial effect, or to comment on the statement, attributed to a doctor in the U.S.A., that the animal's skin secreted some special oil that helped asthmatical patients. The publicity given to this story resulted in a number of breeders receiving enquiries for Chihuahuas for people suffering from asthma. We have not heard if they found that an improvement resulted from the presence of a Chihuahua in the house.

Those who sell Chihuahuas do not, however, use these 'powers' as a selling point. Their consciences would not allow them to raise what they believe might well be false hopes in the minds of people who suffer from a distressing complaint. They have in mind, too, the fact that there might be individuals who would buy a dog for its possible curative effect, and not because the dog is wanted for itself alone, and nobody should acquire a sensitive little animal like a Chihuahua unless they long to make a pet of it and to offer it a loving home.

The eminent authority on Chihuahuas, Mr Charles Wall, tells us in his comprehensive booklet that the Aztecs, valuing their tiny dogs in the dual, if oddly assorted, capacity as items of the larder and for their religious rites, took some with them when persecutions forced them to retreat into the mountain regions. The Techichi or Chihuahua seems to have gone with them in the form of 'a mute, melancholy, mainly sandy-coloured dog' and to have emerged, nearly 500 years later, as a mixed-coloured dog with a shrill bark and an aggressive manner.

It is supposed that many of the little dogs were liberated in the mountains and forced to find for themselves some kind of survival, independent of the hand of man. Did these dogs, then, mix and breed with a smaller, wild mountain canine or rodent? Such a wild animal existed and is often confused with the Tepeizcuintli. It was black and white in colour, and some say it was a rodent, others that it was dog. Tepeizcuintli is the smaller hairless breed of dog, larger than a Chihuahua. They have bare, grey bodies mottled with pink, and some hair on their heads. One who clung firmly to the wild-dog theory was Miss Rosina Casselli, who was unique in that she toured the music halls with a large troupe of performing Chihuahuas, about the beginning of the twentieth century.

Although the evidence is so flimsy, we frankly hesitate to believe or disbelieve the theory, but it is an attractive one, and we wonder if the lady felt that such an unusual background added glamour to her troupe, and the act? An article written by Miss Casselli appeared in a dog publication dated 1904, and in it she says:

Of all the canine breeds, there is probably none so little known or understood as the Chihuahua dogs of Mexico, which were in their natural state a distinctly Mexican race of wild dogs, very shy, and, for their size, very savage.

They inhabit only a limited section of the mountainous part of Chihuahua, whence these dogs derive their name. It is believed that these wild dogs are now extinct, although they are reported by the natives to have been seen up to about fifteen years ago [1889?], and it is barely possible that they might still be found in some undisturbed spot.

These dogs were noted, not only for their extreme smallness, but other peculiarities which they possess.

Their legs were very slender, and their toe-nails very long and strong, and very serviceable to them in making their homes, as they lived in holes in the ground.

Apart from their size, their most striking feature was their head which was very round, and from which projected a very short and pointed nose and large standing ears; there was also a peculiar skull formation, found only in this race. The hair was short, fine and thick and the wild dogs, even when taken young, could not be domesticated, neither could they live any length of time in captivity.

The Indians, however, had a way of taking these dogs and crossing them with the small specimens of the domesticated Indian dog, and in this way produced a domesticated Chihuahua dog which was kept replenished from the wild stock as much as possible.

We do not know whence this lady's information stemmed, whether she had, in fact, visited Mexico and really investigated the origin of her little dogs, or had merely listened to travellers' tales, always known to be somewhat fanciful and highly coloured; nevertheless, everything she writes may well be true, and there are certain aspects of her story one has to consider carefully.

Zoologists and naturalists know that an alliance between different species of animals is not only improbable but usually quite impossible. There are many alleged cases of dog and fox crosses, some of them supposed to have had fruitful results, but such stories seldom stand up to close investigation. If doubts may be cast upon the likelihood of a dog-fox cross, the possibilities of a dog-rodent mating is even more unlikely.

Prior to and during 1950 a Major Mundey was breeding a type of Chihuahua in Mexico. His dogs, for the most part, were quite large, had very long legs, and their heads were distinctive, with enormous ears. He called them Chihuahuenos, and made some claims about their origin that brought him into great disfavour with the Mexican Kennel Club.

Articles by him appeared in the American monthly *Popular Dogs*, also in the *Tail Wagger Magazine*, June 1950 issue, in England.

To quote from the latter article, he wrote:

Many parts of Mexico still today remain unexplored, but it is known that in such regions are to be found animals of a type never to be seen in any Zoological Gardens.

For example, in a certain mountainous region there exists a beautiful new species of wild dog, weighing 3 lb or even less; like the

well-known Chihuahuenos, these dogs are nocturnal, but they have
been seen abroad by daylight also.

It may well be asked, why, once their existence is known, these
dogs have not been caught and domesticated like the wild Chihuahueno; the answer is a simple one.

The natives of the region are very hostile to strangers, and would
almost certainly kill or maim any intruders; some few years ago two
missionaries did venture into the region, but returned shortly afterwards minus their ears. For this reason, any person venturing into
the region has some very good purpose for so doing, and his interest
is not usually in wild dogs.

Indeed, the existence of these dogs was only brought to my
notice by chance. A Mexican friend of mine, on a visit to my house,
saw my Chihuahuenos and remarked that he knew of wild dogs
very similar to my Chihuahuenos, except that the wild dogs were
smaller and their coats longer.

On being questioned further, he said that when shooting for the
pot one day in this mountainous region, he shot a small animal
which he took to be a rabbit, but which he found to be, on careful
examination, a perfect specimen of tiny wild dog.

Being very interested in the tiny creature, he directed his native
guides to trap another dog for him, which they did with some difficulty. Unfortunately the poor little creature was so terrified that it
died almost immediately, and the natives told my friend that these
dogs almost always died if caught.

One interesting point was discovered from this rather unfortunate matter. When caught, the tiny dog had a mouse in its mouth,
and from this my friend assumed the dogs to be carnivorous, as
distinct from the wild Chihuahueno, which is herbivorous.

Major Mundey then goes on to say:

I have recently heard that, although the Chihuahueno is extinct
in the State from which it takes its name, wild Chihuahuas have
been found in another uninhabited part of Mexico.

As these Chihuahuenos take their colour or protective camou-
flage from the terrain in which they live, these dogs are grey in
colour, whereas the wild Chihuahueno was a soft peach-cream
colour, harmonizing with the sandy soil of his habitat.

Major Mundey's views had only to appear in print to cause
a flood of protest from people who did not agree with his

statements. These were contested in an article which came out in the American paper *Little Dogs*, in February 1951, written by Professor Baltran, a well-known and distinguished professor of pre-Columbian history at the University of Puebla, and a lecturer on that subject. Much of Professor Baltran's article is taken up with a personal attack on Major Mundey and his credentials. He begins by insisting that the first Mundey Chihuahua was obtained from the U.S.A., thus implying that the Major's story about his 'wild' Chihuahuenos was a fabrication, and one dreamed up because his unpopularity with the Mexican Kennel Club had led to a ban on his dogs being either registered or exhibited at their shows.

Professor Baltran was 'Director Responsible' of *Mundo Canino*, the Mexican *Dog World*, organ of La Asociacion Canofila Mexicana. Early in 1950 *Mundo Canino* invited all scientists, investigators, historians, and laymen 'to supply them with all known facts, not legends, about the Chihuahua breed'.

During that year they published various letters and statements received in reply. Some came from eminent persons living or working in Chihuahua. One such summarized his findings thus:

Doubtless the little Chihuahua dogs exist in the State of Chihuahua, particularly in the Valley of Allende, that is, in the town of Chihuahua itself and in the villages of the district.

Their origin is not savage (wild) nor do they breed in dens or caves. Their alimentation is the same as that of other dogs, but it is advisable not to give them much meat in the first year of their lives, so that they do not grow large.

They are not rodents.

Also there were references to printed works on the subject:

It is also believed that the origin of the word 'Chihuahua' comes from the imitation of the bark of a dog, and because for a long time past wild 'dogs' have lived in the hills of the State of Chihuahua. They are not true dogs, but rodents, technically known as *Cynomys ludovicianus* and they have been much confused with the little dogs of Chihuahua or Chihuahuenos. We are dealing in consequence with a true member of the 'canine species' whose savage origin is unknown.

There is no record of its (Chihuahua dog) having been seen in anything but a domesticated state.

A lady, living in the town of Chihuahua, whose family resided for many years on a ranch near the Valley of Allende, where they bred and raised many of these dogs, is quoted. One thing she said was: 'They are very sensitive to cold, and if they run loose in the countryside they do not know how to find their own food,' which confirms that they are not of wild origin, but dogs with the handicaps of tameness.

There is also some information about the rodent or prairie dog which some have confused with the 'true' dogs.

Professor Baltran himself writes: 'It is the greatest lie in the world to say that Chihuahua dogs can be captured in Mexico,' and, referring to a picture under discussion which showed a jar, decorated with a design that, Mundey suggested, incorporated a Chihuahua:

'the jar shown . . . corresponds with what the Spanish called barkless dogs' but which were nothing but racoons, an animal previously unknown to them. If you visit our museums you can see these jars by the hundreds, classified as 'coons' and not as Chihuahua dogs. Now get your map and look over Mexican geography. Mundey says 'The Chihuahuenos dig back into Mayan history.' You know where the Mayan Empire was? Yucatan. You know where Chihuahua is? On the U.S.A. border.

All the Chihuahua dogs now in Mexico originated in the U.S.A. The Aztecs never ate Chihuahua dogs. They ate the 'coons', just like the negroes in your Southern States like to do.

Mexico has 25,000,000 inhabitants, and spreads over thousands of square kilometres, and I can swear to you that in all Mexico you cannot find over 100 Chihuahuas. In *Mundo Canino* [the official publication of the Mexican Kennel Club] I published a letter signed by the Governor of the State of Chihuahua, denying that there are any wild dogs in all the territory of the State, an official document.

Major Mundey died some years ago, but stuck to his views to the end.

Arising out of Professor Baltran's article which, in view of his credentials, we have to treat with respect, there are just one or two points to be considered.

One is the fact that although the Governor of the State of Chihuahua has declared that wild dogs do not exist in his province this in no way disproves the possibility of their existence elsewhere, or even the fact that at one time they might have existed in Chihuahua, though doubts have always been expressed that the Chi breed of dogs ever existed there in a wild state. When it became apparent that the little Chihuahua dogs, found in other parts of Mexico, had a great attraction for American tourists, it was natural that they should be brought into that part of Mexico so conveniently situated for visitors from the U.S.A. Acquiring their first dogs in that area, they came to refer to them as Chihuahuas. Doubtless some of the Mexican pedlars, with an eye to the main chance, began breeding the dogs in Chihuahua.

The other interesting fact concerns the journeys which Colonel Harmar, formerly British Military Attaché in Mexico, and now resident in this country, made when he and his wife were endeavouring to secure some rare Mexican hairless dogs. On one of their trips they penetrated into a remote part of the country and found an isolated village which was thickly populated with Chihuahua dogs. Colonel and Mrs Harmar keep and breed Chihuahuas as well as the hairless dogs, and were therefore quick to recognize the type.

If the Chihuahuas flourish in one isolated spot there is no reason to suppose that they do not do so in others. It also suggests that Professor Baltran's statement that in all Mexico 'you cannot find over one hundred Chihuahuas' may not be correct, unless of course he meant officially registered or recognized Chihuahuas.

If we believe that the late Major Mundey was right, then we believe that a dog which sounds exactly like our present-day Chihuahua used to live, and perhaps still does live, the life of a wild animal on mountain slopes in spite of a climate sometimes warm and sometimes bitterly cold.

If the Professor is right then we believe that the first Chihuahuas were bred in the U.S.A. and imported into Mexico. There are various things which discount this theory, and naturally the first thing we ask is—whence came the Chihuahua from the United States; and why, in that country with its well-distributed population, is nothing known of its origin? Which breeds were used to make it?

The Chihuahua is a most distinctive little dog. With its apple head, complete with the curious and uncommon molera, its very small size, the flat tail—the like of which is not seen in any other breed—it has characteristics that are decidedly its own and certainly do not seem to have been borrowed from any other breed of dog.

And when we really know the Chihuahua we realize that it is, in so many ways and some of them very hard to define, totally unlike other dogs. There are times when, in studying Chihuahua behaviour, we find ourselves quite prepared to accept the fact that it may well have more than a little of the wild animal in its make-up.

We know that all our breeds of domestic dog have come down to us from wolves, though the hand of man has twisted the canines into so many and such varied shapes that, in nearly all the breeds he has fashioned, little trace of wolf ancestors is perceptible. These extraordinarily different members of the canine race have been developed by a process of selection, however, and have not been evolved by crossing them with animals of other species.

In the light of this pot-pourri of facts, and when some of the stranger characteristics of the Chihuahuas make themselves manifest, we confess that we wonder if the Chi really was a little wild animal, at least more recently than its other doggy relatives, all of which go back to the wild dog at some stage in their evolution.

The trouble is, nobody really knows. We can only weigh up all this rather scanty evidence, meditate on the strange background out of which these beautiful tiny dogs have emerged, and wonder which, if any, of the stories are true. We can also comfort ourselves with the thought that archaeological discoveries are constantly coming to light in Mexico, and perhaps one day something will turn up to enable us to piece together the history of the world's smallest breed of dog.

For further historical information, see Addendum page 209.

Before we leave the subject of the possible origin of the Chihuahua we must devote a little attention to another breed of dog which is indigenous to Mexico. It is important to do this because it lays claim to a place in its country's early history; also because there are some very conflicting opinions with regard to the available material that refers to the original Mexican dogs.

The Mexican hairless dog of today, or, known .in the Nahuatl language 'Xoloizcuintli' (pronounced 'Shollo-is-quintlie'), does not resemble the Chihuahua in any respect. Yet even now, when Chihuahuas are generally recognized, and although Xoloizcuintli have had quite a lot of publicity, a surprising number of people confuse the two breeds.

If one says 'I have a Chihuahua' one is quite likely to receive the reply: 'They are the dogs with no hair, aren't they?'

The hairless dog of Mexico is medium-sized and never tiny; it weighs about 35 lb. It has fairly long legs, with strong bone, and usually rather flat feet with spreading toes. The head is best described as oval in shape, fairly lengthy, and in no way apple-headed; rather is the skull flattish, with the ears set well on top of the head, usually erect or semi-pricked. It has peculiar dentition, with a lack of premolars.

The dog would be rather undistinguished were it not for the astounding fact that it is, as the name suggests, naked. It is almost unique in the world of dogs for, except for what are believed to be some very close relations, the Chinese crested dogs, the canine race as a whole is covered with hair even though it varies in length and texture.

Although a few harsh, bristle-like hairs can be found on Xoloizcuintli's head, and possibly a very few scattered elsewhere on its body, the dog is really covered with an elephant-like skin that is wrinkled, coarse in texture, and rough and warm to the touch. The colour is mainly grey, but it is sometimes mottled with pink. To remove the harshness its devotees prepare it for showing by rubbing it with oil.

While the Chihuahuas rapidly increased in numbers during the past hundred years, the Xoloizcuintli had almost become extinct until, quite suddenly, a few years ago, some people made a concerted effort to save it from oblivion. Their efforts included excursions into some of the wilder parts of Mexico, to small villages well away from the tourist areas, and in one such settlement a discovery rewarded their optimism—they found just half a dozen hairless dogs. Two of them were taken to Mexico City, and on a subsequent trip others were collected.

Eventually a pair was flown to England, to serve the period of quarantine at the London Zoological Gardens. There they aroused much interest, the more so when, upon their release, they were exhibited at some of the larger dog shows. Although hairless dogs had been brought to England before, in 1912, and again between the two world wars, they did not take kindly to the climate and did not survive very long. Consequently, very few people when they were again introduced had seen anything resembling the animals, which became something of a sensation.

Colonel and Mrs Harmar, who had brought their breeding pair from Mexico, had a busy time showing them to the mass of spectators who mobbed their benches at the shows. The original pair have bred successfully and so there are now several in the country, but the question of an outcross for future matings is causing some concern. Importing dogs is a costly business and even if it can be undertaken, where Xoloizcuintli is concerned, it is not at all easy to find suitable specimens to import. It must also be admitted that at present there is no evidence that they greatly attract the dog-loving public, except as oddities, though the few who own them express pleasure at their agreeable dispositions. Naturally, they are expensive, because of the cost of importing and the scarcity of puppies, and this also inhibits their chance of popularity. Certainly they have become acclimatized very much better than their predecessors, and they seem to be standing up to the English winters quite well; nevertheless they do require more care than coated dogs, and must not be allowed to get chilled or to remain wet.

What, therefore, has this peculiar but interesting animal got to do with the Chihuahua? Nothing—so far as appearance, size, or character are concerned, but a great deal in that there are some admirers of the hairless dog who believe that it was the original dog of the Mayas, the Toltecs, and the Aztecs. Seeing is said to be believing, and they profess to recognize it in the Colima and other ancient models. They feel certain that this was the original edible breed of dog, and the dog of the god Xolotl, with his reputed eerie connections with the souls of the dead. They insist, in fact, that the hairless dog is the subject of the historical effigies and records, and that it is the only breed which has any traces of existence in ancient Mexico. As a matter of interest, doubts are cast on the statement that Xolotl was one of the death gods at all.

The Chihuahua, they say, is the result of merging some small breed of South American native dog with a North American dwarf terrier, perhaps a coyote-type or a rodent, blended into something resembling a breed by the introduction of Amer-toy or English Toy Terrier (Black-and-Tan), (Toy Manchester), blood.

The opposition counter this by saying that much of the so-called evidence apportioned to Xoloizcuintli could, and in fact does, apply just as well or better to the Chihuahua. They point out, with justice, that the hairless dog of Mexico has its counterpart in the crested dog of China, also known as the Tai-tai. This creature is smaller than the Mexican dog, but also hairless, and it is decorated with a tuft of feathery hairs on top of its head. This gives it an almost parrot-like appearance. Hairless dogs were also known in Haiti, Cuba, Abyssinia, Turkey, Southern India, and Paraguay, and it is thought that they probably all originated in Manchuria. There is scant evidence that the present-day type is the 'Xolo' as known in the past.

It was the view of the late Mrs Ida Garrett—one of the greatest of the pioneers of the Chihuahua in the U.S.A.—that Xoloizcuintli stemmed from these hairless dogs of Haiti and South America, and was not really indigenous to Mexico at all.

Mr Norman Pelham Wright, who resides in Mexico, has taken a great interest in the revival of the hairless breed, and is much engaged in promoting and encouraging them. He has often expressed his views on the debatable question of their origin, believing that they are a very ancient breed, and that Chihuahuas are of more recent origin. Mr Wright therefore maintains that the known facts appertaining to the ancient Indians and their dogs relate to the hairless breed.

One thing that emerges from the conflict of opinions is the fact that it is clearly very difficult to prove or disprove the claims of either of the partisans. People seem to see very much what they want to see! Ardent admirers of other, quite dissimilar, breeds of dogs will insist that they can recognize their favourites on the same Egyptian tombs, and these include supporters of Greyhounds, Salukis, Basenjis, Dachshunds, and Cardiganshire Welsh Corgis. They all like to claim that proof of the antiquity of their respective breeds can be found among the carvings, but to the less wishful thinker they are not so easily identified. So look at the picture of the dog found at Colima and compare it with the photograph of Xoloizcuintli, both between pages 32 and 33. Do they look alike? Which breed does the Colima dog represent most closely?

If it is hard to be sure of anything that happened all those centuries ago, of one thing we can be certain. The Chihuahua at some stage in the world's history became a recognizable breed of dog. It found its way to North America to be appreciated, standardized, and gradually bred to a peak of near-perfection. From that huge country it has found its way all over the world, and nowhere is it more heartily welcomed than in Britain, where it continues to flourish and where its promising future is surely of greater importance than its mysterious past.

TWO

HOW THE BREED STARTED IN THE U.S.A.

WHEN we study the history of the Chihuahua we naturally pay attention to the development of the breed in Great Britain, but it would be entirely wrong to ignore its progress in the U.S.A. If the Chihuahua had not been so carefully brought forward and standardized by the breeders in that great country the breed might never have enjoyed the position it does here at the present time. We have such a growing army of admirers of the world's smallest dogs that they naturally want to know exactly how it came to be introduced to us from far-away Mexico. It is distinctly improbable that we could have established the breed in Britain with a type that fits the official Standard of Points if we had been dependent on imports direct from Mexico, without the balancing influence of high-class stock from North America.

Chihuahuas seem to have been introduced into the United States towards the latter part of the nineteenth century. Three gentlemen, Mr Owen Wister, Mr James Watson, and Mr Charles Stewart, seem to be the acknowledged pioneers. Because there is sometimes a tendency to regard this tiny breed as being the prerogative of women, it is therefore especially interesting to record that it was the opposite sex who fell for it in the first place!

Mr Watson was a well-known judge of dogs, and he has stated that he paid about $3 (at that time worth about 10s.!) for his first bitch. She was small enough to travel in a coat pocket but, later, after he had had the misfortune to lose her with pneumonia, he had some difficulty in replacing her with one as tiny. He bought six in El Paso, one of them long-haired, but he admitted that he had great difficulty in getting them acclimatized as, apparently, they did not stand up to the American winters at all well.

About the same time, however, others were becoming interested in Chihuahuas, and they also began to import them into the U.S.A. Very slowly the breed began to make regular appearances at dog shows in various parts of the country, and, as can easily be imagined, through this medium it gradually became widely known. Despite the astronomical registration figures it eventually totalled, its progress was never rapid and it cannot be said to have rocketed to popularity. Once known, however, it proved to have a great appeal to the people of the North American continent, an appeal that was divided between people interested in breeding and showing dogs, and those who wanted to keep one or two as pets.

So far as is known the first Chihuahua exhibited was at the Philadelphia Kennel Club show, held in September 1884. The dog was shown under the name 'Chihuahua Terrier', in a class confined to miscellaneous foreign dogs. It was awarded a 'Very Highly Commended'. It is entertaining to speculate on the reactions of the judge at this show, who must have been quite nonplussed at the sight of this novelty. It has been stated with some certainty that neither that particular judge, nor any of the others who officiated at shows when the breed was in its infancy there, had the slightest idea as to what were the good or the bad points of the breed.

Some years were to pass before a Champion Chihuahua was recorded. When this historic event did take place, the first Champion of Record under A.K.C. (American Kennel Club) rules was a dog named Beppie. He was owned and shown by Mrs McLean, of New Jersey, was born in February 1903, and was about two years of age when he was registered with the A.K.C. Even in 1904 only eleven Chihuahuas were exhibited in the whole of the U.S.A., and then only in variety classes for the most part. The number increased by degrees, but probably the most significant impetus was supplied when the Chihuahua Club of America was founded in the year 1923. This club has been one with a fine record of service to the breed, and it would be impossible to pay sufficient tribute to the founders and the people who have followed them. Their hard work and unflagging interest has brought the Chi to the popular position it occupies in America today.

Of the early breeding establishments the Meron kennel was the most famous. It was actually founded on a long-haired dog called Caranza, one of the first dogs owned by the pioneering Wister and Stewart partnership. A great many illustrious Champions carried the Meron name, the first being Ch. Little Meron, a fawn dog with cream shadings, and smooth-coated. In the main the Merons were smooths, though naturally there were some throwbacks to the original long-haired ancestor.

It must be appreciated that at this time pedigrees scarcely existed at all, and in many cases even the names of the parents were not known. Such pedigrees as could be produced were not all reliable, and seldom extended back for more than the preceding generation.

It was Mrs Ida Garrett who piloted the Merons to fame, and she did much for the breed when it was little known. She can fairly be described and remembered as the Chihuahua's 'fairy godmother'.

Another name to go up in lights was La Rex Doll. The Rex Doll strain was founded when Mrs Dorothy Atwood acquired some stock from Mrs Bertha Peaster. In the nineteen-twenties Mrs Peaster's stock which, in turn, stemmed from the Wister and Stewart imports, had a high reputation, and she is said to have exhibited some very good Chihuahuas. The La Rex Doll line is of interest because it is a solidly smooth-haired strain.

The nucleus of a kennel was gathered together by a Mr Mourman, from purchases from Mrs Garrett and Mrs Peaster. His prefix 'Minitura' is also considered to have played a very big part in the foundation of the dominant strains of the present time.

Other important names are the prefixes Don Rubio, Boo, Perrito, and the later great ones which carried the trade marks La Oro—which came into existence in 1930—Attas, Cola, and Muir, were followed by Don Apache, La Reina, Thurmer, Grudier, and Rhodes.

One of the most dominant of the definitely long-coated lines has come down to us from the first Don Sergio, bred by one Sarah Holland, of Massachusetts. Sergio was a long-coat with chocolate markings on a white ground; he was said to be very handsome, possessing ruby eyes and very good ears. He was small, weighing about 3 lb, and profusely coated. His record was a fine one, considering that he was not much used at stud, for he sired five long-haired Champions. His line eventually produced a celebrated and outstanding show specimen, Ch. Brazilian Brown Joy, and it is said to be the only remaining line that is absolutely pure long-coat. This may be perfectly true, but one would think that, considering the breed's hazy history and its admittedly varied ancestors, this is merely a figure of speech. Even if smooths did intermingle with the strain at some time or another, it seems that a very dominant long-coated strain, long-haired bred for many generations, was established from this source.

One milestone in the history of the breed was the Specialty Show, staged by the Chihuahua Club of America in 1946. The judge was the noted all-rounder Mr Forest N. Hall, and no fewer than seventy-six exhibits were entered for his selection.

Altogether that year was a memorable one, for the registrations at the American Kennel Club totalled 3,359, a rise of over a thousand above the previous year's figures. It was clear that the Chihuahua had arrived, and it was soon to fight for the place it now occupies at the top of the poll—America's most popular Toy breed, and its second most popular breed of dog. The only breed to keep ahead of the Chihuahua so far is the Beagle, and this breed's enormous total is achieved because so many packs are kept for hunting. These hounds have to be registered with the A.K.C., and only a minority are exhibited.

It was in 1946, too, that Mrs Anna Vinyard had the honour of owning the Chihuahua of the year, Ch. La Oro Damisela— clearly a beautiful bitch. Mrs Vinyard has become celebrated, not only for the number and quality of her large collection of Chihuahuas, but for her energy and enthusiasm. There can scarcely be a more widely travelled exhibitor, for she has exhibited her lovely little Champions in no fewer than eight different countries, with conspicuous success; surely a record hard to equal, for some made their titles and were Champions eight times over.

We salute all the early pioneers, even if present-day figures make the original entries seem small indeed. For instance, in 1958 a grand total of 5,685 Chihuahuas were entered at dog shows in the U.S.A. The proportion of this sizeable figure is interesting, because 4,062 were smooth-coated and 1,623 were long-haired. Of this number sixty-nine Smooths and fifty-eight Longs became Champions. Also in this year no fewer than twenty-five C.D. or C.D. ex. degrees—the awards for work in obedience trials—were gained by Chihuahuas.

While we are on the subject of American Champions, it is wise to learn something of their system of making titles, and where it differs from the system we have in Britain. Apart from a very small minority of shows, known as Match shows (which resemble our own Open shows and have nothing in common with matches as we know them in this country), all shows in the States are Championship shows. At such shows, all breeds exhibited can get 'points' towards their Championships, but only if sufficient dogs are actually exhibited in the ring to earn these points according to the rating fixed by the American Kennel Club.

Our own method, whereby the winning of Challenge Certificates gives a dog its title, is simplicity itself, and so the American Scheme seems rather complicated to most of us, not the least to judges from these shores who officiate on the other side. Those who are familiar with the Irish Kennel Club's Green Star system will probably more easily understand the U.S.A. awards, since basically the points are awarded in a similar fashion.

Under the A.K.C. rules the class winners parade before the judge, who then selects the best dog and the best bitch. These are referred to as 'Winners' dog, and 'Winners' bitch. Each will receive points towards the title of Champion, but the number of points varies according to the total exhibits of each sex. This is additionally complicated by the fact that the pair are matched, and one of them is rated 'Best of Winners'. If by the number of bitches entered, say the bitch is entitled to three points, and if, in the same manner, and with fewer dogs entered, the male is entitled to one point, and he is adjudged Best of Winners, he has beaten all the bitches and will automatically take the number of points which the female entry warrants. In the above hypothetical case it is three. But although the 'Winners' dog and 'Winners' bitch entrants cannot lose the points their wins have gained for them, they may not be awarded Best of Breed, for following the award of Best of Winners, the Champions, which may have been entered under the heading 'Specials', come into the ring. Best of Winners is judged against these, and as things work out one of the Champions usually gets the Best of Breed award. This entitles it to compete in the Toy Group, with all the other toy Best of Breed winners that may be at the show, and the Group winner goes on to the final judging for the Best in Show exhibit. If, by any chance, it is the Best of Winners which downs the opposition and gets the Best of Breed award, and if, by further good fortune, it wins the Group, then its points are stepped up if one of the defeated contestants from the other breeds has beaten an entry worth more points than the winner.

To anyone unfamiliar with the system it really takes some working out, especially when it is realized that the breeds have different rating according to their estimated popularity and numerical strength. It is clear, however, that in the American show world the Champions cannot keep the other budding Champs down, as happens in Britain.

Once a dog is a Champion in America he no longer wins 'Winner's points, but can enter only in the 'Specials' class. The next best exhibit can collect points until it, too, becomes a title-holder, is elevated to the company of the 'Specials', and leaves the way clear for its closest rival to collect points.

There is a lot to be said for the American method of awarding Championships, but on the whole I think that it is generally accepted that, at any rate in many breeds, it is easier to make a dog a Champion than it is in our own country. This is not necessarily because actual competition is less strong, although in fact they have fewer classes and, in general, far fewer entries than we do. But it does seem likely that the constant removal to the upper house of the best specimens, leaving the defeated exhibits to become Champions and, in turn, those behind them too, must result in at least some Champions being very inferior to others.

The manner in which the English Kennel Club's rules enable Champions to be made is very different. Certainly our method is not without its faults and virtues. The Kennel Club waits until a breed has substantial registration figures, made within a period of approximately three years, and then it removes the breed from the 'Any other variety' section, classifies it as a separate breed and grants Challenge Certificates for competition. The Certificates vary in number according to the registrations, but in many cases there are four sets allocated for the first championship show year.

A dog must win three Certificates, or 'C.C.s' as exhibitors call them, under three different judges, before it can win the title of Champion.

A judge awards a Certificate only if the exhibit is of 'outstanding merit' and the Certificate does not alter in value if there are few or many competitors.

A breed with registration figures totalling several hundred will probably be allotted C.C.s at twenty or more shows in a year. A dog can win any number of C.C.s, but these do not constitute a further title—they just add to honour and glory, and, incidentally, keep back other aspirants to the title of Champion.

This brief explanation is, however, necessary to explain why there are sometimes more Champions in the pedigree of an American import than is commonly found in the pedigrees of similarly well-bred dogs here.

THREE

HOW THE BREED STARTED IN
GREAT BRITAIN

BECAUSE the Chihuahua has made relatively rapid progress in the past two years it is difficult to appreciate that, after the last world war, it was virtually extinct in Britain.

True, it was never very well known in this country before 1939, but an effort was being made to popularize it, and the dog-showing community were well aware of its existence even if the general public did not know much about it

It is established that the breed was kept in this country really only as a pet, at the end of the last century, and it is thought that a few may have been brought in a good deal earlier; but the farther back we go the harder it is to find any record. A few old photographs have survived, however, and these include dogs that seem to be of definite Chihuahua type. One of them is thought to have been taken in Jersey, C.I., in the early part of the nineteenth century, and is in the possession of Mrs Gloria Hoar, a Chihuahua owner and breeder herself. It is an old-type photograph of a male relative of the breeder, and on his lap is a small dog which looks a typical Chi.

Some of the best evidence of the early imports has come to us direct from the late Miss Viva Montgomerie, who was born in 1879 and died as recently as 1959. Her memory was very clear right up to the time of her death, and she was always interested in Chihuahuas and enjoyed corresponding about them. She kept her first specimens about 1906. They were given to her by a Mrs Swindon, and had been smuggled into the country in the pockets of a sailor. Miss Montgomerie had, curiously enough, already seen the breed when she visited a dog show on Long Island, U.S.A. On that occasion she was told that they were wild dogs from Mexico, and of great value, being almost extinct. They were described to her as being a species of their own, not really true canines at all, excepting for their unusual intelligence. They were said to live in rabbit holes and to climb trees, also to be savage and difficult to catch. Fascinated by these diminutive curiosities, Miss Montgomerie tried to buy one immediately.

Even in those far-away days, however, when the purchasing value of the pound was so much greater than it is today, and when the average price of even the so-called 'valuable' dogs was very small by present standards, the price asked for a Chihuahua in America was the dollar equivalent of £100. Even a half-bred—and apparently such were available, though it is not disclosed what the non-Chihuahua half could have been—cost £25. Miss Montgomerie found the little dogs too expensive and returned to England without one, so it is easy to imagine her joy when she received some as gifts shortly after her return home.

Of course, there was no question of any pedigrees with the Chihuahuas she acquired in this manner, but she bred a number of puppies from them and some she gave to friends. They came in all colours, though fawn was the most usual. Miss Montgomerie describes them as hardy little hunters, and says that they could not be taken anywhere near a rabbit warren or they would disappear underground. Many times they had to be dug out, experiences which their devoted mistress found terrifying, as one can well understand. The original pair, of only 3 lb weight, used to follow behind her bicycle for as much as five miles. One of them, devoted to her sailor cousin, used to wait for hours on the beach, shivering with cold, until his master returned from a boating expedition. Yet they were never any the worse for these experiences. Miss Montgomerie went to great pains to emphasize that her dogs were far from being fragile or pampered, and she had no time for some of the modern Chihuahuas which, she considered, compared unfavourably with her own. She emphasizes how wonderfully clever and teachable her original dogs were. The last tiny one died in 1925 at the age of thirteen. She claimed that one of her little Chihuahuas, called 'Scrap', had seen a ghost, and a story about this incident, and facts leading up to the animal's odd behaviour, got into several of the newspapers.

Viva Montgomerie gave a tricoloured male dog to an aunt, and it was known as 'Tric', for it was hound-marked in black, white, and tan. It was a little larger than most of the others, and was a most devoted pet, never leaving its owner, and was found on her bed when she died. At this sad time it was decided to find Tric a home with a lady in Suffolk, who had just lost her own dog, and by the end of a week Tric seemed quite happy and settled; everybody there loved him, and the arrangement seemed a most suitable one. However, he suddenly slipped out of a side door and vanished, and as it was during a period of bitter winter weather nobody expected to get the little fellow back alive. There was snow on the ground and a biting wind was blowing, and poor Tric had been used to spending most of his time snuggled up in an invalid's eiderdown. Yet, to everyone's astonishment he was found, safe and sound. He had strayed until he made friends with a big dog, whose food and kennel he shared for a day or so, and then wandered farther and farther afield until he had almost reached Cambridge. Exhausted, he followed a woman who took pity on him, brought him to her home, and cared for him until he was claimed by the police. In all he was lost for ten days before he was recovered, but he went back to Miss Montgomerie after these adventures, becoming, she said, 'more precious than he had ever been before'. He lived to the great age of eighteen years. This story certainly supports the belief that the original Chihuahuas were exceedingly tough and hardy.

I am indebted to Mrs Watts-Russell, a well-known breeder of Welsh Corgis, who, knowing my interest in Chihuahuas, sent me an old photograph from her collection of family treasures. It includes several little dogs of marked Chihuahua type, four smooth-haired and one long-coated. The photograph is thought to have been taken about 1908, and Mrs Watts-Russell writes: 'My aunt Alice Hillingdon had more than the five shown in the picture, and certainly her sisters, Lady Musgrave and Lady Sullivan, had the Chihuahuas too. I rather think that Queen Alexandra may have had some, as they were all in the same clique.'

In 1954 Mrs Wells contacted Lady Violet Thesiger who, in a letter dated February 1st, wrote:

. . . about Chihuahua dogs . . . I wish I could tell you more about them—or that I had a photo of the fascinating little lady we brought over from Mexico fifty years ago! I only had her with me for a few months as we really brought her home for old Lady Hillingdon. She was an exquisite little creature and so intelligent and affectionate, with beautifully made, tiny body, huge eyes, and those lovely shell-like, pink-lined ears. Colour a lovely white and fawn, pure bred. Dona Sol of Belamie is exactly like the one I brought over.

This last observation is interesting, suggesting as it does that the type had altered little or not at all in the span of fifty years.

Mrs Watts-Russell's photograph of Lady Hillingdon with her five Chi's does not contain one that really fits the word-picture above. Perhaps they were its progeny, or had been obtained from another source, or had preceded it.

Another early contact with the breed has been made through the Hon. Mrs Gwendolen Bourke, who kindly wrote to the author early in 1960 regarding her experiences with Chihuahuas. Her letter reads:

In 1897 I went to see a dealer about a dog, but I did not like it, and among a crowd of other dogs was this tiny thing, begging to be taken away and climbing on my lap. About 3½ lb—the size of those I saw at the Henley dog show the other day—a bitch, cream in colour. I paid £3 for it, not knowing what it was any more than the dealer, nor where he had got it. One evening we played croquet from 5 to 7 p.m., the little dog in her basket on the edge of the lawn. We went in to dress for dinner, I saw she was not there and sent servants through the village asking everyone if they had seen her. It was not until we were half-way through dinner that the footman told me they had found her, drowned in a small fish-pond hidden in long grass beyond the lawn. A friend of Adele, Lady Essex, of Cassiobury Park, Watford, brought three of these dogs over from Mexico, and she gave me a tiny black and tan with bulgy eyes. I did not care about it, and gave it to my cook who adored it, but it did not live long; I do not think she kept it warm enough.

Mrs John Southworth is known to have brought a pair of Chihuahuas to this country some time prior to the 1914–18 war. She had resided in Mexico for many years, during which time she made frequent trips to this country. At times she smuggled the Chihuahuas in in the sleeves of her fur coat or in her muff, to avoid putting them into quarantine! Modern breeders, do not copy! One of these tiny dogs did not survive very long when Mrs Southworth settled in England, but the other, known as 'Major', had a long and happy life, and those who remember him say that his intelligence and personality were amazing. In the picture that exists of Major, he looks very small and exceedingly dainty. He was white, with a brown head and brown patches on his body.

Mrs Southworth was a relation by marriage of the writer, and it was after she had died that some minute collars and coats which her Chihuahuas had worn were found among her effects.

It can be said that these triggered off the author's latent and ever-increasing desire to own a Chi, for it seemed a pity not to put the elegant little bequests to some use. If they had not been handed down it is possible that there would never have been any 'Rozavel' Chihuahuas.

It was in 1923 that the well-known writer on canine matters, Mr Will Hally, wrote the following in the weekly publication *Our Dogs*:

I learn from Miss Lovett (who has charge of Captain Williams's Leysfield Kennels) that she has a Chihuahua dog in quarantine, due to emerge in February (1924). Miss Lovett is extremely anxious to start this breed in Britain, and she imported three bitches in August last, but they unfortunately died in quarantine. That was a big loss from every point of view, for as Miss Lovett herself says, Chihuahuas 'are expensive little beasts to secure on the other side' and so, unless some enterprising American thinks of sending over some with a view to establishing them here, Miss Lovett fears she will have to remain content with the one dog in the meantime.

I hear, however, that there is another kennel in England which contains two Chihuahua bitches, so a little patience may eventually go a long way.

Miss Lovett's idea is to secure three good bitches, and another dog, while her ambitions include the importation of a brace of unrelated long-haired Chihuahuas.

It would seem that poor Miss Lovett's high hopes did not materialize, because nothing was heard of a foundation kennel until Mrs Powell decided to make a start in the breed.

References to the Chihuahua, over the years, seem to have been scarce, but it must be assumed that it was quite well known to a public of some sort because as early as 1916 a cartoon appeared in an issue of *Vogue* published on December 15th. This was drawn by the celebrated artist whose pseudonym was 'Fish', and it showed a fashionable woman leading a trio of very small dogs, one of which was clearly supposed to be a Chi. It has the exaggerated ears, and is wearing a coat. The caption read:

The only trouble with marrying a rich wife is that, when you sign up for life you are handed a leather leash along with the wedding certificate. Put a metal collar on your neck and a little red velvet blanket around your middle and you might just as well be Yami, or Sing Hi, or Chihuahua, the only three things in the world that your female meal-ticket really seems to love.

We do not know how Mrs Powell came to hear of the breed, whether it was through Miss Lovett, or from some other source, but she was already a dog breeder, with a particular interest in Griffon Bruxellois. Her early imports, consisting of a dog and a bitch, came over from the U.S.A. in 1934. Four days after her arrival, the bitch whelped four puppies in quarantine, and two of these survived.

The late Mr Croxton Smith, a foremost writer on all subjects connected with dogs, and a Championship show judge of many breeds, was always specially interested in unusual breeds. He wrote about the new arrivals in *The Sporting and Dramatic News*, the issue dated October 5th, 1934. Heading the paragraph 'Exotic Little Strangers', he commented upon the breed in general and made special reference to the two puppies that Mrs Powell had just taken out of quarantine.

In the same magazine, and from the same pen, we find yet another paragraph on the breed, this time with a picture of three Chihuahuas owned by Mrs Powell. This appeared in March 1937, and the dogs all look very typical and even in size. One seems to be a red-fawn, one white with either black or dark chocolate and tan markings, the other also white, with light fawn patches. The caption beneath the photograph refers to them as 'the first of their kind seen here for forty years', which in view of what we know about the number scattered about the country towards the end of the nineteenth century and during the first twenty-five years of the present one is a statement that is open to dispute. The dogs are not named in this picture, but one supposes them to be the original imports from the U.S.A., whose names were Idas-conja, Betsy, and Mona II.

There is a slightly later photograph of Mrs Powell's stock, taken on the occasion of the British Dog Breeders Show at the White City, London, in April 1938. The only information we get with the picture is that the dogs are three years old. It shows a pair of Chihuahuas, probably cream or light fawn in colour and, judged by present-day standards, very nice specimens indeed, with extremely typical heads.

It was about this time that Miss J. Macalister was becoming interested in Chihuahuas, and had acquired some of Mrs Powell's breeding.

In the world of dogs it is generally risky to make a statement that an individual has created a record, or was the first to achieve something; someone is almost certain to challenge the claim, dispute it, and profess to have been the pioneer. So we will accept the fact that while Mrs Powell was almost certainly the first person to exhibit Chihuahuas consistently, it is possible that a Chi or two may have been shown from time to time in all-breed classes.

As we have already stated, Mrs Powell was not a novice breeder. She had bred Griffons with some success, and this was mentioned in one of Mr Croxton Smith's articles, when he quoted her as saying that she fed and managed her new

Chihuahua imports on exactly the same lines, and wished to counteract any impression that Chihuahuas were a delicate breed.

However, this lady's hard work and devoted efforts on the breed's behalf were doomed to be terminated in the most brutal and tragic manner. Her home on Clapham Common was destroyed by a bomb when the last war was in progress. All her beloved little dogs perished, and Mrs Powell herself was left a helpless invalid for the few remaining years of her life.

At the end of the war a few Chihuahuas still survived, and they were those which Mrs Powell had bred and sold. One of these was Austral Zorello, born in 1938 and owned by Mrs Gee, a well-known breeder of Papillons. Another was Austral Followon, born April 1st, 1940, a cream-coloured dog by Hechicero Meron out of Betsy. He was still alive in 1948, and was owned by Mrs Wilson, of Burford, Oxfordshire.

Miss Macalister, that enthusiastic early pioneer, also had a bitch called 'Conchita of Manorgreen'. She was very typical, but was disfigured by a wry jaw, caused by a fracture. Efforts were made to mate her with Austral Followon, but the result was a disappointment. 'Chita kept everyone guessing, going through all the motions of a pregnancy, with no puppies at the end of it.

Mrs Dora Wells, whose Belamie prefix is so famous everywhere, was another who was becoming keen on the Chihuahua breed. She succeeded in tracing an elderly gentleman who lived in Hampstead, who had a lovely little white male dog. Hopes ran high, but alas! this little dog suffered from a weak heart, as a result of bombing raids, and would have been a hopeless proposition as a stud dog.

One big setback followed another, and in fact there turned out to be a clean break between the pre-1939 imports, and the stock which eventually resuscitated the breed when hostilities came to an end. Happily, although there were disappointments and difficulties, the later efforts were considerably more successful and the breed was given a secure foothold which was rapidly strengthened and consolidated.

Mrs Gott will always be remembered as one who played a

great part in the building of the Chi in this country. She had a tiny Chihuahua which she had kept for some years, and which she had acquired through a relative who bought it from a foreigner in a London bar. The price paid was £50, which was high for a dog without a pedigree. It was a little bitch, and Mrs Gott was devoted to it. With a view to breeding, it was introduced to one of Mrs Powell's dogs but as the male appeared huge beside the little female, it seems that Mrs Gott was somewhat apprehensive and unenthusiastic about the affair, and when the mating was not achieved she said she felt rather thankful.

She decided, instead, to import some stock, and secured a pair at just about the time that Mrs Wells's celebrated Am. Ch. Mi Pedro Juan of Belamie and Doña Sol of Belamie had been released from quarantine. Mrs Gott's brace came from kennels owned by Mrs Stock, of California, U.S.A., and, like the two which Mrs Wells had obtained, were destined to go down in the breed's history, for they all four proved to be of great value as producers. Their names are still found in the pedigrees of many present-day winners, and some of the leading Champions are descended from them.

It was actually in March 1949 that Mrs Gott bred the first registered bitch puppy, Una of Phoenix. The name is such a prophetic one that we wonder if it was specially chosen? It presumably came from Phoenix Cottage, the name of Mrs Gott's home. The phoenix is the bird that rises from flames and ashes, and surely the first Chihuahua born out of this long era of devastation and destruction was truly named. Mrs Gott was the first of the postwar owners to have her dogs on television. Her daughter, Mrs Secker, appeared with them in the programme 'Picture Page', presented by Leslie Mitchell and Joan Gilbert.

But Mrs Gott had decided views about the future of the breed. She visualized it as rare and exclusive, as indeed it was at that time, and she did not want it to become too popular. Consequently, she never sought much publicity for the tinies.

Mrs Wells held opposite views. She felt that there were several good reasons why efforts should be made to bring the breed's attractions to the public notice, and she had hopes that it would become widely appreciated. To this end, she never missed a chance of writing to the papers about Chihuahuas, or of doing anything that could bring the breed the attention and admiration she felt it so rightly deserved.

During the last war Mrs Lydia Cross had the good fortune to come upon a black-and-tan bitch, which she got from a Canadian officer. She was a little larger than average, and had a natural bob-tail, something very rare indeed. For some time, Mrs Cross was quite unable to find a mate for Palace Bambi, as she was called, and it was not until the summer of 1949 that she bred her first litter by Mrs Gott's dog, Sunstock Jollo.

Suddenly, it seemed, things were beginning to move fast, for in the spring of 1950 Mrs Horner managed to import three. The anticipation and excitement with which these new arrivals were met was tremendous, and what an encouragement it was to the little band of enthusiasts who felt that at last they were overcoming some of the many handicaps which had to date bedevilled efforts to establish the breed on this side of the Atlantic.

It was not to be all plain sailing, however, for a sad blow was dealt when Miss Macalister died in the summer of 1949. She had just been instrumental in helping to form the new British Chihuahua Club, and had accepted the position of Honorary Secretary. Her death was the sadder because she passed on just as her work for the breed was bearing fruit, and the results of her hitherto depressing and often frustrated efforts becoming really encouraging to her and her associates.

The formation of a club for the breed in Britain took place in May 1949, and marked a great step forward in Chihuahua history. Even so, numbers, both of interested parties and of individual specimens, were still very low, and about this time Mrs Wells felt obliged to appeal yet again through the medium of the late Mrs Phyllis Robson's columns in the weekly *Dog World*, for news of any Chihuahuas that might be in the country.

As was feared and rather expected, the response served only to emphasize the fact that there were still few Chihuahuas available. The breed was by no means in a healthy position, and breeders were going to remain badly handicapped unless things altered rapidly. At that time the outlook was not cheerful, and it speaks much for the tenacity and steadfastness of purpose of the club's foundation members that they never ceased in their efforts to assist and promote the breed. That these efforts brought results is now apparent to all, but newcomers who are unfamiliar with the details of the early struggles might fail, if the facts were not stressed, to appreciate how much is owed to these people. Many of us who get untold pleasure from owning Chihuahuas might never have done so but for them.

FOUR

THE FOUNDATION STOCK

SINCE 1950, when importations of Chihuahuas into Britain began to increase, two or three have come from Mexico, and quite a number from the U.S.A.

The first long coated specimens to reach this country were Ch. Cholderton Little Scampy of Teeny Wee, and Ch. Nellistar Schaefer's Taffy Boy. Until they arrived, all the imported stock were smooth haired.

Mrs. Gott might fairly claim to be the first real post-war breeder. Her favourite was a handsome apricot-fawn bitch, acquired from Major Mundey's kennel in Mexico. Tarahumara, as she was named, was a gentle creature, different in type from the modern Chi, but excelling in the size of her ears and her beautiful, luminous eyes. Unfortunately, she proved to be a non-breeder.

The other Mexican import in Mrs. Gott's kennel was a male named Tolteca, a white fellow with fawn patches. In contrast to his lady friend he was a prolific producer and a great stud force. He also had a fiery Mexican temper and was a savage little devil, a veritable 'wild dog', which seemed to boost Major Mundey's theories.

From the Sunstock Kennels, owned by Mrs. Stock of California, U.S.A., came Sunstock Jollo and Sunstock Systy. Jollo was not as good-looking as the bitch Systy, and he sired only three litters before retiring to live with Mrs. Gott's sister in Sussex. Systy, however, was destined to have quite a far-reaching effect on the breed. She was an excellent brood bitch, and numbered among her progeny Mrs. Forster's Jofos Millinita and Mrs. Fearfield's Bowerhinton Margareta. These two did particularly well when mated to Bowerhinton Chico of Belamie.

59

It was a little later that Mrs. Gott began to register her stock with her own kennel name 'Munsun', the prefix being a home-made one, a mixture of the words 'Sunstock' and 'Mundey'. Both Millinita and Margareta were, directly and indirectly, responsible for several Champions, some of them of the very best type even though neither of the above-named sisters was a beauty.

Even with this valuable material, however, Mrs Gott did not have an easy time of it with her dogs. She suffered some tragic losses when her stock was ravaged by an epidemic of hard-pad at a time when inoculations for protection against the viruses common at that period were unreliable and often ineffective. Disease was rife among dogs and it was, unhappily, very easy to pick up infection at shows.

Mrs Wells's brace came from the U.S.A. and had a rather mysterious and romantic origin. They arrived in October 1947, and had previously been the pets of Lady T. A. Wernher in New York. She had had Doña Sol from puppyhood, direct from the breeder, Mrs S. Febles, of N.Y., but, it was afterwards thought, did not bother to have her registered. The breeder died, and it was never possible to trace Dona Sol's pedigree, as her name was chosen for her by her original owner and was not recorded at the American Kennel Club. Following Doña Sol, Lady Wernher acquired Am. Ch. Mi Pedro Juan, already adult and a Champion. Following her death her husband and daughter came to England, bringing the little dogs with them. Just about the time they were due to be released from quarantine, Sir D. J. Wernher also died suddenly and tragically. The poor little dogs were left in boarding kennels for most of the rest of the year, and seemed to be nobody's interest or responsibility until Mrs Wells heard about them and persuaded Miss Wernher to sell them to her. She was promised the pedigrees when they came to light, as they were said to be stored away in a warehouse. In spite of repeated applications over a period of years, however, Mrs Wells was unable to trace Doña's ancestry. It was established that Pedro was in the American Kennel Club Stud Book, and eventually, in a most complicated and roundabout way, Mrs Wells succeeded in obtaining his pedigree. In the meantime, both had been

Ch. Raygistaan Toy Train

Ch. Rozavel Hasta La Vista

C. M. Cooke

The bitch winner, Ch. Bowerhinton Isabela, and the dog winner,
Ch. Rozavel Diaz, are awarded the first Challenge Certificates—
the author on the right

Three generations in one photograph. All are Champions and/or
parents of Champions

Fox Photos

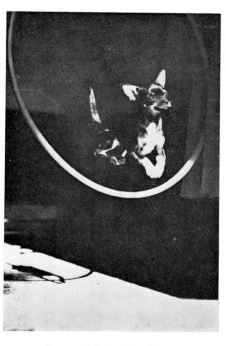

Sport and General

Rozavel Mambo shows
her paces

Ch. Rozavel Tarina
Song

Two Chihuahuas take a swim in the lake

Am. Ch. Mi Pedro Juan of Belamie, Tizoc of Belamie, and Doña Sol of Belamie

Thomson Picture Service

Ch. Rozavel Astra

C. M. Cooke

registered with the English Kennel Club as 'pedigree and particulars unknown', but it was possible to correct this in the case of Pedro. They were no longer young when they passed into Mrs Wells's hands, and she bred only one litter from the pair. There were two dogs and a bitch, and it is easy to imagine how the latter was treasured, and how great was the shock and disappointment when she died from distemper at the age of seven months.

It was miraculous that Tizoc did not succumb. Chico had already gone to Mrs Fearfield, so these two great stud forces were preserved for the benefit of the breed. They were the first two dog puppies to be registered at the start of the surge of progress that took place in 1949, and in due course their progeny dominated the prize lists for a considerable time. It is probably safe to say that either or both appears in about 75 per cent of all the pedigrees we see.

Mrs Wells also obtained another bitch of some consequence, Linda Mia II of Belamie. She bought her from a returned 'G.I. bride' when Linda had already been through quarantine, and it took her a year to persuade the owner to part with her. Even then, it was made conditional that Mrs Wells should buy all her other dogs as well, because she was ill and could no longer keep them, so to obtain the Chihuahua she also became owner of a Dachshund, a Miniature Poodle, and an American Cocker Spaniel, none of which she really wanted. Linda came from a well-known kennel owned by Mrs Pearl Robinson, of San Antonio, Texas, one time Secretary of the Chihuahua Breeders Association out there.

Mrs Lydia Cross who, it will be remembered, had obtained a bitch from a Canadian officer, overjoyed at having discovered a mate for Palace Bambi, took her to Sunstock Jollo, and the result of this long-awaited union was a charming red bitch, named, in the first instance, Chicata. She was undoubtedly the best bitch of her time, and as such was a well-known prize-winner. She later became the property of a new recruit to the ranks of Chi enthusiasts, Mrs M. Rider, who added her kennel prefix 'Rowley' to Chicata's name. Unfortunately, she was not a prolific breeder, but mated to Ch. Rozavel Diaz she produced two red dogs, and one of these, Bronze Idol of

Rowley, is found in some pedigrees and perpetuates her name.

Palace Bambi was also mated to Tizoc of Belamie and was the dam of the noted winner and winner-producer, Jofos Ferronita; also of Palacecourt Queen Zamira. The latter is known to us as the dam of one of the most successful brood bitches we have had in the breed to date, Mrs Ellis-Hughes's black-and-tan Mixcoac.

Of Mrs Horner's original imports, the stud dog Pepito IX is probably most noteworthy. He was sired by a dog which rejoiced in the short and snappy name of Jiggs, reputed to be the smallest stud dog of its day in America, whence came Pepito IX; so it is not really to be wondered that he earned a name for himself as a sire of small, smart stock. His most noted son is undoubtedly Ch. Denger's Don Armando, which Mrs Wells bought as a young puppy and had the pleasure of showing to his Championship.

The first-ever Chihuahua registered with the Kennel Club, then at its premises at 84 Piccadilly, London, was a bitch named Topsy, described as 'sable' and classified as 'Foreign Dog—Chihuahua'. The registration date was July 25th, 1907. Topsy's date of birth, breeder, and parentage were not disclosed, and she was owned by Mrs I. Boddy, of Southsea, Hants. Pure supposition, of course, but Southsea is near Portsmouth. Was Topsy another brought in secretly in a sailor's pocket? We will never know.

Although we hear of other Chihuahuas kept as pets, also bred, over the period, they apparently went unrecorded because no more were registered until seventeen years had elapsed, and then it was a black-and-tan male that was registered by Mrs Kovett, of Buckinghamshire, in 1924. He was called Sorta Solo.

One year later two bitches were registered by Mrs McColl, of Earls Court, London. Rather more is known about this pair, because one, a black-and-white, was sired by Tula Nigger, out of Tula Palma, and her name was Kinaultrae Lula. She was bred by Mrs R. Bedford (not to be confused with Mrs M. Bedford whose Cholderton prefix is so much to the fore at the present time).

The other was a fawn, Kinaultrae Novia, bred by Mrs Adams, and by Nigretto out of Tula Nowada.

It is rather astonishing, really, that following the registration of these two bitches, yet another gap ensued until Mrs Powell's importations began arriving. In fact, throughout the lengthy period extending from the year 1907 to 1940, only thirty-nine Chihuahuas were registered.

The sparsity of these registrations, especially during the last six years of the gap, may have been due to the fact that Mrs Powell in no way suffered from the 'complaint' which is often referred to as 'kennel-blindness', an imaginary affliction which prevents people from seeing faults in their stock. On the contrary, Mrs Powell had set herself a standard, and knew exactly what type of Chihuahua she wanted to breed. If any of her puppies fell short of her ideal, she gave them away as pets, making it conditional that they were not to be used for exhibition or breeding. Consequently, a proportion of the youngsters she bred were thus discarded and not registered at all. Thus, in 1949, only eight Chihuahuas were registered, and this entire number by only two owners.

Quite suddenly, however, the position altered. When the increase began, the registration figures soared. Five hundred and thirty Chihuahuas were registered in 1957 alone, and between 1949 and 1957, inclusive, the total was 1,500.

In 1953 the writer imported a bitch from the La Oro Kennel owned by Mrs Anna Vinyard, in Cincinnati, Ohio. U.S.A. This was Rozavel La Oro Sena de Oro, a daughter of the fabulous Eight-countries International Champion La Oro Alino de Tortilla de Oro. Mrs Vinyard had just secured a dog called Salender's Darro Pharche for outcross breeding purposes, and Sena was mated to him before she flew to England. The litter, awaited with almost breathless anticipation, was born in quarantine kennels at Hatfield, Hertfordshire, and consisted of three males. This was something of a disappointment since bitches were still almost unprocurable in England, and anyway a female of this special breeding would have been a great mainstay to the newly founded Rozavel family of Chihuahuas. Still, in view of the many hazards which accompany the importation of a bitch in whelp, it was exciting to have got the trio of sturdy little boys.

Their future was eagerly anticipated, and was not unjustified since one of their number became Britain's first-ever Chihuahua Champion, Rozavel Diaz. The slightly larger brother, Rozavel Juarez, was unfortunately a less productive sire, and the smallest and most exquisite of the lot, a very tiny apricot with a marvellous head, proved a non-stock-getter. Very soon afterwards, Rozavel La Oro Memoria de Ora came over from the same American kennel. She was also mated before shipment, but alas! she was found to be not in whelp when she arrived. The third mated bitch from La Oro was Rozavel Irra Pettina. She produced one dog puppy in quarantine, also by Salender's Darro Pharche, and what her litter lacked in quantity it made up for in quality, for this single puppy grew into Ch. Rozavel Francisco.

Just about this time Mrs Jean Rawson, of the Brownridge Kennels, Yorkshire, received a very small chocolate-and-tan dog, named Brandman's Modelo, from the kennels of Mrs Thelma Brandman, New York. This strikingly attractive little fellow made a very good start in the show ring, his successes including the Challenge Certificate at the West of England Ladies Kennel Association's Championship show at Cheltenham, in the late spring of 1954. Tragedy followed, however, for very shortly afterwards he was run over and killed by a lorry in the drive just outside his home. What made this loss even more disastrous was the fact that he had mated only one bitch since his release from quarantine, and then only one puppy resulted. The puppy, named Rozavel Miguel, did however survive to allow his ill-fated sire to make some impact on the breed, because many good winners were born by him and he did a great deal of winning himself. Miguel proved to be one of those interesting dogs whose grand-children and great-grand-children appear to be better than the immediate progeny, and such sires, taking the long view, are very valuable to a breed.

Now, the imports were really arriving fast. Mrs Cross, who had a well-known kennel of Yorkshire Terriers under her prefix 'Kelsbro'' (and who, incidentally, is no relation to Mrs

Lydia Cross of the Palace Court Chihuahuas), created a great sensation by bringing over two American Champions. The tiny chocolate-and-tan Dugger's Spice, and a sable-red male. Both were bred by Mrs Cecilia Dugger. Spice got off to a good start and did a tremendous amount of winning, at one time holding the record for the number of Challenge Certificates won by a Chihuahua, but Mrs Cross was disappointed in the dog and sent him back to the U.S.A.

Following her spectacular show career, Spice was sold to Mrs K. Stuart, who had founded her Kaitonia kennel of Chihuahuas not long before. Unfortunately, none of her owners ever succeeded in breeding from Spice, which left the breed the poorer, since she could have passed on some of her many virtues.

Mrs Huxham, better known at the time for her winning Toy Poodles, brought over a bright red dog called Emmrill Son-Ko's Red Rocket. Rocket was consistently in the cards, but it was as a sire that he excelled, proving himself a most dependable producer of puppies with exceptionally good heads, and, usually, of very diminutive size. Rocket died accidentally while still a young dog, and his death was a most serious loss to the breed. Mrs Huxham tried to replace him by purchasing a golden-fawn dog, Emmrill Buck's Peppie, but she had very little luck with this one also. He showed great promise as a sire, and several of his sons and daughters are winning very well indeed, but he was not the most reliable of producers, and at times concerned his owner by seeming to feel the recurrent effects of his spell in quarantine. He died suddenly of heart failure after only about two years in this country, and in view of the quality of his best son and daughter, he was yet another loss to British breeders.

Mrs Vinyard, learning of the disappointment caused by Memoria's failure to produce a litter in quarantine, kindly presented the Rozavel kennel with a promising bitch puppy by the great Alino-La Oro Medida de Ora. Medida proved a very bad whelper, however, and although one of her sons is used at stud from time to time she did not produce anything of note.

In 1955 the writer was asked to judge Chihuahuas at a show

on Long Island, U.S.A. A tour of some of the kennels out there inevitably led to temptations, and seven bitches, five of them mated before dispatch, were flown over and put into quarantine. It typifies the handicaps of importing breeds, and the snags that beset the importer, when it is recorded that from this entire team of bitches, five mated to carefully chosen stud dogs on the other side, only one live puppy emerged from quarantine, and this was a dog that proved to be sterile. The star of the septet was undoubtedly Canadian and American Champion Rozavel Char-Els Cissie Maria, a bitch with a fine record of wins in two countries, and destined to considerable success over here. She was bred by Mrs C. Dugger, but was a disappointing breeder, whelping only one bitch puppy (itself malformed and impossible to mate) before undergoing an operation which precluded her having any more puppies.

Karlena's Chocolate Chips, a tiny and lovely-headed white with chocolate markings, was sold to Mrs Twining of the Hacienda Chihuahuas shortly after her release from quarantine, and she has been breeding from her with some success. A fairly large white bitch, Rozavel Karlena's Bambi, was the only one of the party which was not a top show specimen, but she had been specially acquired because she was bred on similar lines to the late lamented Brandman's Modelo, and it was hoped it might be possible to try a scheme of planned line-breeding. She did in fact produce some winners by Modelo's only son, and by other sires. Rozavel Virginia's Pumpkin, a most gorgeous-headed white bitch, never bred, although every possible thing, including artificial insemination, was tried.

It was the blue, white, and tan imports, however, which really created the biggest sensation, especially when they made their Championship show début at Cruft's. They consisted of Ch. Rozavel Shaw's Violet, a beautiful tiny bitch which always distinguished herself by her wins in Variety classes, including several Best in Show awards in very strong company. She has not been a prolific breeder to date, but her sister, from an earlier litter, Rozavel Shaw's Constance, while not a Champion, but a very good winner, has already had considerable influence for good. Constance is the dam of Ch. Rozavel Humo, Amondso Rozavel Justo, and one or two others.

For some time Mrs Rawson had been hoping to replace Brandman's Modelo, and from the same kennel she purchased Brandman's Modelo's Memory and his sister, Brandman's Brownridge Chatito II.

The pair were rich reds, and have already made names for themselves through the winners they have produced, among them the beautiful tiny bitch that has done so much to make Chihuahuas known in Sweden—Int. Ch. Aku Aku Brownridge Birthday Toy.

Miss Russell-Allen's importations merit almost a chapter to themselves. They number, in all, about seventeen, a few of which unfortunately died in quarantine, and some after release. In 1951 Dalhabboch Chichimeca Mundey, bred by Major Mundey and a full sister to Tolteca, followed her brother to this country about six months later. Another from the same breeder, Quetzalcoatl Mundey, sister to Mrs Gott's Tara, was imported in 1953. Two 1954 imports both died in quarantine, but six came over in 1955. These were Dalhabboch Luce's Blue Snuggle Bunny, Anneray's Lady Magnolia, Luce's Lady Blue, Seko King, Luce's Little King Blue, and Grosarts Corky. The last three are especially notable, Seko King for stamping his progeny with marvellous heads and producing some very tiny specimens, including two Champions; King Blue for siring the hard-to-get blues to a few of his bitches; and Corky who has produced one Champion to date. Anneray's Blue Dahlia joined the Dalhabboch kennel in 1956, and in 1957, came no fewer than six long-hairs, all from the Anneray's kennel.

Lady Margaret Drummond-Hay imported a white dog, Kirstie's Little Strutter, and a bitch, Pearsons Angela La Ora, which whelped a litter in quarantine, sired by Am. Ch. Allen's Snowball. A dog puppy from this litter, Int. Ch. Seggieden Jupiter, did a great deal of winning and sired the well-known Int. Ch. Seggieden Tiny Mite.

Many of the imports and their progeny were, as was to be expected, bred to dogs and bitches of the strongly line-bred and inbred Tizoc, Chico, and Dengers lines, and the results in many cases were good. Early in 1960 Mrs Forster's importation, Am. Ch. El Juguete's Ringmaster, was released from quarantine, a small golden dog bred by Mr J. Brown, U.S.A.

He is the first male Champion to be imported from the U.S.A., apart from Mrs Cross's dog, which did not remain in this country, and Mrs Wells's dog which was not known to be a Champion till after it had died.

In spite of the fact that perfection was still a long way away, it became clear at this point that the overall standard of quality was improving. It was realized that at last a wide selection of varied bloodlines was available, and that breeders had only to use these wisely to establish the breed on the same plane of excellence as other breeds in England, the acknowledged land of skilled breeders of livestock.

THE LONG-HAIRED CHIHUAHUA

Some of the very earliest references to Chihuahuas include both smooth-coated and long-coated varieties. This rather negatives the recurrent suggestion that the 'longs' have been produced by crossing 'smooths' with another breed—and the dog named is usually the Papillon.

It is very probable that this breed and Chihuahuas have some basic connection, perhaps as far back as the Spanish conquest, for we are told that dogs with similarities common to both the Papillons and the fluffy Chi's were known in that country in past centuries.

The two coats have been consistently interbred, but it is curious that the early smooth imports of the nineteen-thirties, and those of the more immediate post-war period, threw no longs. The more so because most of the smooth lines sometimes produce longs from time to time in these days, and there have been many long-coats born from two smooth parents. It was a great surprise to owners when these longs began popping up in what were expected to be solidly smooth-coated litters, and they began to do so only when the rush of importations started in about 1955, and after. It has now become quite common for a fluffy puppy or two to emerge from a mating between two smooths.

Some long-coats have been imported, the best known by Mrs M. Bedford, Mrs Erskine, and Mrs Frei-Denver.

The first long-haired exhibits to achieve real distinction were Mrs Erskine's Ch. Nellistar Schaefer's Taffy Boy, and Mrs Bedford's Ch. Cholderton Little Scampy of Teeny Wee. Both males were imported from the U.S.A.

The two types of coat were not, for a time, recognized as separate varieties by our Kennel Club, although the American Kennel Club long ago sanctioned separate classes for smooths and long-coats.

Eventually, the Kennel Club acceded to the wishes of the breeders and, deciding that long-coated Chihuahuas were being registered in sufficient numbers to justify the move, gave them a separate register. Breeders had to return all registration cards to Clarges Street, indicating the coat type and the variety under which each animal should be recorded. Although much of the effort to get the Kennel Club to make this change came from long-coat lovers, supporters of the smooths welcomed the division. Many were of the opinion that it was hardly fair to judge their exhibits in the same classes as the longs, since the faults on the smooth are so easily seen and are so impossible to hide. During this major upheaval within the breed's circle, a new club was born with the interests of the one variety at heart—and it is known as the Long-coat Chihuahua Club.

The first Championship show at which the two types had separate sets of Challenge Certificates was Crufts 1965. One important matter had to be settled, and it concerned the question of inter-breeding between the two coats. Breeders wondered, rather anxiously, whether smooth to long matings, and vice versa, would still be permissible. They also wanted to know what would happen when long-coat and smooth-coat puppies appeared in a single litter—a very common occurrence. The Kennel Club decided that, puppies must be registered under the heading of the variety they most closely resembled, and that Chihuahuas would, at any rate for the time being, be included in the small list of breeds which were permitted to interbreed. In so far as there is a preference for one variety as opposed to the other, most breeders include both in their kennels, and only a few specialize. Those who prefer the smooths have a point when they say that they can see no great advantage in having a dog cluttered up with hair when the same thing is available sleek and tailored. The long-coat lovers retort by saying that the smooths appear, to them, rather naked looking! and that they admire the profuse feathering of the heavy coated type.

At one time it was commonly thought that long-coated Chihuahuas had too great a resemblance to the Papillon breed. Some Chihuahuas are white, marked with black, tan or fawn patches and this colour combination is shared with the other toy breed and constitutes a resemblance. It is also true that a bad long-coat Chihuahua, particularly if it is marked like a 'Pap', can look like one. Certainly the smooths are more distinctive, and although in the breed's formative period it was sometimes said that confusion could arise between black and tan Chihuahuas and English Toy Terriers (see picture between pages 64 and 65) the improvement in Chi type has done away with this allegation and nowadays the only similarity lies in the colour.

At the present time a good deal of—permissible—interbreeding is taking place between the coats, since one variety has much to offer the other. So far results are very encouraging, and there is no indication that the introduction of some smooth bloodlines is having any detrimental effect on the profuse coats of the longs. There have been one or two cases of over-dense coats on smooths, however, and while this need not cause immediate concern it should not go unnoticed as it would be a pity if these soft, short, thick coats—not typical of either variety—became common.

Now that we have two separate breed standards (the same for both varieties except for the section relating to coats) judges will be expected to pay more attention to coat.

A long-coated puppy will rarely carry a heavy coat, and will need time to grow fringes and feathering. A mature long-coat should have sleek, soft body hair as long as possible, with ample feathers on ears, legs and tail, together with fluffy 'panties'. The coat should not be of a 'stand-off' texture, nor so heavy as to conceal the body shape.

Some specimens come into full coat earlier than others, but most long-coated Chi's are seen in perfect coat by the time they are three or three and a half years old.

FIVE

PROGRESS AT THE SHOWS

IN AN issue of *Dog World*, published in 1949, the well-known all-breed judge, Mr J. W. H. Beynon, stated that 'Chihuahuas were first shown in this country at Cruft's in 1936', but this statement is incorrect. A Chihuahua is known to have been exhibited at a Ladies Kennel Association dog show held in Regent's Park, London, in the year 1897, and it seems likely that this happened on other occasions.

The mild sensation caused by Mrs Powell's exhibits when he began showing them in 1936 suggests, however, that Chihuahuas had not been seen at shows for a number of years.

The first post-war exhibitor is thought to have been Mrs D. Wells, in 1949, who expended much time and energy in gaining publicity for the breed. Her Doña Sol of Belamie and Tizoc of Belamie were most successful.

Shortly after, Mrs M. Fearfield had acquired Bowerhinton Chico of Belamie and was doing great things with him. He was among the winners, and one of his most important early successes was at the 1950 Cruft's, where he won First prize in the Any Variety Not Classified, Novice class, against the strong competition provided by 23 other exhibits of various breeds. The judge on this occasion was Mr H. G. Sanders, who described Chico as 'a fearless tot who put up a grand show; quite the smallest dog ever to win a First at Cruft's'. This was the type of win, and the type of judge's critique, bound to help in putting the breed on the map.

Mrs Gott was responsible for taking the largest team to Cruft's, where she benched four, and at this time Mrs Watkinson and Mrs Twining, who both had dogs of Mrs Gott's breeding, were swelling the little band of pioneers.

Bowerhinton Chico of Belamie continued to notch up wins, and it was a tremendous thrill when he was judged Best in Show, at an Exemption show at Sherborne, Dorset. He was the first Chihuahua to win a Best in Show, and if the event was one of modest size, the importance of Chico's success is in no way diminished.

About this time Mrs L. Cross began a series of fine wins with her home-bred Chicata. Up till then wins were all in Any Variety classes, but dog show secretaries were becoming aware of the breed, and especially of its power to draw and attract the general public. Some more enterprising dog show committees began to interest themselves in providing breed classes for the Chi's, and it seems that the credit of being the first to do so must go to the Metropolitan and Essex Canine Society, in October 1950, the Ladies Kennel Association and the West of England Ladies Kennel Society following in that order. Another pioneer supporter was the Bournemouth Canine Society which also started classes for the tinies.

It may be wondered what kind of support was forthcoming for these shows, in view of the paucity of both Chi's and exhibitors: the Metropolitan and Essex Society had an entry of nine for the judge, Mr Jas. Saunders, to sort out, while at the Ladies Kennel Association show Mr T. Corbett, who made the placings, had eight entrants in the class. It is interesting to note that both these judges picked the same winners and placed them in identical order, viz: Mrs Wells's Tizoc of Belamie was First, Bowerhinton Chico of Belamie was Second, and Chicata was Third.

It was at the Metropolitan and Essex show that Mrs L. Cross exhibited a litter of three puppies by Tizoc out of Palace Bambi. The little creatures were surrounded by fascinated spectators, and photographers were much in evidence. Mrs J. Forster, whose kennel prefix 'Jofos' was to become such a great name within the breed, secured one of these puppies, a black-and-tan bitch, and registered as Jofos Ferronita she grew up to be the breed's 'First Lady' of the early post-war era, for she won often, and produced some winning progeny.

Mr J. W. H. Beynon judged two classes at Cruft's in 1951, his winners in the Novice class being Bowerhinton Chico of

Belamie, Doña Sol of Belamie, and Mrs Fearfield's Bowerhinton
Margareta, in the order named. Margareta was of Mrs Gott's
stock. The Open class was headed by Tizoc of Belamie, with
Chico in Second place and Chicata Third, positions frequently
occupied by this trio.

Richmond Championship show was held in July that same
year, and the schedule included a class for the Chi's. Mr
L. C. Wilson was the judge.

Even one or two Open shows—always chary of providing
classes for any breed which was not sure to come up with a
paying entry—began to put on Chihuahua classes. Apart
from anything else, they were always a popular attraction for
public and Press.

Mr T. M. Corbett was the judge at the 1952 Cruft's,
and we sensed that considerable progress had been made by
the fact that there was both an increased entry and new names
among the winners. There were seventeen entries, and one
First-prize winner was Bowerhinton Rosita, owned by Mrs
Fearfield, while Mrs Gott secured a Third with Munsun
Nacon. Jofos Ferronita topped the Open class for Mrs Forster,
a position she often filled about that period.

The West of England Ladies Kennel Society's show at
Cheltenham in 1952 was an event of some importance because
the breed was judged by a visitor from the U.S.A., Mrs
Brewster-Sewell. From sixteen entries, she selected Jofos
Ferronita for First place, and next to her came a couple of
new names, both owner and exhibit, Mrs Beeson, with Sun-
stock Joanna of Beckanbee. Joanna was another typical
import to come to this country from Mrs Stock's kennel in
California. On this occasion Chico stood Third, and Chicata,
Reserve.

Mrs Brewster-Sewell was most popular, and was destined
to judge the breed again in this country, in 1957, when she
drew a very large entry at Blackpool Championship show.
It must have been a most interesting experience for a judge to
find herself in the position of being able to study the progress
of a breed, ranging from two such extremes—the modest early
entry and the greatly increased one five years later. Writing

her report of the Blackpool show, Mrs Brewster-Sewell expressed herself 'most pleasantly surprised with the quality of the dogs' which she had seen in 1952. Exhibitors were happy to note that their first overseas judge was elected an Honorary member of the British Chihuahua Club as a token of their appreciation.

However, to revert to 1952, an important transfer had taken place, and Bowerhinton Chico of Belamie had become the property of Mrs Forster, making a very attractive brace with her other black–and-tan, Ferronita. Chico continued to be well to the fore at the shows, together with Mrs Wells's Tizoc, and another of her charmers, Primo of Belamie, a small black-and-cream dog of great quality. Other current winners were Mrs Gott's Allens El Rey of Sunstock, Mrs Cornelius's Don Juan, also Mrs Shaw's Jofos Ferdinand. Mrs Wells began exhibiting Perla Pequena of Belamie.

Among the enthusiasts recruited to Chihuahua ranks in 1952 were the writer, who bought Denger's Don Lorinel from Mrs Beeson, who had originally acquired him from his breeder, Mrs Horner. Mrs Mooney was already getting the breed well known in Scotland with Jofos Cactus and Angelita of Winterlea, and Mrs Betty Smith was laying the foundation of her Yotmas Kennel. Mrs Rider succeeded in charming Chicata away from Mrs L. Cross, and like so many other breeders who had previously specialized in much larger dogs, completely fell for Chihuahuas and virtually ceased breeding and exhibiting her Alsatians in order to build up a kennel of Chi's.

With such an increase in the ranks, it was only to be expected that many more shows would take an interest in the tinies, and there were classes at Bath, where Mr J. Garrow judged. He gave the Best of Breed award to Primo of Belamie, an important win for Mrs Wells because it carried with it a Challenge Cup, presented by Mrs Gott, and enabled her to win it outright. As Primo's sire Tizoc had won it no less than ten times in the course of his show career, it was a well-deserved and popular award.

Mrs Bagshaw, by now very interested in the Chihuahua, was instrumental in arranging for classes at the Paignton

Championship show, but unfortunately the classes were not well supported; no doubt the exhibitors in the London area, by now numerous, were deterred from entering because of the long journey entailed.

Since it first began to be shown, the breed had been judged by all-rounders, so it was a milestone in the history of the breed when the officials of the Bournemouth dog show gave the British Chihuahua Club the option of selecting a specialist judge of its own choice. Mrs Fearfield was invited to judge, and nine Chi's were entered.

Nineteen fifty-four brought further progress, since most of the shows increased the classes scheduled to three, and upwards of nine shows catered for the breed in their classifications.

As the table of registrations shows, it was not just the shows that were indicative of the breed's mounting popularity. Breeders were meeting with continuous successes, and numbers increased until at last the total reached that which the Kennel Club considered necessary for a breed to be given separate registration and Championship status. This pinnacle was reached in 1954, and gave a thrill to everyone connected with the breed, and especially to the early pioneers whose hard work had led to this triumph. It was a spur to the enthusiasts who had come into the breed more recently, and a great encouragement to all. The first Challenge Certificates were put on offer for the 1954 Cruft's, and exhibitors began to prepare their dogs with eager anticipation and to plan to show them under the appointed judge, Mr Macdonald Daly.

It was a sorry anticlimax, therefore, when the great Cruft's Show—the biggest event of its kind in the world—was cancelled at short notice owing to a strike of electricians. People who had prepared to exhibit their best dogs at the best and biggest show were naturally shocked and disappointed, but by far the most downcast were the Chihuahua owners for whom this show was to have been a milestone in the history of their breed—its first Championship show with Challenge Certificates offered.

Only six sets of Certificates were allotted for the first year, and as Cruft's had not been held the distinction of being the first show under the new status fell to Glasgow. The judge there was Mr A. Murray, who drew a good entry of the breed in spite of the fact that the geographical distribution of Chihuahuas over the British Isles suggests that at that time the largest proportion was domiciled in the south. Inevitably, some exhibitors who could have shown their dogs at Cruft's were unable to travel to Scotland to do so. Probably the Cruft's entry would have been bigger still had the show taken place as arranged.

Excitement was tense when the Glasgow awards were made, for everybody showing Chihuahuas longed to be the first to win a Challenge Certificate, and with it, to have 'one leg' towards the crown of Champion, which three Certificates under three different judges would bring.

In the event, the first-ever dog Challenge Certificate was won by Rozavel Diaz, and the same award for bitches by Bowerhinton Isabela. Diaz was owned and bred by the writer, being imported in dam and born in quarantine to Rozavel La Oro Sena de Ora, in whelp to Salender's Darro Pharche, shortly after her arrival in this country. Isabela was bred by Mrs Horner, being a daughter of her Denger's Don Carlos and Denger's Doña Maria, and at the time of her great win she was owned by Mrs Fearfield.

Mrs M. Mooney had the distinction of owning both the Reserve Best of Sex winners at this show. These were Jofos Cactus and Angelita of Winterlea, a brace which had won many awards at earlier shows. Both these exhibits were by Bowerhinton Chico of Belamie, Cactus being Mrs Forster's breeding from her now famous Jofos Ferronita. Mrs Mooney herself bred Angelita from another Jofos bitch, Cholula, who was in fact Chico's daughter, successfully mated back to her sire.

Cheltenham was the next excitement, an outdoor show held on a beautiful country site. Unfortunately, the weather was extremely cold and wet. Very few of the Chihuahuas did themselves justice under these conditions, but the judge, Mr A. Demaine, had a nice entry. Mrs Rawson's chocolate-and-tan import, Brandman's Modelo, made his first appearance at a big show although he had already won some lesser events. He won the Challenge Certificate for dogs, with Rozavel Diaz taking the Reserve. Bowerhinton Isabela won her second C.C., followed by Angelita of Winterlea, which placements repeated the Glasgow awards.

Bright sunshine and a park-like setting at Blackpool enabled the Chi's to parade to better advantage. Mr T. M. Corbett chose Rozavel Diaz for his Certificate winner, and Mrs Forster's Jofos Sadie for the premier award in bitches. Sadie was a chocolate-and-tan import from the U.S.A. Isabela stood Second to Sadie on this day, while Reserve to Diaz was a dog of which a lot was heard later—Mrs Wells's smart little black-and-tan, Denger's Don Armando. He did not have to wait long to hit the headlines because it was at the next, and fourth, Championship show for the breed that he was top dog. The writer was the judge, and placed Armando First in the Open dog class, with Mrs Forster's Jofos Trino next. Amando, as his prefix denotes, was bred by Mrs Horner, from Pepito IX and Denger's Doña Carmencita. Trino was owner-bred, a cream dog out of that great winner-producer Jofos Millinita, and sired by Bowerhinton Chico of Belamie. The bitch winner at Leicester was Mrs Ellis-Hughes's sound and attractive black-and-rich-tan, Mixcoac, bred by Miss Mundey from Pepito IX and Palacecourt Queen Zamira. Zamira was by Tizoc, out of one of the very first imports, Palace Bambi.

The fifth Chihuahua Championship show of the year was at Birmingham, an indoor winter event. Mrs Fearfield, one of the founder-members of the British Chihuahua Club, made the awards on this occasion and confirmed the Leicester choice by putting Denger's Don Armando at the head of a strong Open dog class. Next to him came Lady Margaret Drummond-Hay's American import, Kirstie's Little Strutter, a small white dog. Strutter's story is a sad one, for he promised to have a distinguished career until it was cut short by his swallowing a small ox-tail bone which lodged in his throat; but this was not before he had met with some considerable success.

There was a new and very lovely little face among the top bitches at Birmingham, a cream puppy called Adella of Bendorwyn which won the C.C. for its owner-breeder, Mrs

Benvie. In second place came Mrs Bostwick's six-year-old import, Blaycroft Bruce's Lickie.

The excitement was now really reaching its peak, for there was only one more Championship show before the close of the year. Rozavel Diaz and Denger's Don Armando had won two Challenge Certificates each, and so had Bowerhinton Isabela. Brandman's Modelo, sad to say, had been run over and killed shortly after his great win at Cheltenham, so it seemed likely that either Diaz or Don Armando was certain to be the breed's first Champion dog. Isabela had a clear lead over her competitors as she was the only one of her sex with two C.C.'s, three other bitches having won one each. The atmosphere was charged with excitement at the Ladies Kennel Association show at Olympia, where Mr A. W. Fullwood had the task of handing out the prizes, and it was a breath-taking moment when he awarded the two coveted Certificates to the owners of Rozavel Diaz and Bowerhinton Isabela, the first Champion dog and the first Champion bitch to be made in Britain.

Meanwhile, the breed registrations climbed steadily up and up, and it was a matter for breeders to congratulate themselves when the number of Championship shows for the Chi's jumped from the six held in 1954, to ten in 1955.

Nothing occurred to stop Cruft's that year, and Mr Macdonald Daly started the show year by judging a very good entry, resulting in a fine win for Ch. Rozavel Diaz, which annexed his fourth C.C., and in a triumph for Mrs Rawson's pretty cream bitch, Brownridge Jofos Paloma, which headed a strong entry of bitches. The Reserve Best of Sex winners were, respectively, Jofos Trino and Adella of Bendorwyn. Paloma, who had rocketed to the fore at this event, was bred by Mrs Forster and was another winner by Chico out of Millinita, and owned by Mrs Rawson. This was a very popular win, since everyone felt keenly for her when she lost her imported dog under such unfortunate circumstances the previous year.

Glasgow came round again, and this time we saw Mr A. Demaine pick Kirstie's Little Strutter, with Reserve best of sex to the writer's Rozavel Gringo (a puppy from one of Ch. Diaz's first litters, ex the imported Rozavel La Oro

Memoria de Ora). Paloma, in fine fettle following her Cruft's successes, gained her second Certificate, with her litter sister, Mrs Benvie's Jofos Lucia of Bendorwyn, in second place.

Then the summer shows began, and at Bath, Mrs Wells had the pleasure of making Denger's Don Armando the second dog Champion, for Mr J. Saunders made him best of his sex, with Jofos Trino next. Trino was by this time considered to be an unlucky dog, since he so often occupied the Second position, probably because he did not enjoy shows and scarcely helped his handler to win. Mixcoac, the Leicester winner, won the bitch Certificate, and Second to her was another of Ch. Diaz's early progeny, Rozavel Mantilla, litter sister to Gringo. It began to look as though it would be a neck-and-neck finish between Mixcoac and Paloma for the honour of becoming the second Champion bitch as, at this stage, each of these excellent bitches had won two C.C.'s.

Blackpool provided a change, for a judge from the U.S.A. officiated. This was Miss Lydia Hopkins, a celebrated breeder of Poodles with an interest in Chihuahuas. Mrs McHale had travelled all the way from Ireland to exhibit her Denger's Don Guillamo, yet another of Mrs Horner's breeding from her successful stud dog Pepito IX out of her Denger's Doña Sandra. (It is a matter of interest that Sandra was a Pepito daughter, a point to note by students of close in-breeding.) It was Guillamo which caught the judge's eye, for Miss Hopkins awarded him the C.C. with Cisco Kid of Winterlea winning the Reserve. Cisco Kid was a white, with flashy orange-red markings, which Mrs Mooney had bred from imported parents and had just started to show with great success. This puppy had had an eventful start in life, since his dam was travelling from the U.S.A. to Britain when she gave birth to the puppies on the journey. Fortunately, two survived and came safely through quarantine, and one became Ch. Cisco.

It was at this Blackpool show that Miss Russell-Allen, who had been steadily gathering together a large kennel of Chihuahuas at her home in Cheshire, scored her first big win. Her white bitch, Lucinda Sue Dalhabboch, won the bitch C.C. Her owner had bred her from Munsun Chickenitza, a son of

Tolteca and Sunstock Systy, and was out of one of Systy's daughters.

Leicester came next, with Cisco Kid winning his first Certificate under Mrs Fearfield, and Paloma gaining her third, and with it the sought-after title of Champion. The Reserve C.C. winners were Rozavel Gringo and Rozavel Jofos Onlyone.

Mr T. M. Corbett judged the City of Birmingham show, a crowded outdoor event, and he chose Rozavel Gringo— with Trino Second once again—and Gringo's litter sister, Rozavel Mantilla, followed by Adella of Bendorwyn.

The important autumn show at Edinburgh, marking the close of the summer picnic shows, brought Cisco Kid his second C.C., with a very showy white dog next, Mrs Shiffner's Bowerhinton Aguadero. This latter dog was bred by Mrs Fearfield by Denger's Don Carlos (a son of Tizoc) out of Bowerhinton Margareta. An up-and-coming young star, Maria Carmello of Wytchend, won the Certificate in bitches. Her breeding is of interest since she was sired by Ch. Diaz, the first male Champion, out of one of the two first bitch C.C. winners, Mixcoac. Unfortunately, Mixcoac was never able to get her third and qualifying green card, but if the Champion's crown escaped her she certainly earned for herself a position in breed history as a most outstanding brood bitch. Next to Maria, on this occasion, came Mrs Currie's corky little black-and-tan, Yotmas Angel's Kiss, bred by Mrs Smith, by Pablo of Winterlea out of Consuelo of Winterlea.

In the corresponding period of the previous year, the breed's supporters had had only the Ladies Kennel Association show ahead, but in this year the last pair of Certificates for 1955 were to be won at the Birmingham National Show. At the L.K.A., Mr W. S. Hunt, an all-breed judge, whose own kennel of Cocker Spaniels under the 'Ottershaw' prefix had been very successful, made the awards. His Open dog class winner was Rozavel Miguel, a black-and-tan dog, the only puppy sired by the late lamented Brandman's Modelo, out of Rozavel La Oro Sena de Ora. He was owned and bred by the writer.

Mrs Benvie was successful this time with her Adella of

PROGRESS AT THE SHOWS

Bendorwyn, who had been waiting almost a year for her second C.C. Second place was filled by Rozavel Jofos Onlyone, another of Jofos Millinita's winning daughters, and bred, of course, by Mrs Forster, but owned by the writer, who had had the good fortune to acquire her at eight weeks of age.

As the show year closed with Birmingham, we saw Rozavel Gringo take the Certificate and, for the first time, a long-haired Chihuahua—Mrs Erskine's American import, Nellistar Schaefer's Taffy Boy—near the top. Until this show, all the C.C. and Reserve C.C. winners had been Smooths. It was another U.S.A. import which led the bitches, for Mrs Cross's Kelsbro Dugger's Spice started what was to be a most impressive run of wins when she took her first Certificate at this show. Mrs Cross was already well-known for her Yorkshire Terriers, and had bought Spice from Mrs Cecilia Dugger. The Reserve C.C. went to Belamie Chantico of Brome, owned by Mrs R. Johnson, who also kept some fine Welsh Corgis (Pembroke) at her home in Yorkshire, and who had fallen for the charms of the Chihuahua fairly recently. Chantico was a pretty black-and-tan, and, as her name suggests, had come from Mrs Wells.

Breeders who looked back on the year's ten important shows could note the number of new names among the C.C. and Reserve C.C. winners. Some lively arguments took place as to whether this indicated a lack of uniformity of opinion among the judges, or if it merely indicated that many Chihuahuas being shown were of more or less equal merit.

On the whole it would probably be true to say that, however experienced they might be with other breeds, many of the people who were judging Chihuahuas were still at the 'learner' stage where these distinctive little dogs were concerned. In the same way, a considerable proportion of the people breeding them were still at an experimental stage and gathering knowledge from day to day and from show to show. After all, the breed, though historically old, was still virtually new to Championship shows. It still varied in type, and many of the breed points considered essential were missing in the competitors, even the winners. Often these important points were found in specimens that were not the soundest movers, the best conditioned, or the most spirited performers in the ring, and these things all combined to make the Chihuahua a difficult breed to judge.

But the entries had been satisfactory, and exhibitors looked forward to further progress when the new show season opened in 1956. The breed was thoroughly established and was attracting new adherents all the time. It was clear that competition would become increasingly strong, and that this in itself would help to improve the breed.

It would not be right to conclude a section on progress in the dog-showing calendar, without making some reference to the series of highly successful shows held by the British Chihuahua Club. Even the Kennel Club's allotment of Challenge Certificates to a breed does not entitle a breed to hold a one-breed or 'specialty' show—the latter being a term much used in the U.S.A. The breed has to reach an even higher numerical standard and must have a record of good entries at shows before it can obtain permission for a show of its own.

The first memorable occasion for the Chihuahuas, therefore, was on April 18th, 1958, when the British Chihuahua Club held its first Open show in Manchester. The writer was honoured by an invitation to judge, and there was an entry of 123 Chihuahuas. The Best in Show award went to Ch. Don Silver of Wytchend, and the best opposite sex winner was Ch. Bowerhinton Ollala.

In November of that same year the Club held another Open show, this time in London, Mr D. Cady being the judge. Best in Show at this event was the writer's Ch. Rozavel Uvalda Jemima, and best opposite sex, Ch. Cholderton Little Scampy of Teeny Wee. Chi entries were 131. The following spring another northern Open show took place at Manchester, with Mrs M. Fearfield judging a smaller but still very high-class entry of 104. Int. Ch. Seggieden Tiny Mite was the Best in Show winner, and Mabelle Carlita the leading bitch. Also in 1959, another winter show took place in London, judged by Mrs J. Forster, which had 124 entrants. Her choice for Best of Breed was Ch. Rozavel Bienvenida, with Ch. Cholderton Little Scampy of Teeny Wee, Best Male.

The high-spot of the British Chihuahua Club's show programme was still to come, however, for the Kennel Club allotted Challenge Certificates for a breed Championship show to be held in April 1960, to be judged by Mr Leslie Perrins, in London. There were 113 Chi's entered, and once more Ch. Rozavel Bienvenida was Best of Breed, with Int. Ch. Seggieden Tiny Mite best of his sex. It was a memorable day, for the Chihuahua was by this time well established as one of the leading Toy breeds in the country.

Since then the Chihuahua has gone from strength to strength. With new breed clubs joining the parent club in running highly successful shows, leading up to a major event in 1965—Cruft's Championship show, where both varieties had separate classes, and, for the first time, a pair of Challenge Certificates for the smooth-coats and a pair for the long-coats. The former were won by Int. Ch. Seggieden Mighty Dime and Tinkerbell of Glenjoy. The latter by Olijon Teeny Roddy and Int. Ch. Aztec Ita Stardust.

Finally, the breed's greatest triumph came when the 3 lb. long-coat bitch, Ch. Rozavel Tarina Song, won the Toy Group at Crufts, 1971, and went on to be Reserve Best in Show, thus defeating an entry of 8,431 dogs. This all-time record breaking Chihuahua also won the Toy Group at the Scottish Kennel Club show at Glasgow, went Best in Show at Paignton Championship show, and Reserve Best in Show at the Ladies Kennel Association Championship show where she was placed above 7,975 other dogs.

A remarkable record has been set by Mrs M. Moorhouse, whose beautiful home-bred smooth-coat bitch, Ch. Molimor Talentina has smashed the breed record by winning 40 Challenge Certificates, an achievement unlikely to be easily matched. Talentina was sired by the Ch. Rozavel Chief Scout son, Ch. Molimor Rozavel Talent Scout, her dam, also a Chief Scout daughter, being Molimor Grageo Salome.

Another outstanding winner breaking records is Mrs E. King's Ch. Raygistaan Toy Train, bred by his proud owner from Raygistaan Golden Train and Zaleti Piacoxicola.

In the relatively short space of time since it was reintroduced into this country, the Chihuahua has certainly made its presence felt—and understandably, people in other countries are falling for these charming little dogs.

SIX

CHOOSING A CHIHUAHUA

THIS subject may be regarded from two different view-points: choosing a dog as a pet, and selecting foundation stock for breeding or showing. In one respect, however, the two aims are identical: the dog must be strong and healthy; if it isn't, it is a liability. If the dog is bought from a reliable breeder it is extremely unlikely to be in anything but perfect condition. That is why it is much better to buy from a private kennel than from a dog shop.

There are some very well-run pet stores, but scarcely any of the proprietors breed their own stock, which means they must buy all the dogs they sell and, of course, they buy them from the breeders. A shopkeeper has heavy overheads and other costs to meet, and to meet these he must add a sum, usually substantial, over and above the price he has paid for the dog which he is offering for re-sale. This means that the customer will pay a good deal more than if he had bought direct from the breeder in the first instance. Apart from this, whenever there is a constant flow of incoming and outgoing dogs from different kennels in different parts of the country, the risk of infection cannot be ignored.

It is advisable, therefore, to buy your dog direct from a well-known kennel. The Kennel Club will supply names of breeders in your area, or sell you a copy of *The Kennel Gazette*, in which you can find addresses. There are, also, the weekly dog publications which usually contain plenty of advertisements. If you do not know a breeder of Chihuahuas, you may know somebody actively interested in another breed. Such a person, who gets out and about to the shows, would know which were the best and most successful kennels to contact: so have a word with them.

For a variety of reasons, a great many people buy dogs without having seen them first. They do so after negotiating by post or by telephone, and the transactions are usually quite satisfactory. But there is nothing like seeing for oneself, and it is far better for buyer and seller if the deal is a personal one. Acquiring a dog, which may well be your best friend for the next fifteen years or so, is something important, and if it entails a long journey—what of it? Make the effort, see the stock on offer, and choose a Chihuahua that appeals to you. Ask to see the puppies on the floor, not cuddled up in somebody's arms. Do they seem bright, interested, and strong on their legs? Many Chihuahua puppies, especially those bred in country kennels which do not see many strangers, will not run to every caller. But an aloofness and lack of interest in new faces is not the same thing as nervousness, and it is not always a good sign if a puppy remains in its bed or hides in a corner.

Chihuahuas, even at an early age, are very individual little animals. They become most attached to one or two persons in a household and will adopt an indifferent attitude to people whom they do not know.

While some are friendlier than others, it is very possible that the puppies you see will not want you to pick them up or handle them. They recognize you as someone new, and will make friends with you only in their own time. So use your own judgement, and try to differentiate between the nervous puppy and the one that shows normal breed characteristics, taking its time to size up a newcomer.

The puppies should have clean, glossy coats, smooth and flat or, if long-haired, a coat that is soft, very fluffy, and with distinct signs of feathering. A rough, staring coat is usually a sign of malnutrition or worms, or both.

The eyes should not be deep set, and should be bright, clean, and free from any signs of mucus discharge. They may look slightly moist, but any sign of watering should be clear and slight. Chihuahuas' eyes do tend to water, for reasons which are not entirely explained, but in most cases due to the fact that they are very close to the ground and if they run around the dust is bound to be thrown up about them. Ears may be up or down, and the latter is not detrimental at any time under five months old, though naturally the pup looks most attractive when they are up. A puppy should not be lean, nor should its ribs or backbone appear prominent. On the contrary, it should have a well-rounded little body, well covered with flesh which is soft and pliable to the touch.

If the kennel has been soiled, any motions should be medium brown in colour, and slightly or entirely formed. The stool varies according to how the puppies are fed, and is usually softer when a milky meal has been consumed than after solid food. Some puppies tend to have rather relaxed bowel movements following a milk drink, and this must not be confused with diarrhoea.

A feed given too warm or too cold can also cause a puppy to scour; or a greedy feeder can gobble more than its share and temporarily upset its stomach in the same way. It will probably be normal again by the next mealtime. The demeanour of the puppy is the best guide. Some slight cause of loose motions will not depress it, but a puppy suffering from a real departure from normal health will be quiet, worried-looking, and unhappy.

Ask the breeder if you may pick the puppy up, and on receiving permission, hold it firmly, making allowance for the fact that it may wriggle, and carry it a short distance away. Put it down carefully on the ground, and see if it moves in a jaunty manner, strong on its legs and showing no signs of weakness. Never allow a puppy to jump off your lap or from a height. It is not unusual to get a variation of size in a litter of Chihuahuas. There may be one or two very tiny puppies, and one or two that are much larger. Often, they are all equally strong, and it is probably a case of some taking after tiny father, and others favouring a strapping mama. But sometimes a puppy is extra small because it is backward, developing much more slowly than its brothers and sisters. This is not a good choice, because although it may very well catch up if given extra care, it could remain rather delicate. If it is not just as good on its legs and as lively as the rest of the litter, it is better not to take it.

Some people have decided ideas as to the sex of the dog

they propose to buy. Others are undecided, and need advice as to the most suitable choice.

A bitch comes into season twice a year, and will be 'on heat' for about three weeks on each occasion. She is not usually very attractive to male dogs for the first, or the last, few days, and will generally growl and snap angrily if they try to flirt with her. But there are exceptions to this rule, and it is wise to take great care of the bitch throughout the entire period.

The disadvantages of a bitch are much reduced in such tiny creatures as a Chihuahua. Bitches of larger breeds do, it is admitted, present their owners with problems, since there are often neighbours' dogs which can become persistent suitors and make nuisances of themselves especially when the bitch is at her most attractive—about the eighth to fourteenth days as a general, but by no means infallible, rule.

A Chihuahua bitch is the same as any other, but because of her diminutive size, it is far easier to keep her safely confined during the heat period. She can be provided with a little pen, papered with newsprint, or if she is too fastidious to use it, she can be carried out of doors and put down in some secluded and isolated spot.

Finally, if by some mischance she escapes supervision and meets a male dog in the garden, she is so tiny that it is unlikely that any neighbouring stray would be able to mate her. But strict supervision throughout the three weeks is strongly advisable and, with a tiny bitch, usually quite easily arranged.

Chihuahua dogs make delightful pets. They become very devoted to their owners, and seldom stray or wander— common characteristics in male dogs of many other breeds, and one of the reasons why so many people choose bitches for companions.

Male Chihuahuas have, for many years, cost very much less than bitches, and for this reason they appeal to a wide section of the pet-loving public.

Having decided on the relative merits of dog and bitch, or perhaps having come to the conclusion that both are so nice that it does not greatly matter which it is going to be, the next question is one of age.

There is a lot to be said for taking a puppy as soon as it is ready to leave the mother. It is fun to watch it develop from the early stages, and it can be trained to fit into the household from the beginning. That is why so many people settle for a puppy of eight or nine weeks old, in spite of the fact that, generally speaking, at four to six months old it is often easier to teach and very much less trouble all round.

One cannot get away from the fact that a baby puppy is oozing with charm, and however attractive the finished product may be, a dog at the gangling, in-between, stages is less appealing. Their cherubic chubbiness has been left behind, distinguished good looks are something in the future, and they are going through a plain, or at any rate, plainer, stage. That explains the reason why some buyers whose homes are not entirely suitable for a very young puppy will choose one because they cannot resist its charm, although they know quite well that they would find an older dog easier to instal and manage.

Sometimes, too, a half-grown dog or young adult will cost less than the eight-week-old puppy. This seems very odd, considering that the breeder has had to feed and care for it for a much longer period. But so many puppies look very promising at a few weeks old, and a price in proportion to such good looks is warranted. In two or three months' time, however, they may have become disappointments. From the point of view of the person who is buying a dog purely as a pet, the defects developed probably do not matter very much. Ears or eyes too small, feet too large, elbows not tight to the ribs, toes turned out, these are but a few of the failings which in no way affect a little dog's future as a pet, but make it far less valuable to the critical eye of judge and breeder. It has become a rather ordinary specimen, instead of the potential Champion it promised to be in its early stages and is, therefore, not worth so much as it was when younger.

On the other hand, it is well known that some puppies which do not show exceptional promise, alter and improve in an almost miraculous manner, and eventually grow into beautiful show prospects. The really ugly ducklings, however, seldom if ever grow into swans, and it would be unwise to acquire one in the hopes that it will be anything than a rather indifferent specimen of its breed. But such a puppy, not good enough for the breeder to keep or to sell as a show proposition, may make a wonderful companion, so if that is what you are looking for, do not be too critical when you go to pick your puppy.

Some Chihuahuas are exquisitely beautiful. Some are plain, to the extent of being almost comical in appearance. Each one has the same enchanting characteristics, the same brilliant intelligence, the amazing capacity for bestowing love and fidelity even upon the most undeserving of us all. Every Chihuahua is lovable, something to be treasured and prized and cherished. Those privileged to own them, be they Champions or 'just Chihuahuas', are fortunate indeed.

We have dealt with most of the problems that the prospective owner of a pet Chihuahua has to face, but the buyer seeking stock for showing or breeding, or both, has many more things to think about.

One thing, however, is plain, simple fact. If funds permit, without question, the best way to make a start is with a really high-class young bitch, not less than six months of age. If she is well up to Championship show form—and at that age her merits should be discernible—so much the better. The new owner can get off to a good start, gain some experience, and begin making a reputation for himself and his stock by showing his first acquisition while waiting to breed a litter from her.

Such a promising young bitch will not be bought cheaply. She will probably cost anything from £100 upwards, and could very easily cost much more. Really outstanding Chihuahua bitch puppies, especially some which have been shown and have proved themselves winners at an early age and in good company, have been sold for hundreds of pounds.

A younger bitch, say a puppy of two or three months old, will cost a minimum of £75 to £150, according to the promise she shows at the time. She can grow into a Champion and prove a wonderful bargain, even at that substantial figure. Or she can turn out a bad buy, and grow into an ordinary specimen and be of little consequence against the strong competition prevailing at present-day dog shows.

There are any amount of people in dogs, and this applies to all breeds, who are fired with enthusiasm and who have bought puppy after puppy in a frantic effort to obtain something to show in top company, yet have never secured a worthwhile winner at all. These same people, asked 200 or 300 guineas for a fully developed young adult of outstanding merit, would recoil in horror, yet at the end of it all they have paid as much or more for their disappointing succession of puppy failures, and have not even got a good one to show for their outlay. Still, let us accept the fact that lots of us like a gamble. Plenty of fortunate people have struck lucky straight away, and in buying one puppy have found that they have been blessed with a Champion or a Champion-producer.

It is a matter for great congratulation if fate is so kind, but there is really no doubt that it is better and surer to play for safety. Whenever possible, pay the price that a good half-grown or grown youngster commands, and see exactly what you are getting when you buy.

But what if we cannot pay the big price for a potential 'flier'? Lots of us find it difficult to do so. And equally, those of us with low bank balances also have high ideals. We want good dogs. We have 'ideas above our stations'. We want to 'go in' for Chihuahuas and we find, to our dismay, that they are expensive little creatures. We cannot possibly aspire to buying one of the top-price adults, and in fact, we even feel that the cost of a good young bitch puppy is really out of reach.

How, then, can we make some sort of a start in this captivating breed?

We will have to be gamblers, on a large scale, too. We must try to get hold of a good stamp of bitch or bitch puppy, with as few faults as possible. We must accept the fact that we cannot expect to get a show-ring star. We *might* get one worth taking to the occasional little local show, but she will probably not be suitable. With a limit to our purse, we must be prepared to take second best and feel stimulated by the challenge she presents, for we will have to exercise our skill and try to breed winners from her.

In every case, when a beginner makes a start in a breed, pedigree is of the utmost importance. It is even more so when the foundation bitch is not first class in appearance or some other respects. Even with excellent parents it is rare to get a whole litter of puppies of equal merit. The dream puppy which grows up to become a Champion usually has a less glamorous, or sometimes downright plain, sister. The Cinderella of the family, if well-bred and intelligently mated, may not only breed something very much better than herself, but she may even breed far better quality puppies than her beautiful sister.

So, if we are buying on a budget, we will grab the second puppy and leave the obviously superior one to somebody who can afford it.

If a brood bitch is our aim, there is a good deal to be said for getting one that has already bred a litter. It is clearly a help if we can find out a little about her puppies, and see if they were promising and what faults and virtues predominated.

If her progeny were really worth while, however, it is no use our expecting to buy her cheaply. If she is a good brood bitch she is very valuable, and nobody in their right senses is going to part with her for a song. But we might be lucky enough to get her for a reasonable figure, especially when she has just left her litter. Most breeders are limited by the numbers they can keep conveniently, and if they have chosen a good bitch puppy to run on for future shows, they may have to part with the dam. She should cost less at the early stage, rather than later when she may have been mated again. A good mated bitch is 'in profit' as it were, and this always pushes up the price.

A good brood bitch can prove herself a treasure, and, if near season or mated, can turn out a wonderful buy. Obviously she can provide a flying start in the breed. Provided she has a litter, the worst that can happen is that the puppies turn out to be of pet quality only, and in such a case they can usually be sold to good homes at moderate prices. These sales may not recoup the entire purchase price of the bitch, but will certainly bring in a substantial part of it, and the dam is still there to breed from another time, to a different sire, with the prospects of getting something much better. Luck comes into it again; there may even be one outstanding puppy or more, in which case the future is indeed a rosy one.

Sometimes beginners want to start, not only with one or two bitches, but with a stud dog as well. This is occasionally unavoidable, for instance, when breeders overseas are starting Chihuahuas in a country where the breed is either very scarce or totally unknown. There may be other reasons which make the purchase of a stud dog advisable, but in the main it is a step to be avoided like the plague.

Most successful stud dogs are hard to buy. The cost of one is very substantial. If it is not, the chances are that for some reason the dog is not worth having. While the stud dog may be a useful source of income in its experienced owner's hands, it is by no means certain that it would do as well with a beginner, in which case it might not pay for itself. But the real danger lies in the fact that once the dog has been added to the new kennel, the temptation to use it on all the bitches is almost irresistible. Since it is very unlikely that it is the best and most suitable mate for them all, the disadvantages are obvious.

A far better policy for the novice is to spend every available penny on good bitches, keeping back a sum to meet the stud fees charged for the top stud dogs in the breed. For a moderate outlay—at the present time the highest Chihuahua stud fees are only £30—the most suitable dog can be chosen for each bitch, and puppies secured for a few pounds, by a sire that has proved his worth in the show ring, and/or by the quality of his existing progeny. Such a dog may have cost its breeder hundreds of pounds to produce. It is easy to see how much better the chances of breeding winners must be when this procedure is followed.

We have talked this matter over on the assumption that the beginner would in any event consider investing only in an absolutely first-class dog. But it is unfortunately true that a number of people completely sabotage their chances of success by purchasing a second- or third-rate dog for stud purposes.

They muddle along, breeding litter after litter from a dog that to the knowledgeable eye looks most unlikely to produce good stock for them or for anybody else, wasting precious time and money, and finally ending disillusioned. Sad to say, there are a few such unfortunates who cannot accept the fact that they have failed by their own mistakes. They will grumble away, saying that the big breeders have all the luck, that the beginner hasn't got a chance, ignoring the fact that all the successful exhibitors and kennel owners were beginners once, and that everybody starts equal in the race to breed good dogs.

It is all very sad, and often some good and enthusiastic recruits to a breed are lost, and to save other newcomers from the same fate we advise them not to buy a male dog at the start. As experience is gained and successes come along, it may be possible to breed a really good young dog, or eventually the time may come when it is wise to purchase one; but for the present, forget about it. After all, many successful and long-established breeders do not keep stud dogs of their own. They prefer to make use of the cream of the sires available all over the country, carefully choosing one for each bitch with due consideration for its bloodlines, its own show record and that of its winning progeny, and this is undoubtedly the likeliest road to success. Why not do the same yourself?

Whether we take this advice or not, however, we must now consider choosing a Chihuahua for breeding purposes; and 'choose' is the word, for we must be far more critical and exacting than someone who is looking for a dog which will never be bred from or taken to shows. We will, however, go along with the prospective pet owner to this extent: we also want a robust puppy, full of health and vitality, but we must have one that fits the Standard of Points in so far as is possible.

The Standard can be found on page 105, and it should be read and re-read, also the drawings studied at the same time. To get a mental picture of the ideal Chihuahua, however, this should not take the place of visits to shows to watch the judging and to spend time looking at the winners in the ring and on the benches. All available breed literature should be collected. This includes club pamphlets and Year Books, and especially the illustrated supplements published by the two dog weeklies at Christmas-time. The kennel reviews, with their photographs, are extraordinarily helpful in developing an 'eye'.

Both on the printed page and at the shows, the same kennel names will crop up over and over again. These are the names to watch. The prefix or affix is being applied to dogs that are winning or otherwise making names for themselves. Visit the kennels whence these good ones are flowing. Have a talk to the breeders, tell them what you would like to buy, ask the prices of any individual Chihuahuas that appeal to you, and ask for advice as to the most suitable for foundation stock. Most breeders are generous about imparting the knowledge they have gained to others still at the bottom of the ladder, and their experience can be very helpful to a beginner. You must expect to be fairly closely questioned about the methods you plan to use for housing your Chihuahua, and your previous experience with dogs, so do not take offence if you find that the seller is particular as to where the dogs are going. Breeders take great pains to produce good, sound stock, and in the process get extremely attached to their dogs. They will not let them go unless they feel confident that they will receive the same loving care in their new homes.

SEVEN

JUDGING THE CHIHUAHUA

EVERY Chihuahua breeder and exhibitor has to be a
judge of the breed. This does not imply that he must
undertake the judging at dog shows, but rather that,
if a kennel is to turn out first-class stock the owner must be
capable of appraising the good and the bad points of a dog.

The most successful breeders are always those who are
most conscious of the failings of their own dogs. The people
who cannot see anything wrong with their animals are said
to suffer from 'kennel blindness', a hypothetical affliction,
and probably the greatest handicap to progress in the world
of dog showing. Not only beginners, but enthusiasts who
have been breeding for years, suffer from it.

It is right and natural to take a pride in one's home-bred
stock, but coupled with it there should be a faint dissatisfaction,
an awareness of slight imperfections, a longing for something
even better. We may delight in the puppy with the beautiful
head, yet at the same time realize that it could be straighter
in front. If we continually seek to produce something better—
better even than the best—we shall come close to finding it.

Every dog show is full of people who spend time and
money campaigning second-rate dogs, with results that
disappoint them. It never seems to occur to them that they
just do not have dogs good enough for the prevailing competition. They will complain that the judging is 'unfair', that
theirs—the best exhibit—was overlooked, and they will
point out the faults of the dogs which have defeated their own.
If only they would try to look at their treasures with an un-
biased eye, evaluate it point by point, and admit that it could
be better, they would be more likely to correct the faults in

95

the subsequent generation and would soon find themselves at the receiving end for prize-cards.

To judge a dog, one must first have some knowledge, however scant, of anatomy. Buy, borrow, or beg a book on the conformation of the dog, or a veterinary book which includes diagrams of the skeleton and the muscular formation. Study also the breed standards set out by the Kennel Club, reproduced at the end of this chapter. The bones vary in shape in the different breeds, all of which have been bred to varying sizes, length, and especially heads and length of limbs, but the basic skeletons are very much the same. It is particularly valuable to compare charts of these different breeds and to pay special attention to such points as the shoulder blade, and its position, also the hind legs with the specific bones which supply straight hocks or sweeping angulation.

Many Chihuahuas are straight in shoulder, and this affects the movement of the front legs. A correctly placed shoulder enables the dog to lift its legs high enough from the ground to take long strides. The badly placed shoulder limits this movement, and the dog walks with a short, choppy action, moving its front legs in an irregular, stirring motion, usually referred to as 'plaiting'. A straight shoulder is frequently, though not always, accompanied by a very short neck.

 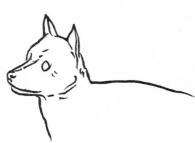

Good head with round skull, large ears, and short foreface. Elegant lengthy neck and level back

Bad head with flat wedge-shaped skull, small ears, and long foreface. Short neck and roached back

Another prevalent Chihuahua fault is a weak movement of the hind legs. This can be caused by a straight stifle, perhaps by an over-long bone running from the foot to the point of the hock, or by a malformation at the point where the hip bone fits into its socket, or at the patella—the dog's knee-cap.

It does not take a very experienced eye to see whether or not a dog has a level back. When the back rises in a hump, it is a glaring and ugly fault. It not only looks horrid but it also affects the propelling qualities of the hind legs, and roach-backed dogs never move well. Nor should the back dip, either in the middle or just behind the shoulders. The back can and should be quite straight. Avoid, like a plague, breeding stock which produces these hump backs, for the fault is strongly hereditary.

Gentle handling of the body reveals the rib conformation. Slight, narrow Chihuahuas are often slab-sided; they lack spring of rib or 'heart room', and however much their owners try to condition them and to pile on extra weight, they never look nicely rounded or substantial.

Where adult dogs are concerned, good and bad points are likely to be fairly permanent, but with puppies, many changes take place. Beautiful youngsters grow, if not into 'ugly ducklings', then into very plain ducklings indeed. Rather unattractive 'ducklings' can grow into beautiful swans. Really poor quality puppies may improve somewhat but are unlikely to turn out very well, yet it is wonderful how some, which at one stage do not look at all promising, can blossom with age and maturity.

Most experienced breeders have known bitter disappointments. Puppies can look wonderful at a few weeks old, but instead of growing into Champions may finish up as pet quality which, while they may give someone great pleasure in that capacity, are heartbreaks to those who had hoped they would be future stars.

There is often a chance that some faults will disappear or at least become much less apparent, but there are also certain defects which are unlikely to alter for the better. Take ears, for instance. If a puppy has very small, pointed, kitten-like ears, they will never become large, rounded, and flaring. But soft, drooping, or badly carried ears may remain unsatisfactory or with luck can be well carried by the time the dog has cut its second teeth. Uncertain ear carriage at ten months of age gives rise to some anxiety, but this has been known to correct itself as late as at twelve or fourteen months of age, but if the ears are not perfect by then they are generally hopeless. Teeth should fit in a scissor-bite. Slight deviations may collect themselves as a puppy matures. A badly overshot or undershot jaw is a serious fault in a show animal; but the degree to which imperfections of this type are penalized depends on the judges. Some overlook a small dentition fault. Others will not consider a dog for a top award unless the teeth are perfect.

Another fault, a slightly roached back, will often level

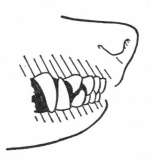

Correct scissor-bite

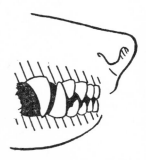

Imperfect edge-to-edge bite

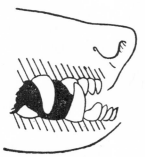

Faulty undershot jaw

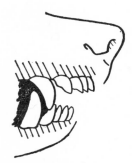

Faulty overshot jaw

out by the time the puppy is three-parts grown; loose elbows may tighten a little or a lot. Even wobbly pasterns or hocks can strengthen and become firm, especially with ample exercise. But a badly roached back is usually a constructional fault, as is a really crooked front, and neither will be completely eliminated.

An over-long body cannot shorten, but may appear much less obvious with maturity and extra weight. The dog with too-short legs can only become more mis-shapen and dwarf-like, for it will fill out and deepen as time goes on and its increasing heaviness will only emphasize the fault. At the other end of the scale, the dog with unusually long legs, although the actual length of legs will never decrease, will look far more in proportion as it thickens and deepens in body and chest.

A good Chihuahua is a balanced dog, and proportions can be assessed only by experience. It is helpful to study pictures of the top winning Chihuahuas, past and present, but better still, to look at good dogs themselves, and by practice, develop an 'eye' for the right length of body and the length of leg that is correct. Chi's are not short-backed little dogs,

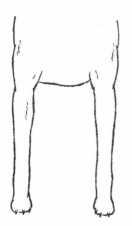 

Good straight front legs—not too long or too short

Bad front legs—crooked, and also too long

although the males are usually more compact than the females. They should have bodies of medium length, that is, the length of the back from the top of the shoulders to the root of the tail should be slightly more than the height of the dog from the ground to the same point on the shoulders. An altogether four-square outline is, however, preferable to a snaky, drain-pipe, Dachshund-y Chihuahua.

The front legs should be straight, from any angle. Starting at the elbows, which should fit neatly to the sides, the legs extend down to the feet, with the pasterns very slightly sprung. A bad front can consist of straight legs with loose or wavy elbows, of legs which turn outwards at the 'knee' joint or at the pasterns, or legs which are completely bowed.

The feet should be small, neat, more oval than round, with clearly defined toes, but thick and well-knuckled up, never flat or spread.

The neck should be fairly lengthy and slightly arched. A short, thick neck is very ugly, and is all too often seen. The head is one of the most important breed features. It should be round, looking like a ball from all angles, which means that the skull must be high, with a deep, rectangular stop. The head must be rounded between the ears, and rounded from the back of the skull to the point where it joins the stop between the eyes. If the skull slopes gradually forward to the point where the muzzle joins the head, it is not good.

The muzzle itself is moderately short, not 'Pug like' and not as fine or as pointed as the Pomeranian foreface. The eyes are round, medium to large, not deep set but neither bulgy nor protruding. Small, boot-button eyes, or almond-shaped eyes, give the dog a 'foreign' expression, and are not typical. The eyes are generally dark brown and very lustrous. White, cream, and pale fawn or apricot Chihuahuas often have the beautiful, luminous 'jewelled' or 'ruby' eyes so peculiar to the breed. In certain lights, the eyes glow like precious gems. The paler-coated Chihuahuas sometimes have light-coloured eyes, noses, and eye-rims, which are permissible, and must not be penalized when judging the breed at shows.

The Chihuahua's large, flaring ears are one of its most striking characteristics. They are set low on the side of the head, are big for the size of the dog, and usually rounded at the tips. When the dog is in repose, the ears are held out at an angle of about 45 degrees, but when alerted it holds them up more stiffly. When apprehensive or frightened, the ears are laid back against the neck. They must never be carried straight up on top of the skull.

Good head, with round skull, deep stop, and short foreface. Medium-sized, round eyes, and large, well-set, flaring ears

Bad head, with flat skull, shallow sloping stop, and long foreface. Small almond eyes and small high-set ears

Many Chihuahuas have the famous 'molera', a small opening on top of the skull which approximates to the 'fontanelle' which human babies have at birth. With the human child, the space closes within the first year as a rule, but most Chihuahuas keep this peculiar depression for the whole of their lives. It was originally supposed that the molera was a sign of 'pure breeding', but in recent years this has been discounted. All in all, it has come to be considered a doubtful asset and it might be a good thing if it were to disappear altogether, since it only makes the head more vulnerable to damage.

If there is one, more than another, particular Chihuahua characteristic that points at a pure lineage, it is the curious flat tail, and breeders now consider that this has assumed the importance that was held by the molera in the formative years of the breed. The hair on the tail grows sparsely on the top and the underside, and is bushier at the sides. This gives a tail of most unusual shape and is a most distinctive Chi breed point. Young puppies have round tails, but as they grow older the tail usually flattens, and it puts a very neat and attractive finish to a typical Chihuahua.

If the Chi is made right, it will move right. It should travel freely and evenly, covering a good deal of ground with every step it takes, and never move with a short, jerky or proppy action. The front legs should not turn in or out, and hind legs should be straight with a medium space between them, for dogs can move with legs too wide apart or too close together, and neither extreme is desirable. When the dog stands still, the hocks should be at right angles to the ground and in line with the root of the tail; not in, nor under, the body, or out away from it.

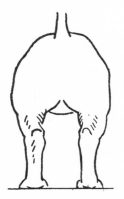 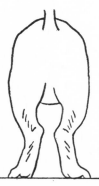 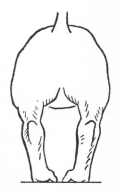

Good level hocks   Faulty 'turned-in'   Faulty 'turned-out'
hocks   hocks

Very naturally, the breeder of Chihuahuas is searching eagerly for the best points in the stock, but it is wise to look for faults at the same time. It is in such cases as these that skill and judgement play such a great part in the production of winners. The decision to sell one puppy or to keep another, is always a hard one. Even experienced breeders make mistakes, so clearly the beginner who has to sort out an even litter has no easy task. Countless people have sold as a pet what they thought was the least promising puppy, and retained what appeared to be a potential winner, only to find within a few months that their pride and joy is far less good-looking than his discarded brother. Because of these hazards, if two puppies show equal promise it is wise to keep the pair until such time as it is possible to assess the finished products and to make a choice, for eventually one will probably outstrip the other in overall merit.

The study of one's own Chihuahuas, and of those belonging to others, is not only fascinating but the best training for any embryo dog show judge. How does one become a judge? There is, in fact, and contrary to what many people believe, no definite point where the rubicon is crossed. Like Topsy in *Uncle Tom's Cabin*, as a judge, one 'just grows'. If a newcomer displays great interest in a breed, is distinguished by regular attendance at all the important shows and some of the lesser events as well, if such a person becomes an enthusiastic breed-Club member, and in addition begins to exhibit a continuous flow of high-class stock, sooner or later an invitation to judge at a show held under Kennel Club rules will be forthcoming.

The appointment will be subject to Kennel Club approval, but apart from this, arrangements will be between the individual concerned and the show management. Breed-class judges officiating at the smaller shows do not generally receive a fee, and are often invited to judge free of all expense to the society which is promoting the show. Most show secretaries, however, are authorized to pay travelling expenses.

The embryo judge will be sent a schedule of the show and should arrive in time to start judging punctually. Exhibitors have usually risen early in order to have their dogs ready in the ring, and it is bad manners to keep them waiting. It should also not be necessary to remind judges that it is their duty to be courteous and polite, even though handlers can be tiresome at times.

A very small minority of judges suffer from an unwarrantable conceit and an exaggerated idea of their own importance. They take it upon themselves to order people about, to rebuke exhibitors, and even—the most damning of all—to handle the exhibits roughly. Such judges do not receive support from Chihuahua exhibitors for very long.

As a matter of fact, the judge is not nearly as important as are the dogs. If the judge failed to turn up and the dogs showed up in force, people would still pay to see them. But if the dogs stayed away, who would pay to see the judge? The judge is there to satisfy the owners by placing the dogs in the correct order to the best of his ability and to do so quickly and purposefully, yet paying attention to each and every dog shown so that every handler leaves the ring feeling that he has had a fair chance, win or lose.

If, after judging is finished, a disappointed entrant stays to ask why a dog was not put higher, the judge should try to give a concise and candid reply. It is better to say, 'I thought it was a little long in the head,' than to prevaricate and say, 'Of course it is absolutely beautiful but I just liked the winners better.' When this advice is followed it may well be countered by, 'I showed it last week to Mr Knowitall, and he told me it had a wonderful head,' in which case it is best to bring the conversation to a speedy close since one can never win this type of argument. Terminate matters by saying, 'I do advise you to show it under Mr K. next time he judges, when I expect you will do well.'

In the main, dog-show exhibitors are good losers and excellent sports. They take their defeats well, and though everybody who shows hopes to win and is disappointed when luck is out, there is always another show coming along and a different judge, offering the hope of better things.

If a judging invitation comes along, accept it and see if it proves an enjoyable experience. If it is not, and if it proves worrying with its accompanying sensation of rising panic as each big class files into the ring, be comforted by the thought that even the most celebrated judge had to start once. Certainly no one, least of all the judge of livestock, is perfect, and there can be few who do not make mistakes—only the fools who think they do not!

If there were no judges, there would be no dog shows, which would make the world a dull place for the people who enjoy them.

on the rabbit-hutch principal, with the entire front barred, and there are others which have a boarded compartment for sleeping at one end, and a barred run at the other. The little kennels are on legs, some are single, others can be had in two or three tiers, and these are useful space-savers. They have the additional advantage of keeping the dog well up off the floor, so are especially good if the weather is chilly.

The best kennels of this type have the floors covered with zinc trays. They are sanitary, and easy to keep clean. Ordinary wooden floors get very smelly, and urine tends to drip down on the floor below or into the kennel beneath, which is disgusting. If the trays are kept covered with newspaper, this can be rolled up and burned when it is soiled. If a cloth is wrung out in warm water and disinfectant, and the zinc surface wiped, fresh paper can be spread out and everything is spotless and sweet-smelling again.

No matter what type of kennel, pen, or box is used, the Chihuahuas will need little beds. Cardboard boxes are quite useful, but the dogs enjoy chewing them, also if soiled they cannot be cleaned, and the cardboard becomes soggy. They do not have a long life, but can usually be obtained free from the grocer so may be renewed frequently. Small wooden boxes are better. These can be made by any handyman, who should bind the edges with heavy tin, because even little Chihuahuas, with their easily dislodged, gramophone-needle-like teeth, can gnaw and seem to like doing it. Herring boxes, from the fishmonger, are an ideal size. They will be wet and smelly when they arrive, but one or two good scrubs and a day in the fresh air with a good breeze blowing will remove the smell. The boxes in which greengrocers receive tomatoes from Italy, and grapes from Spain, are also very suitable. Some shopkeepers give them away free and seem happy to find someone who is willing to take half a dozen or more. Others charge a few pence for them.

The chain stores sell little plastic knobs costing 3d. each, and these make lovely little feet for the beds. Screw one at each corner, taking care that the bed stands firm when it is nicely raised off the floor, and it will be dry and warm.

The boxes are usually improved if well rubbed down with

sandpaper, and they look better if they are painted. A plastic emulsion is recommended. Some paints contain lead and are lethal if an animal sucks or chews the surface. These little sleeping-benches are really far better than elaborate baskets or special dog beds costing twenty times the price. They are so cheap that if they get chewed, stained, or shabby, the little 'feet' can be unscrewed and used again on a new box, and the old one used for firewood. This is advisable if there has been any illness or infection in the kennels, for it is so much better to destroy a sick animal's sleeping-box than to have to go to the trouble of fumigating or disinfecting it.

Even more up to date are the brightly coloured plastic bowls which the chain stores sell for domestic use in sinks. Many of these make wonderful tiny dog beds, are easily wiped clean with a damp cloth, and are very hygienic, not to say reasonable in price.

Tiered kennels are usually made of plain wood and are much improved if painted inside and out, the colour scheme being a matter of taste. White or cream is bright, and any dirt can be immediately noticed and sponged clean, so a light shade is best for the interior. Pastel shades or bright colours look equally smart on the outer surfaces. New wood soaks up the paint, so an undercoat of pink primer followed by two coats of enamel or high-gloss paint will give best results. But do enquire, when buying paint, if it contains any lead, and reject it if it does.

Whitewash is not suitable for kennels; it flakes, and rubs off on the dogs, and it cannot be washed down. Distemper is almost as bad, even the kind described as washable. Glossy (non-lead) paint is by far the best. It is not cheap, but if carefully applied is long-lasting, and should last at least two or three years.

Whether the dogs are to be kept in tiered 'flats' or 'hutches', or on the floor, some sort of floor cover must be decided upon. Plain concrete is fairly easy to keep clean, but it stays damp for a long time after being swabbed, and even when dry it is very cold to little feet, especially puppies. If a concrete floor is to be put down, it is well worth while consulting one of the firms specializing in the construction of farm buildings. There are modern methods of introducing air ducts beneath the concrete which are successfully adopted for cow-sheds and piggeries, and which result in a much warmer surface. Even more recent is the heating of tiled or concrete floors by electricity, and an enquiry into this is also suggested, since such an installation would be a big problem once the floor was laid and could more easily be supplied when the surface was under construction.

Special plastic dressings are used on cement and concrete floors. It comes in drums, is painted over the surface, and prevents the continuous collection of dust which never fails to form, and it looks attractive when it is finished. Quarry tiles are easy to clean, but rather cold, and probably other floorings are better for small dogs. Plastic or linoleum tiles, fixed with a special adhesive, will adhere to almost any surface, are lovely to look at and easy to mop. Ordinary linoleum always looks good and the mottled or jaspe patterns do not show paw marks or mud, as do the plain colours. It goes down well on boards, but has a rather brief life if laid on concrete. Vinyl flooring is the newest type, and is worth investigating as it sounds as though it might be very suitable for a kennel floor.

Sawdust, such a useful essential for the larger breeds, is not as suitable for the Toys. It gets in their eyes, scatters about, makes the place untidy, and can be really dangerous if puppies drop food in it. So long as the newspaper in the pens is regularly renewed and the floors well washed, a mop and bucket and some disinfectant will keep the flooring spick and span, regardless of the surface. Always use disinfectant according to makers' instructions. Mix carefully, and choose one that is non-poisonous and recommended for animals.

The bedding, whatever kind is used, must be changed at least once a week, even daily if the dog happens to soil it. It is surprising how much dust, grit, and hairs can collect in a sleeping-box, and how fusty it can smell even with the Chihuahua, which is one of the few breeds of dogs known to be free from doggy odour.

The safest and most labour-saving method of heating kennels is by electricity, and an enormous number of different methods and appliances are available. The local electricity board will willingly send a representative to advise on the best and most economical way to heat a room or building, and it is a good idea to take advantage of this service and obtain expert advice. Tubular heating is used by many owners of kennels. Some people like the plug-in oil-filled radiators, others use convector heaters, either free-standing on the floor or attached to the wall. Ordinary electric fires with exposed elements are not recommended for animals. If any kind of stove or heater is used at ground level, great care must be taken to see that the cord is protected so that it cannot get bitten or wet. Accidents can happen, and for this reason it is not wise to allow amateurs or do-it-yourself enthusiasts to fit electrical appliances. It is a job for the expert, and it is far better to be safe than sorry afterwards.

Lastly, there are the infra-red lamps which have become so popular in recent years. Whereas the various ways of heating described above will warm the entire room, the infra-red lamps have to be suspended over individual sleeping-benches or boxes. Breeders speak very highly of these, for they give out gentle warmth just where it is most needed, and being suspended well above the floor, they are safe. They are, however, no use when the dogs are kept in boxed-tier kennels.

They are inexpensive to instal and to run, and although it has been suggested that they have certain disadvantages if dogs are kept beneath them for long periods, there is no real evidence that they are anything other than a useful way of warming the open-top type of dog-bed.

It is not everybody, even in these enlightened times, who can make use of electricity, however. Those who cannot, often instal a solid fuel stove which burns day and night and gives out a good steady heat. It needs regular attention, the fuel, which may be coke or anthracite, has to be fetched and shovelled, and it creates a good deal of dust. Again, it is most important to have such a stove installed by a specialist fitter, who will pay proper attention to the stove pipe and the ventilation. A few years ago, some dogs sleeping in a scullery were suffocated by fumes from a stove. To be really ideal, the stove should be outside the dog room or building, and connected with pipes which will efficiently warm the dog's quarters. This type of installation is widely used in greenhouses and can be successfully adapted to heat a kennel.

Finally, there are all sorts, shapes, and sizes of oil heaters.

These are economical to run, costing less than almost any form of electric or solid-fuel heating. They are also messy to fill, the wicks are capricious, the paraffin runs out at most awkward times. Some of the blue-flame type of radiators have long-lasting absestos wicks, will burn for forty-eight hours on one filling, and are heavy and difficult to upset, and so are very safe. Only heaters of this type should be used where there are dogs, even though Chihuahuas are so light and dainty and unlikely to knock a stove over. A bare-flame heater of any kind, always carries a risk of fire, however slight this may be with some of the excellent modern heaters now on the market. Left in a draught, they can flare up. One over-careful owner, afraid to put an oil stove on the floor lest the puppies should upset it, placed it on a table well out of reach. The heat emerging from its open top set the ceiling on fire, and a bitch and her puppies perished. There are one or two makes of oil heater which are specially manufactured for use in kennels and poultry houses, and these are probably the least dangerous, but even these stoves have wicks that need careful maintenance and adjustment. They can easily start to smoke, and give off harmful fumes.

All forms of heating consume the oxygen in the air so that the carbon dioxide can become very toxic. A heated room containing animals should have some ventilation.

If electric light can be fitted in the dog building it will be of enormous assistance during the winter months when it is dark in the mornings and by early afternoon. Work with the dogs is thereby made so much easier.

Where a number of dogs is kept, it is an asset if a separate place can be provided for whelping bitches, and some kind of isolation section if any of the kennel become ill.

This special accommodation should also be warm and well lit. It need not be large, as it is unlikely that it will be required to hold many dogs at a time, but it should be conveniently situated, perhaps adjacent to the attendant's bedroom, so that the invalids can be given constant care at all hours.

KENNEL ROUTINE

The management of the Chihuahua, whether it is one huose-dog or a sizeable kennel, is much the same as the routines recommended for any other breed and follows the lines found suitable for other members of the Toy group. One or two companion dogs will be required to fit in with the rest of the household, and their timetable established accordingly. But regularity is important. So far as mealtimes, exercise periods, and so on are concerned, it does not matter much when the dogs are fed and taken out so long as you fix their programme and stick to it.

Adult dogs should be put into the garden before breakfast. If there is no garden, they must be taken out on a lead. In either case, the dogs must not be out long enough to catch cold, especially if they have just come out of a warm sleeping-box or from the underside of someone's quilt. They should be brought in again the moment they have done both their jobs, and Chihuahuas learn to oblige very rapidly since they dislike being out in the cold. If the owner watches them while they are outside, it is a very good way of checking any indisposition. Loose or constipated motions are noticed and can be dealt with promptly.

In mild weather, the Chihuahuas will enjoy romping in the garden or in a large wired enclosure, and while they are exercising their pens can be cleaned, and puppies, if any, fed. The Chi's should always have a small kennel or wooden boxes in their run, so that if they feel chilly they can pop inside out of the wind.

If their room has a floor that needs washing it should be mopped over with warm water containing a little disinfectant. Any dirty newspapers can be rolled up and stuffed into a bucket with a lid, later to be burned on bonfire or in boiler.

The floors or trays of pens must be well washed or scrubbed, and if necessary put out in the fresh air to dry. The windows can be opened while the work is in progress, and when the trays are dry, they can be slid back and fresh newspaper spread over them in each little kennel. If many Toy dogs are kept, it is quite difficult to keep up supplies of newsprint, and certainly the household's intake of Sunday and daily papers is not enough. Many newsagents sell bundles of papers by the hundredweight, and dog owners who use these in quantity are glad to be able to buy them. Most people have friends who save papers for them, and it is worth asking the neighbours to do so, as some people only throw them away and are pleased to find a use for them. The little beds should be taken outside and well brushed out with a stiff handbrush. Blankets, if not dirtied, can be shaken and aired. Soiled blankets should soak in a bucket of soapy water to which a little disinfectant has been added, prior to washing, drying and airing.

A bucket and shovel, with a small, stiff brush (*not* the one you use for the beds!) should be used for going over the surface of the run, or that part of the garden where the dogs exercise. A plastic bucket does well and is easily washed. An ordinary coal shovel with a wooden handle is the best, and all excreta must be removed and burned or buried. The bucket must be well disinfected after use and the shovel rinsed. This is a most important part of kennel routine, yet one that is often neglected. Careful attention to cleanliness does much to prevent worms, and even more serious infections and illnesses.

Grass, gravel, and concrete can all get into a disgusting state if not subjected to regular bucket-and-shovel drill throughout the day. In long spells of dry weather it is nearly always necessary to swill or hose down concrete with water and disinfectant, and to soak other surfaces by means of a watering-can fitted with a spray. A word about disinfectant. There are dozens of brands, some derived from tar, others with a pine-oil base. One good make is generally as effective a deodorant as another; some are not quite such efficient germ-killers. Most well-known manufacturers make products which conform to a standard, and so the choice really resolves itself into a preference for one particular fragrance. Always, however, ascertain that a disinfectant is non-toxic.

A veterinary surgeon will probably tell you that hot water containing plain household washing soda is the best possible disinfectant but even so, most people like to add something with a pleasant aroma. Always use disinfectants in the recommended proportions advised by the makers, for very strong solutions are seldom more effective than the correct, and weaker, dilutions. The smell of very strong disinfectant can be overpowering when used indoors.

After kennels and runs are spick and span, water bowls

must be rinsed, wiped with a clean dishcloth, and refilled. Chihuahuas drink relatively little but like to have cold, fresh water within reach should they feel thirsty. During summer, drinking vessels should be placed in shady spots, and the water must be changed two or three times daily.

Bitches in season or with litters, or any dog confined to its pen, should have small individual bowls of clean water so that they can help themselves.

All the time the kennel work is in progress, the dogs will be running about or sunning themselves outside. Once everything is done, call one dog in at a time, and look it over carefully before it is placed in its pen. This is the time to notice any signs of bareness on the ears, skull, or hocks; eyes that require bathing, teeth or any other minor items that need attention. The coat should be roughed up the wrong way a few times, so that if the dog has collected a flea from the grass, it is immediately detected. It can be removed with a fine-tooth comb or, with a little practise, nimble finger and thumb. There is nothing shameful in a dog picking up fleas. Country dogs are extremely likely to do so. What is disgraceful is neglect of these parasites, which should be dealt with promptly and not allowed to multiply. If numerous, it may be necessary to give the dog a medicated bath. Anal glands—at the root of the tail—may need attention occasionally. Ask a vet to show you how to deal with these.

When the dogs are all back in their places, they will settle happily for a while until it is time for a meal. This will be followed by another brief spell outside. The early afternoon is a good time for the walk. Although Chihuahuas can do quite well with very little exercise, they love their outings, and will look forward to them about the same time every day. They begin peering through the window, barking in eager anticipation, and are terribly disappointed if the walk does not materialize, so much so that every effort should be made to take them out, even if it is for only a few minutes. Chihuahuas have such expressive little faces, to disappoint them is just like disappointing a child. The alteration in them is immediately noticeable; they can change, like sunlight into shadow, in a moment. When the brightness is gone, the little creatures look downcast and dull.

Chihuahua puppies begin to enjoy walks at quite an early age, and at three or four months can trot about the garden. At five months they will probably follow the older dogs, and it is a fact that a normal, sound Chihuahua will walk as far as its owner, and come back fresh and full of life even if 'two legs' is worn out. Not everyone is able to take a pack of Chihuahuas out loose. It is wonderful to see them fly past in a wild rush, streaming up the path and into a field, but a conducted ramble round the garden is better than nothing at all, and the dogs love it.

When they are back in their runs or pens again, it is time to spend a few minutes with any youngsters that are being trained to walk on a lead, or learning to stand and be handled at shows. It will be feeding-time again when that is done, for the puppies, nursing mothers, and any other 'priorities' such as dogs requiring extra weight and condition. The dogs are then coming towards the end of their busy day. Some or all of them will be anxious to join the family for an evening round the television; then will come the last run of the day, followed by another comfortable night snuggled up in cosy beds.

Chihuahuas thrive as individuals, and wilt without human companionship and love. They should be included in the family circle whenever possible. This is not always easy if there are many of them, but even so it should be possible to give individual attention to each in turn. Take one or two out shopping. Have half a dozen in the kitchen for an hour or two, and bring some others into the dining-room at meal-times. Let the old favourites take it in turns to occupy all available laps during television viewing times.

And do not aspire to have the biggest kennel—only the best—otherwise you may find that the dogs do not receive the personal attention they need and deserve.

NINE

THE STUD DOG

W E HAVE dealt very fully, in another chapter, with the question of selecting breeding stock, and therefore it is unnecessary to continue to stress the importance of keeping stud dogs of only the highest quality.

A great many small breeders—and this applies not only to Chihuahuas but to all breeds throughout the country—never keep a stud dog of their own. It *is* one more dog to feed and care for, to house and to exercise, even if the labour and cost involved in looking after a Chihuahua is small. Such people prefer to have a wide choice of stud dogs at their disposal, and to mate their bitches with the best dogs owned by others.

Admittedly, a large proportion of Chihuahua breeders *do* keep their own studs. This would seem to be, in the main, because such tiny animals are so little bother; and whether one keeps four Chihuahuas or six is of very little consequence. It feels nice to have no stud fees to pay, and it is certainly convenient to be spared the trouble of taking or sending the bitches away when they are in season. It would in fact be advisable for every breeder to have a stud dog, if there were enough stud dogs of outstanding merit, and if genetics ran to a pattern and one dog suited any bitch. Unfortunately, this is not so. There are few really 'plus dogs' in the Chihuahua breed, or, for that matter, in most of the other breeds; and the best dog in the country does not suit every bitch he mates. The result of it is that there are a lot of people keeping second-rate, third-rate, and worse, stud dogs, detrimental to the breed as a whole and spelling doom to their own kennels. We will not dwell on this point further, except to say again—and it cannot be too often emphasized—that the only stud dog worth keeping is the top-quality one. The other kind are a waste of time and money. The dog that consistently sires pet puppies is just not good enough. The market for pet Chihuahuas is not sufficiently developed to make it profitable to breed deliberately for the companion trade. After all, even the breeders, whose aim is to produce nothing less than Championship show winners, still get a proportion of puppies which are nothing like good enough for showing. These make delightful pets, and there are plenty of them about; there is certainly no need to set out to breed them.

Having rammed this point home, we can now assume that the new breeder has either bought, or bred in one of his early litters, a dog destined to become the stud force in the kennel. It is likely that it will be used for breeding on the home stock, and offered at public stud in the expectation that it will earn some revenue in the form of stud fees.

How early in its life can such a dog be started on its career? Nature takes care of this question, as the dog will not be capable of serving a bitch until such time as it is right to let him do so. If the dog appears keen and able to mate, it will probably do him no harm to let him serve one bitch, even if he is still young. He should, however, be very carefully and patiently handled and every precaution should be taken to make sure that he is not hurt or frightened. The bitch must be restrained from throwing herself about or snapping at the dog.

Dogs vary greatly in their approach to the reproductive act, and some mature much more rapidly than others. We get the cocky little fellow that will ape his elders by lifting his leg when the other puppies are still babyish, and he takes an interest in the girls at four or five months old. But the puppy should be at least eight or nine months, and preferably ten or eleven months, before his precocity should be utilized. Some youngsters are well over a year old before they take an interest in the opposite sex, and require a lot of patient manipulation so that they can successfully serve a bitch for the first time.

A normal dog will eventually mate a bitch, but may take his time about it. A very keen young puppy may, equally, go about the job with the skill and aplomb of an old hand. Yet another may refuse bitch after bitch, yet suddenly decide to mate one which, so far as can be seen, is no more receptive or attractive than those he has rejected.

It is tiresome if a dog remains apathetic over his bitches when it is specially desired to mate him, but as long as he is entire, he is almost sure to oblige at some time. The exception might arise in a very exceptionally small male dog, one weighing under $2\frac{1}{2}$ lb. Such dogs are not often prepotent sires, and some never succeed in mating a bitch at all.

When possible, choose an experienced brood bitch as a beginning for the young male. She is almost sure to be more amenable and easier to mate than a maiden bitch. Furthermore, if there are no puppies as a result, you will know that, while it may be 'just one of those things', the bitch is a proven breeder and so it might be the fault of the dog. If a maiden bitch and an untried dog are mated unfruitfully, it could be that either the bitch or the dog is barren, but as both have not previously produced young there is no guidance as to where the blame lies.

The ideal bitch to try with an up-and-coming stud dog is one of his own kennel companions. He will not feel strange with her; and with both animals on the spot, you will be able to put them together when the bitch seems perfectly ready. A youngster can mess about and waste much of his energies and enthusiasm trying to mate with a bitch that is not just right.

If the first bitch has to be one from outside the home establishment, an experienced owner will probably manage to bring her when she is standing to a dog and at just the right stage in her oestrum or heat. A beginner in the dog-breeding game may make the mistake of coming too early or, worse still, too late, especially if there is no male dog handy that can be used to try out the bitch so that her demeanour can be noticed. It is not at all easy to know the perfect time to take a bitch to the sire, but it is better to err on the early side.

A quiet spot must be found for the service, well away from the other dogs. If the same place can be used every time it is an advantage, as very small things such as unaccustomed surroundings can put a dog off.

Do not embark on the task in the dining-room, although I know people who always arrange the stud work there. The stud

Int. Ch. Seggieden Jupiter and Int. Ch. Seggieden Tiny Mite

Bigo's Zoranna of Winterlea and her son, Ch. Cisco Kid of Winterlea

R. Horgan, Scotnews

Ch. Rozavel Chief Scout   Ch. Rozavel Larkwhistle Nutkin

Ch. Rowley Perito of Sektuny

C. M. Cooke

Ch. Cholderton Little Scampy of Teeny Wee

Ch. Rozavel Wolf Cub

Ch. Rozavel
Bienvenida

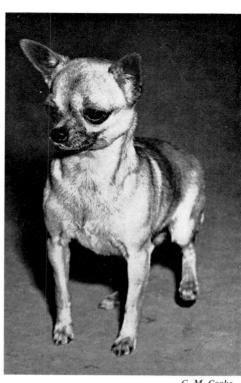

Emmrill Son-Ko's Red Rocket

C. M. Cooke

dog should be able to run about and lift his leg if he wants to; it is the natural thing for him to do when he is courting a bitch, and it would be very unkind to scold him for what is the normal behaviour.

To begin with, the dog will feel more relaxed upon the floor, but later you will require him to mate his bitches on a large table, at a height which is much more comfortable for the handlers and enables one to see what is going on.

Let dog and bitch play together for a minute or two, but keep a sharp eye on the bitch in case she is going to growl and snap. When they seem to be getting on well together, put a collar on the bitch so that she can be held when the dog mounts her. If she is inclined to collapse under his weight, put the other hand gently under her tummy. If she keeps sitting down, the dog will wear himself out and get discouraged. As you support her, see if she is the right height for the dog. If she needs to be raised up a little or if the dog needs an inch or two under his feet, arrange a little platform. This can be a few thicknesses of towelling, a folded sack, or a book wrapped in some non-slip material.

Should the bitch seem very fidgetty or snappy it is best to get a second person to help. In fact it is just as well to have two pairs of hands at any time, for one person can hold her by the neck or collar and soothe and talk to her, while the other can look after the other end, hold her tail to one side, keep her standing firmly on all four legs and get ready to hold the little dog in position once he gets going. If the dog does not seem to be managing his task, try inserting a small spot of petroleum jelly, on the tip of the little finger, just inside the opening of the bitch's vaginal passage. This may make all the difference and things will be easier for the dog.

Once the dog looks like making contact, do hold the bitch firmly. If she jumps away she may spoil everything. When the dog has 'tied' inside the bitch, he can either remain where he is, on top of the bitch, or be allowed to slide gently down. Help him to lift his leg over so that he can stand comfortably. In this position he may need something beneath his hind legs, especially if he is much smaller than the bitch. If the difference in size is very marked, it is better to leave the dog resting on the back of the bitch. He will usually need a supporting hand under his hindquarters. The 'tie' can last for a minute or two, or for the best part of an hour. Puppies occasionally result when there is no tie at all, but the chances are not quite so good, and it is considered to be a satisfactory service if dog and bitch are locked together for upwards of ten minutes.

When they part, lift the dog down, take hold of the bitch by her rear end and lift it up so that you are holding her with her hindquarters higher than her head. Keep her in this position for a minute. Then gently carry her to her kennel and leave her quietly for at least an hour before letting her out to relieve herself. Passing urine immediately after mating can prejudice the chance of puppies. But the stud dog should have a good run and be allowed to make himself comfortable before he, too, returns to his kennel. It is better not to put him in a pen or run with other male dogs, even if they are ordinarily good friends. The scent of a bitch in season will be very noticeable, and it may result in his being attacked by jealous competitors for the hand—or should it be paw?—of the lady. A few hours later he can go out with the others as usual and it will no longer be obvious to them.

Some breeders like to give bitches two services on different days. Other people, and among them are some veterinary surgeons, believe that one good and normal mating is sufficient. This is a matter of opinion, but if the first effort has been in any way unsatisfactory, it is best to try again two days later. Leaving a day in between gives the dog time to rest and recuperate, especially if the first service has been difficult or exhausting for him.

Cnes own bitches are almost invariably far easier to manage than those belonging to other people. A visiting bitch is often nervous and uneasy, and under a strain she will snap at anybody or anything. There have been instances recorded where promising youngsters have had a stud career cut short before it even began by unfortunate early experiences when bitches have frightened and upset them.

From this extensive advice it will be seen that there is more in the mating of valuable dogs and bitches than most people think. It is commonly supposed that all that is necessary is to put them together in a run and leave them alone for the rest of the day. Apart from the uncertainty of not knowing if a service has taken place, the dog can be seriously injured if he effects a tie with a restless bitch. It is not only unwise but cruel to leave, without a skilled attendant, the dog with a bitch in season.

Great care must be taken of any visiting bitches that may be brought to the dog. Other people's animals are heavy responsibilities; never accept them without making sure that there is safe, suitable accommodation prepared for them. It is not sufficient to shut the strange bitch in one of the rooms in the house; someone may go in and let her slip out and away, or leave the door ajar. The bitch cannot be turned loose in the garden, for she will almost certainly be impossible to catch even if she does not scale the fence or dive through a hole and run away. A visiting bitch should be exercised in a carefully wired enclosure, and if she is allowed off a lead the wire should be at least six feet high or more, or covered over the top. The fencing should go down into the ground to a depth of several inches.

Surely, you may ask, a gentle little Chihuahua could not scale a high wall or dig under a fence? The answer is that many can, and will do so if they have the chance. Some Chihuahuas climb like monkeys, will run up chain link, balance on the top, and drop down on the other side. Most are quite capable of digging underneath. A bitch in season, disliking her strange surroundings and anxious to find her way home, also torn by the strange urge to find herself a mate, is quite likely to try to escape.

Even exercising a strange Chihuahua on a collar and lead is not without risk. A nervous bitch can slip backwards out of a collar with alarming ease, and although a harness is not recommended wear in the normal course of things, it is safer to use if a strange dog is taken for walks.

A proportion of visiting bitches will be brought by the owners and taken home again, especially so if the stud-dog's home is in a locality easily reached by road and rail. These are the most welcome visitors, but only so if they are brought on the correct day. When bitches are sent unaccompanied, at least they can be kept until ready, and mated at the stud-dog owner's convenience, which is some recompense for the extra care and attention they require.

How often can a stud dog be used? This is a difficult question, because some dogs are more robust and fertile than others. Also, stud work is never regular. One reads or hears expressions of opinion such as the one that a good stud dog should be able to serve a hundred bitches in a year.

In the first instance, it is very unlikely that the dog will ever be offered so many. In the second, even if the dog was patronized as extensively, he could manage this number only if they were regularly spaced, two per week, with two or three days between each. Things being what they are, it never works that way. Although bitches come into season all the year round, there are periods when a lot of them come in about the same time. This is especially true of the weeks beginning in late December and extending into April. But at any time, a popular stud dog can have applications from owners of four or five bitches, all of whom want to use him within the space of a few days. Then there may be a gap of three weeks or more when there are no further applications for his services.

It is therefore not possible to be dogmatic about a stud-dog's capabilities. What we can say is that a vigorous youngster in fine condition should be able to manage three or four bitches within a week, provided none of them is especially difficult to mate, also provided the dog can be rested the week before and the week after this busy period. If the dog *has* had a struggle to serve one of the bitches, and it has been a long and wearing business, then it is questionable whether he should be allowed to try again until he has had some days of complete rest.

The above applies to the mature dog. A puppy embarking on its career at stud should not have more than one or two bitches per month until it is about fourteen months old when, since the Chihuahua is an early-maturing breed, it can take on a little more work. After a healthy dog is eighteen months of age it should be perfectly capable of dealing with any normal number of applications for its services.

Stud fees are charged for the use of a dog, and such fee covers the actual act of service, not the result, as many people suppose. There is a moral responsibility on behalf of the sire's owner to do everything possible to ensure a fruitful union. The dog should be fit and well, never overworked, the mating attended to by competent persons, and the bitch given every care both before and after the coupling.

If there are no puppies as a result of the visit, the stud fee is not returnable either in whole or in part, but most owners give a free service at the next heat, and this is regarded as customary even if it is not obligatory. It is as well to ask for details of the conditions under which bitches are accepted for stud. The dog's owners should provide these, either printed on the pedigree card or on a separate sheet. There can then be no arguments.

The amount charged for the fee must be based on the current scale of stud fees common throughout the breed, the merits of the dog himself, and the estimated prices his puppies can be expected to fetch. The sire's show successes enter into this, also the quality of his pedigree. For instance, a dog whose bloodlines include very scarce and sought-after strains may command as high a fee as a reigning Champion, even if he has not done as much winning himself.

Never make the mistake of charging too little. We have not minimized the trouble, work, and responsibility that is attached to the care of a stud dog and his visitors, nor the fact that it can be time-absorbing and even occasionally worrying. In view of this it is obviously better to accept, say, ten bitches at fees of 12 guineas each, than all the bother of fifteen at 8 guineas.

If the dog is really outstanding, and if he is doing well at the shows, the stud work will probably come along of its own accord. Most owners, however, like to advertise their dogs, and they can do this in dog weekly and monthly magazines, local newspapers, or in the breed society's handbooks. Advertisements in dog-show catalogues are yet another channel, though these have rather a small circulation and are not seen by as many people as the Press announcements will be.

It is generally thought that a regular small advertisement attracts more attention than an occasional splash in the paper. The publishers of the two dog weeklies produce attractive illustrated supplements at Christmas time and these are in demand all over the world. Space in either or both, preferably including one or two good photographs, is an excellent way of bringing one's stock to the notice of a wide public.

Enquiries are sure to include requests for the dog's pedigree. This takes time to copy, so it is best to have a quantity duplicated, or to order some printed cards with the breeding on one side and a picture of the sire on the other. There are printers who specialize in work for dog breeders, and they can be relied upon to submit samples of various types of attractive stud cards and folders.

It is a fact that a fashionable stud dog can be a great asset, but it is very doubtful if anybody lives a life of luxury by the earnings of their dogs. At best, the stud fees are a great help towards the running expenses of a kennel. Even when the dog is in good demand, it is still unwise to bank too much on the duration of his popularity. A rush of stud work is encouraging, but cannot be expected to continue throughout the lifetime of the dog, and it is actually likely to be a comparatively short spell of activity and prosperity. A little thought on this subject makes the reason for this abundantly clear. If the dog is a first-class stud force, it means he is siring very good puppies. Included among these are some fine young males, and these will appear at the shows and do their sire credit. Breeders notably incline to run after the latest winner as soon as he makes a spectacular appearance, so directly a dog is in the news there will be many people anxious to make use of his services. It is a matter of opinion whether it is best to stick to the sire of the new star which has proved that he can sire fliers, or to breed to the young sensation which may well be superior to his parent but which may or may not prove as successful a sire. Naturally there will always be some breeders who will want to mate their bitches to the older dog, and he will continue to get some fees from time to time. But many owners get so assured when they find stud fees are rolling in that they are misled into thinking that this happy state of affairs will continue for the rest of the dog's life. Alas, this is not so, as has been explained above.

There is, then, one other side to the question. There may be a rush to use the big winner, but this will rapidly cease if he does not sire top stars in his early litters. The stud-dog owner's chief concern is to get some of his progeny into the ring as winners, otherwise people are not going to patronize the dog. But if the dog sires winning sons, they are going to draw some of the stud fees away from the sire, so, on the whole, it looks as if we cannot win either way. Perhaps the most profitable stud dog is the one that produces a succession of Champion daughters. He can thus make for himself a reputation as a wonderful winner-producer, and at the same time does not produce sons as good or better than himself to snatch the fees.

Before leaving the question of fees, we must not forget the 'puppy arrangements'. All owners of stud dogs are asked from time to time if they are willing to take a puppy from the prospective litter in lieu of a cash payment at the time of mating. A few owners, and particularly those who do not do much breeding and who have few if any bitches of their own, will come to some such arrangement. Others, especially those who prefer to sell their own home-bred stock, reared to their own specifications, refuse to do this. The advantages of such agreements are of doubtful benefit to either of the parties concerned, and the probable outcome is always a gamble. The breeder of the litter is usually required to promise to give up the pick of the puppies, or at least the second choice, at about two months of age. This means that he cannot sell any of the puppies until the dog's owner has made his selection. It also means that what is probably the best puppy in the litter has to be given away, and in the normal course of events this is worth a good deal more than the fee. When the time comes, the breeder finds himself wishing that he had paid the money and was in a position to keep or sell the outstanding specimen in the litter.

It is by no means such a one-sided arrangement for the stud-dog owner, either. If the bitch 'misses', there is no puppy and no fee. If the litter turns out to be mediocre (and even the best sires cannot be expected to sire outstanding puppies every time) the pick of litter may be worth less than the fee. This is particularly likely in a breed like Chihuahuas, which have small litters as a rule and do not offer a very wide choice. While admittedly any reasonably good bitch puppy is worth more than the largest stud fee, an all-dog litter may well contain puppies that are only pets and not likely to command much of a price.

Finally, there is always an element of risk, however slight, in taking a baby puppy from a strange kennel. Some owners are less careful than others, and pick-of-litter transactions usually take place when the puppies are still too young to have received immunity against prevalent dog diseases. It generally means bringing home an uninoculated puppy which may be a potent source of infection.

It is rather difficult to make puppy-in-lieu-of-fee arrangements with one applicant and not with another. Arrange it once, and the next person is asking for the same concession, and if refused, says: 'Oh! But you did it for Mrs A.' So by and large it is best to take a firm stand. Fix a sensible fee, and refuse to mate a bitch on any other terms. If a particularly good bitch is brought to the stud dog, it is perfectly easy to ask her owner if a puppy may be booked from the litter, and this is a straightforward and far more satisfactory arrangement.

If a stud dog is kept, it is as well for him to have an understudy. Many dogs have strongly individual ideas and may refuse to mate an apparently ready and willing bitch. It may be too late for the owner to rush her to a different place and dog, so it is useful to have another male handy, preferably of equal merit, of course. Apart from anything else he is useful because he can be shown the rejected bitch, and if he, too, is disinterested it is obvious she is either not ready or has gone over. If he is keen and anxious to mate, then it is clear that the first stud dog just does not fancy her for reasons best known to himself, and she will probably mate with number two without further difficulty.

Because this is a situation that can always crop up, it is just as well to get things clear with owners of unaccompanied bitches, since not everyone is on the telephone, and delay at such a time serves only to complicate the matter. Ask the owners, if, in the event of the chosen sire refusing to mate, they are agreeable to the bitch being tried with another dog.

Keep a record of the bitches sent to the stud dog. Printed

books of stud service receipts, with counterfoils, are satisfactory, and leave room for the most important details—
registered name of bitch, dates of service(s), name and address
of owner, etc. It is as well to add the bitch's sire and dam, also
if the service was easy or in any way complicated, for such
information often comes in useful afterwards.

In conclusion, if you are lucky enough to get a good male
puppy by your beautiful stud dog, do not be persuaded to part
with him too easily. So many people live to regret the fact that
they have dwelt overmuch in the present without giving
sufficient thought to the future. It is good to have another
young stud dog growing up, however much the sire's reputation may be booming, and there is nothing sadder than to see a
kennel fading out of the limelight because it has failed to produce a succession of good dogs to keep it to the fore.

TEN

THE BROOD BITCH AND HER LITTER

IF A good stud dog can be a useful source of revenue, then a good brood bitch is a pearl above price. She can build an entire kennel, and because of her importance much thought must be given to her selection. She is to be the rock on which we build.

Very tiny Chihuahuas are delightful little things, and if good in the essential breed points are sure to do well in the show ring. But they seldom make the best breeding propositions.

The possibility of whelping complications is very real where the tinies are concerned and, as a rule, a maximum of one or two puppies per litter is about as much as one can hope for.

It is the larger bitches that have litters of up to five puppies on an average (although seven and eight puppies have been recorded, this is not usual) and are much more likely to whelp naturally and easily.

Whatever size she is, the brood bitch should be typical, and she should excel in at least some of the more important breed characteristics. While we speak of her as a larger size, we do not mean that she should be in the seven or eight-pound range. In fact it is not desirable to breed from the really outsize dams, since even if they produce small daughters, the very fact that their characteristics are hiding in the background, means that the likelihood of the little bitch throwing big puppies, with consequent complications, has to be faced.

A bitch within the standard weight is a wise choice; one about 5 to 6 lb is ideal. There are certainly plenty of much smaller bitches used for breeding, many of which are prolific

natural whelpers. But a large proportion of the bitches under
4½-lb weight require veterinary assistance, and the beginner
usually gets off to an easier start with a rather larger foundation
brood.

The bitch should be maintained in good condition. She
must be carefully fed and exercised, never allowed to get lean or
ribby, never overfed to the stage of getting podgy and fat.

She will come into season some time after she is six months
old. There is something to be said for mating a bitch at her first
season, provided she is mature enough and not less than ten
months of age. Chihuahuas do develop early and whereas a
big breed would still be very immature at this age, some of the
toys are already quite adult. There is an idea that the muscles
are pliable in a very young female, and that this enhances the
chances of easy parturition. Many people believe that the
bitch should not be bred from until her second heat, when it is
certain she is fully matured.

If there are differing views about this, however, everyone is
unanimous in agreeing that it is folly to wait until a bitch is two
and a half to three years old or over before she is mated for the
first time, and definitely risky to begin breeding from a bitch of
four years old or so.

Chihuahuas are not always the easiest of bitches to get
mated owing to some difficulty in deciding upon the best day
for the visit to the stud dog.

In a majority of other breeds, bitches are willing to mate
about the tenth to thirteenth day, following the first signs of
oestrum. But many Chihuahuas will accept the dog on the
seventh or eighth days, and are showing an obvious decline in
the heat period by the time the thirteenth day is up.

This makes it rather trying for the owner of the bitch to
know what to do for the best, especially if he has no male dog
available to keep him informed. It also greatly complicates the
lives of the stud-dog owners, since they cannot be certain of the
days when their dog's services will be required, but have to try
to keep him reserved for the booked bitch over a period of
several days.

Because of this uncertainty, owners should always make
arrangements to take a bitch to the selected dog well in

advance of the day when she is expected to be ready. It is best to write or telephone when the first signs of a red discharge are observed. If a likely day is fixed, perhaps the 9th, this can be put forward or postponed when the bitch's behaviour gives a clue as to the way things are working out.

Most bitches show a decided swelling of the female organ, the vulva, for one or two days, and then this is followed by a discharge which resembles blood. This can be observed for a few days or for over a week, and then it will be seen to have changed in colour; it will no longer be bright red, but a sort of watery pink. At this stage, or very soon after, it is most likely that the bitch will be ready and eager to mate, and she should be introduced to the dog without further delay.

Some bitches discharge less than others, and many are fastidious in their habits, constantly licking and cleaning themselves which makes it hard to check their progress. It is a help to provide a clean white towel or piece of old sheeting for a bed-cover. Then every spot of discharge will be noticeable, and if the cover is changed daily and a fresh piece of material supplied, the subtle alterations in the colour and consistency of the mucus can be carefully checked.

While a bitch is attractive to the other sex from the first day to the last, she is unlikely to accept the dog for the first few days, nor is the dog very determined about serving her until she is nearly or completely ready. But there are exceptions to every rule, and it is best to be sure rather than sorry, so keep the bitch under careful supervision right from the start. She should not be allowed to roam in the garden unattended, even if it is fenced. Strange dogs are remarkably determined when they are aware of a bitch in season, and are quite capable of jumping over a wall or digging underneath.

The risks of accidental matings with Chihuahua bitches are less serious than with the larger breeds, because it is unlikely there will be many strays about anything like as small. But misalliances have been known, and there have been cases when bitches have mated with dogs quite considerably larger than themselves, so it is best to be cautious. Keep the bitch shut up in her pen and behind doors, exercise her regularly but only on a lead.

If several bitches live together they will play about, and when the bitch on heat shows every sign of flirting with them she is probably getting ready to visit the dog.

If the breeder can travel with the bitch it is always the most satisfactory arrangement. The mating can be supervised, the whole thing may be over within an hour, and the bitch taken home. This is often a help to the owner of the stud, who is thus relieved of the responsibility of boarding and dealing with a strange and frequently nervous and hard-to-handle visitor.

It is by no means always possible for owners to drop everything and take off at short notice for what is often a long journey, and when this cannot be done then the bitch must be sent by train.

The stud fee, with the sum to cover the cost of the return carriage, should be posted directly the bitch has been put on rail.

The dog's owner will have been advised of the day and time of arrival, will collect the bitch from the station and attend to the mating. After she has been rested and fed she will be returned by the same route, the owner having been notified that she is being dispatched.

When she is home again the bitch must still be very carefully guarded for the remainder of her season, which may last another week or ten days. Some bitches go off very quickly after being mated, others do not.

There is no need to alter the routine of the first month. It is a mistake to begin stuffing a bitch with extra-nourishing foods too early, for she will only get fat, which is something to be avoided at all costs. After four or five weeks there should be signs of pregnancy. There may be an obvious swelling of the abdomen, or a slightly rounder appearance which an observant owner detects immediately the animal has had a meal. At this stage the swelling becomes rapidly more obvious, and the protein in the diet can be increased. If the bitch enjoys raw meat there is nothing better for her at this time.

Some bitches become very hungry when they are in whelp; others, which previously had good appetites, become rather indifferent feeders. The latter must be pampered and tempted with delicacies, because the bitch needs plenty of nourishment to enable her puppies to develop inside her without exercising a drain on her bodily resources; she also needs to build herself up so that she will have plenty of milk for the babies when they are born.

About the beginning of the last week the bitch should be offered a light, milky breakfast in addition to her solid food. If she is getting uncomfortably distended she may like to have her meat divided into two small meals rather than one large. It may be advisable to give her a small dessert-spoonful of liquid paraffin daily for the last week only.

Extras, such as calcium, bone meal, and so on are not necessary for the normal Chihuahua bitch. These supplements are given to bitches when it is desired to build heavy bone and large size. Neither is required in a Chi, and such extras only serve to make the puppies big and coarse, and possibly thus complicate the whelping.

The exception is the bitch that is likely to suffer from eclampsia, a calcium deficiency condition which causes alarming convulsions that have been known to prove fatal. A vet is the best person to advise treatment, which should be prompt; and who will also prescribe the best methods to try to avoid a recurrence of the trouble.

The gestation period for the dog is sixty-three days, but Chihuahuas frequently whelp early, and the puppies can arrive alive and well any time from the fifty-seventh day. Puppies up to six days early usually do well, but any born eight days early have a poor chance of survival.

The whelping box should be prepared well ahead of time, and the bitch should be invited to sleep in it for a week or two, then she will not feel strange when the time comes for her to settle down and have her puppies.

A quiet spot is essential. Many litters have been lost, especially when the bitch concerned is young and inexperienced, because other dogs have been allowed to interfere, or well-meaning humans have been too persistent in their attentions.

The whelping box does not need to be elaborate. A small wooden kennel or box with plenty of ventilation and a hinged side and lid is satisfactory. The best place for the box is in a warm room, near a good fire, where the owner can sit in comfort and attend to the bitch from time to time.

The first signs vary, but probably the bitch will become fidgety, wander about, sit down and lick herself, and whine. She may ask to be let out, and will then want to come back again almost immediately. She will try to pass urine frequently, and look rather uncomfortable and worried. In between times she will tear at her bed, scratch it into heaps, and it is best to take away cushions, rugs, or blankets and to line the bed with a piece of clean bath towel on top of some thick newspapers.

The uneasiness and bed-making can go on for an hour or two or for most of the day or night. They are sure signs that labour is about to begin, and eventually the bitch will start to strain. She will become less excited, and may curl up in her bed. Straining will become more definite, and if all goes well the slimey, bluish tip of a puppy's nose will appear. Another heave and a grunt from the little mother, with perhaps a quick cry of pain, and the puppy falls out with a 'plop' on the floor of the box. A sensible bitch will seize it and in a most expert way chew, suck, and lick at the unattractive membrane which envelops the puppy, pulling it away from it and finally biting off the cord. The puppy, bounced about and pushed around, fills its tiny lungs with air and utters its first cry. If the bitch is at all slow about this she must have help, otherwise the puppy will die. With the corner of a towel wipe the mucus away from the puppy's mouth and nose, and take a piece of sewing silk, dipped in Dettol or iodine. With this tie the umbilical cord securely, about half to three-quarters of an inch from the tummy. Then cut the cord with clean scissors, rub the puppy dry and either return it to the mother or put it in a blanket inside a cardboard box, and keep it warm. If the jelly-like 'afterbirth' or sac does not come away with the puppy, try not to break the cord until it is all pulled gently away. Watch the bitch and see if she has expelled it. Retained afterbirths are very dangerous, usually fatal.

Any Chihuahua bitch, and especially one whelping for the first time, may have difficulty in expelling a puppy. If straining persists for over an hour and a half, or two hours, and there is no sign of a puppy, telephone the Vet and seek advice.

If the head of a puppy appears it should be possible to take hold of it, masking the hand and fingers in a piece of clean towel so that a firm grip is ensured, and to pull firmly downwards until the puppy emerges. Do not hurry this; pull slowly and, if possible, time it for the moment when the little mother is straining.

Sometimes puppies come tail and back legs first; this is known as a 'breech' presentation. It is often more difficult for a bitch to expel a puppy in this position, and it is also harder to help her as there is not much to grip.

If a puppy is protruding, or if it can be felt with the tip of a very well scrubbed and greased finger, it needs to be born quite quickly or it will die. If the birth does not progress and if it does not seem possible to assist, a Vet should be called, because delay at this stage is dangerous. Not only may the puppy stop breathing, but others behind it may suffer a similar fate from the hold-up.

When the puppies are all born the bitch will usually settle down and lick and feed her family. If it has been a tiring whelping for her she will probably curl round and go to sleep. This relaxed attitude is generally a sign that there are no more puppies to come and that she has finished. The size of the bitch herself is no real indication, because she may look quite distended for some hours and it takes a little time for the swollen uterus to contract and for her figure to return to something like normal. She will welcome a long drink of warm milk and glucose.

Professional fingers, however, can tell if there are any puppies still to come, so where there is any doubt at all it is wise to ask the Vet to call. If there is a chance of a puppy having remained behind, or if it is uncertain whether all the afterbirths were expelled with the puppies that have been born, the Vet will give an injection to contract the womb and expel its contents. Anything of this type left in the uterus will set up septicaemia, and many bitches have been lost for want of a little extra care. Some breeders like to remove afterbirths, others allow the bitch to eat them.

If the Vet has not been successful in getting the puppies by normal methods, it will be necessary to resort to either forceps or a Caesarian operation. Most Vets are reluctant to use the former, since with a small animal it is a difficult and dangerous business groping round in an effort to grasp the slippery pup and yet not pinch the delicate organs inside the bitch herself. When forceps are used, it generally means a tight grip on the puppy while it is extracted, and more often than not it is badly injured.

A Caesarian operation is a better proposition, modern anaesthetics and antibiotics having greatly minimized the dangers which made it necessary to avoid this in years gone by. At one time the chances of a bitch surviving the operation were not always good, but now the whole thing is over in a couple of hours and the bitch should progress well and take good care of her puppies. She will probably be given one or two daily injections of penicillin, and will have her stitches taken out in a fortnight.

If the bitch having had a Caesarian operation was a maiden and has not had puppies previously, she is apt to come out of her deep sleep to regard with horror the little monsters which are squeaking all around her. She will shrink into a corner of her box, the expression on her face being one of utter revulsion. She may growl at the puppies. Not having had them naturally, she has no idea that they are hers. Get someone whom the bitch loves and trusts to hold her, and try to get the puppies to suck. Hold them, one by one, to a teat, press the little mouths open and encourage them to hang on by themselves. It may be necessary to keep on doing this at regular intervals until the bitch accepts her litter. If she can be persuaded to lick them the battle is won, and it may be a help to squeeze out some milk from her teats on to the puppy, or to smear it with a little butter.

Once the Chihuahua takes charge of the puppies she will be a model mother, but even so it may be a matter of hours or even a couple of days before her milk flows freely. It often comes down slowly after an operation, or even when the birth has been normal, especially if the puppies are premature. But even if the teats seem dry it is still important to keep on trying to get the litter suckling, because this stimulates the milk flow.

Help the little mother by keeping her warm. Baby puppies require warmth—they have just come from a snug, dark, cosy place into a chilly and draughty world—and if a new-born whelp is allowed to get cold it is extremely difficult to restore heat to the tiny body. Because of this, many breeders like to take each puppy as it is born and to place it in a flannel-lined box by the stove, preferably with a well-covered hot-water bottle under the blanket for the puppies to crawl and lie upon. When the bitch has finished and has been given a clean, dry bed, she can have all the babies back again. A few bitches, however, become agitated and upset if the puppies are removed, in which event one should be left in the whelping box and the others kept warm out of her hearing.

Be sure to let the bitch out to make herself comfortable; she will want to do this every few hours, for she will be most anxious to avoid soiling her bed and her precious babies. Do not let her stay out more than a minute or two; you do not want her or the new family to catch cold. The mother will not require her normal exercise until the puppies are beginning to grow up, but as soon as they leave the nest and start to toddle around she will tend to be less solicitous, more prepared to leave them for short intervals, and will probably enjoy a daily walk. It will not hurt the pups if she is away from them for twenty minutes or so, and it makes a change for the dam.

As the puppies are weaned, so will she spend longer and longer periods away from them but, unlike bitches of many other breeds which become bored with their offspring at a very early stage, the Chihuahua mother will usually remain devoted to them for weeks or months, often for ever. She remains interested in her puppies, appears to know them and to single them out for attention even when she has been away from them for a considerable time. She will run to them, push them with her nose, lick them, and show every sign of delight at being reunited with her treasures.

Many bitches, especially those which have been properly and generously fed, will leave a litter, looking in perfect show condition. Others, and this is not necessarily any reflection on the care they have received, come away from their puppies looking very thin and poor. These seem to pass on all the nourishment to their puppies without retaining enough for themselves, but they soon regain condition when lavishly fed and provided with a tonic. In all cases it takes a few weeks for the milk glands to dry up and the pendant breasts to tighten, so very few show bitches are ready for the ring until some time after they have left a litter.

The condition of the dam when she has finished with her puppies must determine the question as to whether or not she can be bred from again at her next heat, and the number of puppies reared has some bearing on the matter. A bitch that rears one or two puppies and looks plump and sleek when they are independent of her, can be mated again without risk of bad effects. Another which has reared four, five, or more and is herself run down when her task is finished, should have twelve months' rest before motherhood is thrust upon her again.

Even when a bitch has fairly small litters and maintains herself in fine condition, it is still a safe rule to mate her twice running and then let her miss at her third heat, so that she can have a really good rest.

ELEVEN

FEEDING THE CHIHUAHUA

WEANING

THE stage at which weaning should begin is dictated by the amount of milk the dam is giving to her babies, and this, in turn, is governed by her own state of health and by the number of whelps she is rearing.

A bitch with a single puppy, irrespective of her own condition, will probably continue to provide milk for it until it is at least six to eight weeks old. One with several puppies may have a rapidly diminishing milk supply at any time from about three-and-a-half to four-and-a-half weeks following the birth of the litter, and this is very likely if she herself is debilitated. As soon as the bitch is conscious that she has insufficient nourishment for her babies she may growl or snap at them, when they try to suck. This is a sign that the puppies must learn to lap, or they will have their growth impeded.

Some bitches start the weaning process off themselves by eating their own food, and almost immediately vomiting it among the puppies so that they may eat it. Unfortunately, if the bitch has been fed meat in fairly large pieces the puppies will choke or make themselves sick when they try to swallow it, so the habit is not one to be encouraged. If a bitch vomits her food for her litter she should be kept away from them for a couple of hours after feeding-time.

Obviously, the perfect time to start weaning a litter is well before they begin to be a drain on their mother, so as soon as they can be persuaded to take an interest in milk and meat these should be offered to them. The best quality raw beef is safest in the early days, and it should be scraped. To do this,

144

take a chunk of meat weighing half a pound or more, and a large, sharp knife. Scrape the meat, pressing the edge of the knife down firmly and drawing it towards you, and as the fine pulp collects along the blade put it aside in a saucer. When there is about a small teaspoonful ready for each puppy, take the babies on your knee, one by one, and gently push the meat into the little mouths. If the mother is still feeding them generously they will not be hungry and will spit out the meat. A little pushed well down the throat may start them eating, but if they are still reluctant, keep the dam away for a couple of hours or so and then try again. Continue to offer the puppies scraped meat in this manner twice daily until they fall on it greedily. The amount can be then gradually increased until they are taking up to a good tablespoonful at a meal, according to size and appetite.

While this is happening the bitch herself will still be having a good milky breakfast, and it is a good thing to try to interest the puppies in her dish each morning. They may not need much invitation, but will stumble into it to see what 'Mum' is finding so attractive. Take the puppy gently, press its little mouth down until it touches the milk, but not too deep or it will get some liquid up its nose. The puppy will very soon learn to drink, and once it gets going it is as well to provide a separate saucer of milk for the litter, both morning and evening, and watch the mother to see that she does not drink her own and take theirs as well.

With scraped meat at midday and at tea-time, and with milk for breakfast and supper, the puppies will be on four regular meals, and soon the second meat meal can be replaced by one of fine puppy meal or rusk, soaked in broth. From this stage onwards the diet will proceed on the lines suggested in the section we have devoted to the feeding of older puppies.

Always keep careful watch for signs of tummy upsets, sickness, or loose motions, and adjust the ration accordingly. Indigestion can generally be cured by withholding one of the solid meals, or by keeping the puppy on milk for a day and giving a little magnesia, or bismuth.

Check the puppy for worms. These parasites are usually present to a greater or lesser degree in all puppies, whatever the breed, and can not only have a bad effect on the health of the dog but, in small toy breeds, can cause death.

A wormy puppy can be consuming plenty of nourishing food, but the worms will absorb much of the goodness and the dog will in fact virtually be starved. It is foolish to feed worms: get rid of them. A worm-infested puppy is easily identified. The signs are leanness; lack-lustre, rough-textured coat; a noticeable tendency to blow up after even a small meal. Loose motions, and motions composed of slimy mucus are strongly indicative of parasites. In bad cases the puppy may suffer from convulsions. Sometimes worms are vomited, often they are passed through the rectum, one or more at a time.

The quality of vermifuges available for dogs has greatly improved in recent years. Our grandfathers dosed their dogs with powdered glass and turpentine. If they killed the worms they must often have killed the dogs as well. Even a few years ago an effective worm dose involved hours of preparatory fasting followed by a violent purge which sometimes proved too much for a puppy already debilitated by the effects of the parasites. Now, however, there are a number of safe and effective preparations that can be given even to very young dogs. Fasting is not necessary, and often the dog suffers the minimum discomfort. It is best to consult a veterinary surgeon about worming a valuable dog; he will advise the correct dosage according to the animal's age and weight.

When a puppy has been wormed keep a careful watch, and if worms are passed, remove them and burn them. Worming is usually repeated after a week or two in case any worm eggs have been left behind and developed since the others were expelled. After this a dog kept under hygienic conditions should remain clear for a considerable time. Most people do not dose puppies for worms until they are at least seven or eight weeks old, unless the symptoms shown make it imperative to treat them earlier. It is politic to dose them if they show definite signs of infestation, as it is quite possible for the worms to kill them. When very young puppies are to be dosed it is more important still that a Vet prescribes the treatment.

Chihuahua puppies are usually extremely tough, hardy, and lively little creatures. While, like most young things, they require warmth and care in the nest, as weaning progresses they grow up to be strong, healthy little dogs; no more trouble to rear than dogs of other breeds and less prone to illnesses than a great many larger members of the canine race. Puppies need opportunities for exercise and should be kept in a roomy pen in which they can play and gambol, preferably on newspaper. This will keep the floor sanitary and spotless since the paper can be rolled up and burned when it becomes soiled.

Freedom from draughts is a prime essential, and the puppies should have a tiny kennel or covered box containing some sort of bedding, so that they can snuggle up and sleep when their games have tired them out. On warm summer days the box and pen can be placed on the lawn, but if the sun goes down or a chill wind gets up, it is time to take the puppies indoors.

By the time they are four or five months old puppies will enjoy spells of freedom in the garden, and will probably take quite long walks in suitable surroundings. Naturally, no puppy should be taken into streets or public parks until fully inoculated. The Vet will attend to this when the puppy is nine or ten weeks of age, using one of the modern injections which protect dogs against the most prevalent canine diseases; there are excellent preparations which give threefold immunization in one shot.

We have been happily assuming that the rearing of the puppies has followed the normal course, with the dam providing for her offspring in the early stages. Unfortunately, however, there are times when things go wrong, and when supplementary, temporary, or even total hand feeding becomes necessary if the puppies are to survive.

If a bitch whelps prematurely for instance, or if she had to have a Caesarian operation, it may be two or three days before her milk supply comes down. While such tragedies do not often occur, it is possible that a bitch may be lost through complications at whelping time, and when any of these things happen the puppies must be kept alive by artificial means.

For the first few hours after they are born the best supplement for the puppies is tepid boiled water containing a little glucose. The puppy will take only a few drops every two hours, best administered by a pipette, fountain-pen filler, or one of the 'Bellcroy' premature baby feeders, the latter being useful when the puppy is strong enough to suck.

If the dam is not ill the puppies should be put to her at frequent intervals. Each puppy, in turn, must be held on to a teat and encouraged to suck. This stimulates the milk glands and helps to promote the flow, and perseverance rarely fails to produce the required result. If the bitch will lick and clean the babies she must be allowed to do so. If there is still no nourishment for the puppies they must be hand fed. So long as the bitch has accepted them and is taking care of them they are best left with her in her bed. Otherwise a cardboard box must be prepared. Wrap up a hot-water bottle in a couple of thicknesses of soft clean towelling and put it in the box. Cover this with a piece of clean blanket and place the puppies on top. Cover the box with another piece of blanket, leaving a little space for air, and place the box in a warm spot, well away from draughts and out of reach of other animals.

There are various milk mixtures that have been used successfully for rearing puppies by hand. One of these is Bengers' Food, made up according to the manufacturer's instructions on the tin. Dried milk, fresh cows' milk, goats' milk, and tinned condensed milk are all used with additions and modifications. It has to be borne in mind that the milk of the bitch is richer and stronger than that of the cow, so that most artificial feeds need to be fortified to make them suitable for puppies.

An extremely good formula was devised and used with striking success by the late Mrs Rider, of the famous 'Rowley' prefix. Mrs Rider kindly gave her permission to reproduce an article which she wrote for the British Chihuahua Club Handbook, and as she achieved with her methods the remarkable feat of rearing a complete litter of seven Chihuahuas entirely by hand, following the dam's collapse with eclampsia when they were only five days old, the method can scarcely be improved upon.

Mrs Rider tells us:

My only worry was finding a suitable feeder. A fountain-pen filler was, I found, easiest, but the end was hard to the mouth so I pulled a piece of bicycle valve rubber over the mouthpiece. This served admirably and the puppies took to it happily after a few tries.

Now for the actual food: it must be remembered that bitches' milk is much stronger than ordinary cows' milk, and should be mixed accordingly.

I commenced with this mixture:

To ¼ pint of Grade A Jersey milk, I added 1 teaspoonful of cream, 1 teaspoonful of dried full-cream milk powder (well mixed), 1 teaspoonful of glucose, 1 drop of Radiostol, ½ teaspoonful of Woodwards Gripe Water, half a crushed tablet of Howards Sodium Citrate, all mixed and heated to a temperature of 100, the normal blood heat of the dam.

This formula was fed at the rate of one fountain-pen fillerful to each puppy every two hours, night and day, increasing the quantity as the puppies demanded. Usually at a week old they were taking two pen-fillersful at each feed, but to the inexperienced, a word of warning—make haste slowly. Feed very, very carefully, and let the puppy take its time and get the taste of the food, thus avoiding indigestion and wind. The puppies must, of course, be kept very warm all the time.

Next comes the job of 'topping and tailing'. As you probably know, the mother normally cleans the puppies up as they feed, so a supply of cotton wool, a bowl of warm water and a jar of 'Vaseline' must be at hand. Firstly, with a piece of damp cottonwool, clean round the puppy's mouth, removing any food which may have spilled. Then gently smooth the puppy from tail towards the tummy to encourage and assist the puppy to pass water and excreta. Afterwards, clean and dry, finishing off with a smear of 'Vaseline' to prevent chafing.

The two-hourly rota continues for about ten days, when the puppies will be taking more food, and the time between feeds can be extended to three hours, and so on, until they start to lap. As soon as this happens, night feeds can be suspended and only day feeds continued, as necessary and until the little orphans feed well and are able to consume scraped raw beef. Food must, of course, be available for them to seek out during the night, once they can lap and hand-feeding has been discontinued. At this stage, cereals such as Farex can be added to the milk. I did not find raw egg a suitable diet for the very young, but I did add beaten egg to the milk to be consumed by the puppies when they were about four to six weeks old.

It can be seen, from Mrs Rider's carefully planned routine, that the hand-rearing of puppies is time-absorbing, tiring, and exacting, and although it is also very rewarding, many people lack the patience and energy to undertake it or, even if they do, fail to carry it to a successful conclusion. Even the weeks of sleepless nights seem worth while when a litter of healthy puppies play happily together, which, but for the toil and trouble of hand-rearing, would have died.

It cannot be too strongly emphasized that any milk mixture fed to puppies must be absolutely fresh. It can be mixed and kept in a refrigerator for short periods, but is best prepared afresh each time a feed is due. It must be warmed. All utensils or feeders used should be boiled between meals and kept under an upturned basin or protected in some other manner from germs and dust.

For the two-hourly interruptions through the night it is suggested that the task can be made less onerous by having a thermos flask, or one of the new gadgets devised to keep babies' bottles warm. Sufficient mixtures can be prepared to last until morning; if too hot it can be cooled easily enough, but in the middle of the night it is more than trying to have to pad round the house in dressing-gown and slippers heating up milk on a stove.

If no help is available there is only one thing to be done— the alarm clock must be set at two-hourly intervals. If the rearing can become a family affair, two individuals can take turns to sit up at night with the puppies; this makes the loss of sleep more easily endured.

Hand-reared puppies are always full of character, and never fail to have outstanding personalities. They have received so much love and attention, have had such gentle handling bestowed upon them from the start, that they grow up with an engaging trust and dependence on human beings. Somehow, this early and prolonged contact with human hands seems to stimulate their intelligence. This fact, in itself, is a further reward for the good-hearted individual who goes to the trouble of rearing them artificially.

But of course it is not always necessary to take the puppies from the mother for good. Sometimes her inability to feed her puppies, and her indisposition, whatever it may be, clears up after a few days, and she is able and willing to accept the babies and to rear them herself. Provided they have been kept warm and have been carefully fed until they go back to her, they should go on quite well for, after all, she is better equipped to look after them than the best-intentioned and most able foster-mother.

There is nothing especially complicated or hazardous about feeding baby Chihuahuas. The main thing to remember is that the tiny stomachs should never be overloaded. The puppy requires ample, first-quality body-building nutrients to enable it to grow and develop, but it cannot take too much at once.

When we start to rear puppies we divide the foods, and give the puppies meals several times a day. In this way the digestive system is not overworked. It deals with one portion and then prepares to receive another. The very early stages of puppy-feeding—that is, the actual process of weaning—has been dealt with earlier in this chapter. We are now considering the puppy from about five weeks onwards, for by this time it will not be getting very much sustenance from the mother. We have no way of telling if the puppy is receiving sufficient until it loses condition and shows unmistakable signs of hunger, and by this time it will have received a severe check in the growth process, which could have serious consequences. Therefore we do not leave things to chance. We begin to supplement the puppy's feeds at an early date, and gradually increase the quantities until it is independent of its dam.

Remember that a puppy is undergoing a transition from a milk diet to a solid one; a milk diet, too, that is served to it at exactly the right temperature, sterile, and of the perfect strength for its needs. From this it is learning to digest milk, which will probably be made up of different constituents, often presented too warm or too cold, and solid foods of various kinds, consistencies, and textures, all too often of variable quality. The puppy's digestion faces quite a task, and this applies to a puppy of any breed. There is no suggestion that a Chihuahua is any harder to wean or more difficult to feed than dogs of other varieties.

It is important to stress that only the best foods are suitable for puppies. Milk must never be anything but sweet; not even 'on the turn'. Meat should be fresh and never tainted, even though the adult dogs will eat it when it is a little high and be none the worse. Biscuit meal should be dry, crisp, before soaking, and have a pleasant smell without a hint of mouldiness. Musty dog biscuits should be thrown away. They are unsuitable for feeding to dogs of any age.

The preparation of the food is also important. Puppies are often greedy little creatures, and especially when more than one is gathered round the dish. The competitive spirit then prevails, and all concerned will grab, gulp, push, end up with all four feet in the dish, and generally try to get as much as possible before the others scoff the lot. In consequence, the puppies will bolt their food and, if it is fed to them in lumps, they will either choke or, if they swallow it, vomit it back again. Meat should be minced or finely chopped. Biscuit meal should be finely kibbled.

Some people feed puppies five or six times a day. Most breeders consider that four meals are sufficient, especially for breeds in which large size and heavy bone are undesirable. There is no rule about actual feeding-times. They should be fitted into the routine of kennel and household. The main thing to remember is that the timetable should be arranged and then every effort made to keep to it. Puppies appreciate punctual meals and do not thrive when fed at odd hours. It is best to space the feeds so that they do not come too close together. Suggested times could be 8 a.m., 12 noon, 4 p.m., and 9 p.m. Very early risers may like to give their puppies a breakfast directly they get up, and, similarly, a lot of people have a look at their stock before retiring for the night, and take the opportunity of doling out the milky supper at bedtime.

The first feed could be milk, mixed with Farex, Pablum, cornflakes, or well-boiled oatmeal porridge. The milk itself can be dried, canned, or fresh. There are one or two well-known and reliable brands of powdered milk sold especially for dogs.

There are also the various makes of baby foods all of more or less equal merit and with little to choose between them even though they vary in price. Some breeders set great store by tinned condensed milk, but care should be taken to dilute it to the right consistency, otherwise it is too rich and will make the puppies sick. Mixed with an excess of water it distends the stomach without providing proper nourishment.

If cow's milk is used, it should be from Jersey or Guernsey cows, as this is much richer, and approximates more closely to bitches' milk than that yielded by cows of other breeds. It is the use of cows' milk poor in butterfat which has given rise to a prevalent idea that ordinary milk is unsuitable for puppies and 'gives them worms'. They do not thrive on such stuff, but the quality product is perfectly good for them.

Goats' milk is wonderful for dogs, but is possibly not as suitable for Chihuahuas as for some of the other breeds, as it seems to promote size and substantial bone.

The puppies' main meal is really the most important of all, for it consists of protein and of nothing else. It can be raw, or lightly cooked, and can be varied with things like fish and rabbit; as these take quite a time to prepare, plain raw meat is probably not only the best food the puppy can have but one that is the least trouble to give.

At tea-time the best meal is a dish of good quality puppy grade biscuit meal, or brown bread rusks, soaked in good broth. If stock is not available, milk can be used, but is not quite so suitable. It is optional whether or not a little minced meat is stirred into this meal or not. It certainly makes the meal tastier, and the puppies appreciate it.

The final meal is the light supper, prepared on much the same lines as the first feed of the day. It can be milk, or milk and cereal. If milk, it is usual to offer the puppy a little hard biscuit or a rusk to crunch as well. These amuse and interest the puppy and are good for the teeth.

Up to now we have said nothing about the actual quantities. This is because Chihuahua puppies vary so much in size and in weight, consequently also in appetite. What would fill a very tiny puppy to the point where it feels bloated and uncomfortable might be barely satisfying for a larger member of the litter. The best guide is to remember that the Chihuahua is a very small dog.

People accustomed to feeding larger dogs fall into two pit-falls. Half find it hard to realize that a Chi eats very little, even by comparison with other toy breeds. They get very worried because they think the little dog is not eating enough. Others go to the other extreme; because the Chihuahua is a miniature they imagine it scarcely needs any food at all, and give it far too little.

Common sense is essential. If the puppy cleans up its dish, looks distended, grunts, whines, and runs round in circles, it has had too much to eat and is feeling very uncomfortable. If, after gobbling its ration, it does not look much fatter than when it started and keeps sniffing round hopefully for more, increase the quantity.

As the puppy grows up, keep a sharp watch on its con-dition. It should be well covered, with a soft, pliable fat. The muscle and hard, solid flesh we like to see on the older Chi-huahua is not right for the puppy, which should be a roly-poly, cuddly little animal. As it becomes more active it will run off much of its fat. A lean, skinny puppy has nothing in hand if an indisposition or other setback comes along. We know that in a breed in which small size is a virtue we are not impelled to push quantities of food into a puppy as we must do if we are to make a good job of rearing the big breeds. But it is entirely wrong to imagine that Chihuahua growth-rate can be slowed down satisfactorily by withholding the nourishing food that a little dog requires if it is to grow up strong and healthy. There are a few foolish folk who think on these lines, and believe that they can keep their stock small and still fit by poor feeding. This policy cannot be too strongly condemned, for it is both short-sighted and unkind.

Far better a bigger Chihuahua, swift-moving, with straight, sound limbs, full of vitality and energy, than a minute, shivering little scrap with hunched back, crooked front, weak hindquarters, and frail constitution: the results of bad rearing, either by intention or through ignorance of the correct methods.

Mention must be made, however, of the owners who, with

the best intentions, err too much in the other direction. Commendably anxious to give their dogs the best of everything, fearful lest they stint them of something that will do them good, they stuff the pregnant bitch and, later, the puppies themselves, with calcium, tonics, vitamins, and every kind of proprietary 'conditioner' and supplement. Such things are not usually necessary for very small dogs, particularly if they are receiving a good and adequate diet, and they only go to produce clumsy bone and oversize. When given to the bitch between mating and whelping, they can even be harmful, for they may well make the embryo puppies too large and cause trouble when parturition take place. Generally, these things are necessary only in special cases and if a veterinary surgeon advises them. Otherwise they are best avoided.

Always keep an eye on puppies when they are eating. There may be a bully, or a puppy could start to choke. In this case a finger can push the food right down the throat, or hook it right out.

Very often a litter contains one puppy that is smaller and less robust than the others. While this can be due to a variety of causes it may simply be that it is being pushed out by the others and is not receiving its fair share of food. It is quite easy to feed it separately until it catches up with the rest or, if there is one pup which is getting the lion's share, feed it alone too, lest it does itself well at the expense of the majority.

As the puppies get older they require slightly more food, but at less frequent intervals. Indeed, they often decide for themselves when one or two meals should be dropped. From greeting their food with great enthusiasm on every occasion they will consume one meal, but seem disinterested with the next. This is a sign that their time-table should be condensed, and it might be a good idea to stop one of the milk feeds, usually supper. Later still, combine the main meal into one solid dinner, but keep offering the milk breakfast until the puppy rejects it, which it probably will by the time it is nine or ten months of age.

From that stage onwards it can be considered an adult, and fed accordingly.

Anyone who contemplates purchasing a Chihuahua for the first time is usually, and very rightly, much concerned as to how it should be fed. This is a sensible attitude, because correct diet is the basis of good health, and does much to determine the life-span of any dog. At best a dog's life is far too short, but if we hope to have one for something like thirteen or fourteen years it is necessary to keep it in tip-top condition.

In this respect the Chihuahua owners have no special problems. Indeed, it is probable that the man who buys a Great Dane or similar large breed has a far more complicated task, for the nourishment of a big animal, the provision of all the essentials necessary to build a huge frame, complete with the compensating strong bones and muscles, is something of an expert's job.

A Chi is easily fed, and the provision of plain, wholesome food is all that is required. It does not in the normal course of events, require extras such as calcium, cod-liver oil, malt, iron tonics, and the like. It has a tiny body, and small size and fine bone are desirable characteristics. The supplements only go to promote increased size and massive limbs, very undesirable breed points.

It is the exquisitely dainty, fairy-like build that gives so many people the impression that the Chihuahua is fragile and delicate, although this is far from being so. Chi's, sensibly kept and reared, are every bit as sturdy and strong as any other kind of dog. Any idea that a diet of pap and minced chicken is a regular requirement should be rejected straight away.

Feed a Chihuahua much as you would any dog. Naturally, the flesh foods will be chopped or minced, and the biscuit meal should be finely kibbled—the grade sold for puppies is suitable. Chihuahuas do best on a diet consisting mainly of meat. Fed raw or lightly cooked it is a natural food and nourishes without producing over-rapid growth or coarse, spongy bone. Too much biscuit distends the stomach without providing salts, minerals, and vitamins necessary to canine good health.

Ch. Rowley
Josephine

C. M. Cooke

Ch. Rozavel Platina

Veronica-Vi
Dalhabboch

Sally Anne Thompson

Ch. Rozavel Humo

Belamie Estrellita and
Jofos Tacuba

R. L. Nowak

'Well, I'll be blowed!
Jemima's pinching
my pudding now!'

Associated Newspapers

Ch. Molimor Talentina

Australian Ch. Rozavel
Contrast

Boiled paunch is relished, but the bleached tripe sold by butchers is not popular with dogs, and the preparation used to whiten it is thought to be harmful, and a possible cause of stomach troubles. Rabbit and fish are always fed boiled, and must be carefully boned. The danger from small bones or splinters of bone cannot be too strongly emphasized. They are exceedingly dangerous, and not only must they never be fed to dogs, but they must never be thrown where a dog might find them.

Your Chihuahua, far from being a fool, is smart as paint. If he smells something tasty in the bucket under the sink he will probably manage to get at it, even if he had to climb on something and push off a lid to do it. If you bury the kitchen debris, bury it deep, or he will dig it up. Better still, burn the bones, or put them in a tall dustbin with a heavy, well-fitting cover.

It is possible to boil both rabbit, poultry, and fish bones in a pressure cooker until nothing remains but a soft mush. This greatly minimizes the danger of feeding scraps of bone by accident. It is difficult to 'fillet' food in such a way as to be certain that no vestige of bone remains.

Large bones—marrow bones, for instance—should be safe for a Chihuahua, however, and there is no doubt that they give them an immense amount of pleasure. Some veterinary surgeons are opposed to bones of any size or type for dogs, so if they are given at all it is best to let the dogs chew them under strict supervision. If a small section breaks away it may lodge in the throat, or if swallowed could perforate stomach or bowel with dreadful results.

As a substitute for bones, most dogs like an occasional hard biscuit to play with and to gnaw, and Chihuahuas are no exception. Indeed, something of the kind is beneficial to puppies throughout the teething periods.

Once an adult reaches the stage when its teeth tend to become loose, neither bones nor hard biscuits are advisable. The dog will still enjoy them, but they will push out the teeth which, while it may not be of great consequence to a pet Chihuahua, could be a major disaster to one still enjoying its show career.

Is *any* kind of meat suitable? This is a question most commonly asked by people who come to buy a puppy. Any fresh meat makes a wholesome meal. Lean beef or mutton, meat from a carefully boned sheep's head, or veal are all good. Pork is rather rich for dogs and is inclined to upset them. A little, fed lean and well cooked, can do no harm, but it is best avoided. Horse-meat from a reliable source is perfectly satisfactory, but if it is in any way doubtful it should be well boiled and not fed raw. The stock or gravy from most meat is good poured on to biscuit meal, but the water in which horse-meat or paunch and tripe has been cooked is best thrown away.

Some owners feed whale meat, and very good it is. It is free from bone and fat, and contains oil which seems to suit dogs and to make the coats shine. It is also relatively inexpensive and is a useful source of protein. A few dogs find it difficult to digest, but most of them like it now and again for a change. Fed exclusively, they get rather tired of it.

Tinned meat, produced specially for dogs, is sold in great quantities and there are many different brands from which to choose. Some brands seem better than others, particularly the tins containing tightly packed lean meat without a lot of watery soup or jelly. Avoid the galantine type, which contain cereals and other things; dogs seem to eat this only if there is nothing more appetizing on offer. Food in tins is always fresh until it is opened, and is most useful when travelling or at shows, or to keep on the shelf in the kennel store cupboard for emergencies. Nothing can really take the place of fresh meat. It is the natural food for the carnivore, and however much the manufacturers would like to persuade us that their canned products are in every way its equal, the results do not indicate that this is so. One veterinary surgeon has stated that he treats an unusual number of cases of enteritis among dogs fed on tinned meat. Even if no harm comes of feeding these products it is hard to believe that the valuable mineral salts, vitamins, and other nutrients are found in a heat-treated product. Nothing can be better than fresh, natural food. Tinned meat may be easier to obtain, and pleasanter to handle, but although it is certainly a useful standby for occasional use it is not recommended as a staple diet.

The same remarks apply to dried meat, which is useful as a reserve, especially in the finely powdered form, but which should be used only when the normal delivery of fresh food has failed. The kibbled, coarse-textured dried meat is not suitable for toy dogs, and is probably dangerous for dogs of any size, for most of it contains pieces of sharp bone which can be lethal. Even when the dried scraps are carefully picked over, bone can be overlooked because it is dark brown and looks like pieces of meat. It is easier to find when boiling water has been poured over it all, for dried meat must be well soaked before it is fed, if it is fed at all.

There are many makes of biscuit, and the famous name and the high price are not necessarily a guarantee of superior quality. Dog biscuits which, like many other things, have enormously increased in price since before the war, vary greatly in cost. It is possible to pay less for a hundred-weight of biscuit meal of excellent feeding value than for other makes which do not seem to be of superior quality nor any more palatable to the dogs themselves.

Dogs undoubtedly show decided preferences for certain kinds of biscuits. Once they take a fancy to a make and get it regularly they do not seem to appreciate a change. They prefer always to have the same brand, especially if it is mixed with something different from time to time. The meat can be served cooked one day, raw the next; boiled sheep's head tomorrow, stewed liver today; a little fish stirred in, or the much appreciated well-cooked rabbit, or paunch.

Use judgement when selecting a biscuit meal. If it is clean, wholemeal, free from dust, sweet-smelling without a trace of mustiness, it is probably a good meal irrespective of the price. White meal, made with bleached flour, is best avoided as is white bread. Do not be dazzled by meals made-up of confetti-like fragments. The colours often mean nothing at all, have no particular flavours, and are put in, as one merchant told me, 'because the owners seem to like them'. They have no advantage over the plain meal. Brown wholemeal biscuits are the wisest choice, but do choose a finely kibbled grade, though avoiding the pin-head type that goes pasty when soaked, which the dogs dislike intensely.

The purchase of dog biscuit meals can be avoided altogether if the owner cares to go to the trouble of making brown bread rusks for the kennel. From wholemeal loaves cut slices about half an inch thick, and spread them on baking sheets in a fairly cool oven, leaving the door ajar to allow the steam to escape. Broken-up and soaked in good strong broth, these rusks make a pure and nourishing food. Most dogs enjoy them; though, as with any other new food, they are best introduced gradually because at first they may have a laxative effect on dogs that have been habitually fed on biscuits. Feed half rusk and half of the usual kibbled meal for a day or two before changing over to an all-rusk diet for the cereal part of the daily ration.

Young Chihuahuas always enjoy the small oval and shaped biscuits sold by leading dog-food manufacturers. These are sometimes coloured, and do vary in flavour, most dogs finding them attractive. The older dogs should have them, just as long as the question of loose teeth is borne in mind. It is surprising how the old pensioners in the kennel, many with one or two teeth or none at all, manage to eat these hard-baked biscuits and will never be left out when they are handed round.

Boiled rice and boiled barley are both quite useful forms of cereal, and mixed with chopped or minced meat or fish are usually acceptable to all but the faddiest feeders.

Opinions are divided about giving dogs vegetables. Veterinary authorities tell us that, in so far as raw vegetables are concerned, they have to be very finely chopped indeed for the dog to derive any benefits from them at all, otherwise they pass out of the system without being utilized by the digestive organs. One school of thought believes that cooked vegetables are of very little value to the carnivores. A few carrots and onions boiled up with the meat and stock certainly help to make it tasty, and a sprinkling of finely chopped uncooked parsley or grated raw carrot may well be beneficial, but dogs seem to get on very well without these things. Potatoes should certainly not be given in quantity, and if a little is fed from time to time it must be well mashed.

Many half-grown and adult Chihuahuas do not care for milk. They will drink it occasionally, but a regular milky

breakfast will be refused. Milk is an easily digested, useful conditioner, and of particular value for a show dog requiring a
little extra weight and bloom. Sometimes a sweetened rice
pudding or custard is popular, and many Chi's are extremely
fond of malted milk in liquid or tablet form.

How much food should a Chihuahua receive? This is not
an easy question to answer, because requirements vary with
the size of the dog. A Chi is a fair eater for its size, but of course
the amount consumed is small compared with the quantity
larger dogs will eat. The Chihuahua eats so little that new
owners are often worried that their pets are not getting enough.
A Chi will eat from two to four ounces of meat per day, plus
a little biscuit meal or other cereal, and one or two small hard
biscuits.

The appearance of the dog is the best guide. If it polishes
the dish with its tongue, yet still looks much the same shape as
it did when it began to eat, it probably needs a little more food.
If, on the other hand, it has finished its meal and it looks blown
out, distended, and uncomfortable, it has clearly had more than
is good for it at one time and only two-thirds of that quantity
should be offered next day.

The good keeper of livestock is very quick to observe such
signs as these. It is far better to be guided by them than to
collect diet sheets and books and to try to be guided by the
written word alone. This is a long-term policy too. If the dog
looks lean, efforts must be made to persuade it to eat more. If
it puts on excess weight the allowance must be scaled down
until it is eating approximately the same quantity each day
and is in ideal condition, firm and well covered but neither
skinny nor fat.

There can be few experienced dog show exhibitors who
have not suffered the maddening defeats in the ring caused—
according to the subsequent critiques from the judges—by the
fact that an exhibit was either too fat or too thin. The first-
named condition is by far the easiest to deal with, and usually
a diet consisting entirely of meat, reduced in quantity with all
titbits eliminated, and plenty of exercise, will put matters right
in a short time. Putting weight on a dog is generally much more
difficult. Young dogs, in particular, can be tiresome about food.

They are upset by all sorts of things: the proximity of bitches in season, by travelling, by strange surroundings, by changes in their menu, even by sounds such as footsteps, doors being opened and closed, traffic, and so on. Whatever the cause, they look at the carefully prepared bowl of food, give it a casual sniff or a look of disgust, and walk away. The accepted procedure is to take the food away and offer it again the next day, and to repeat until hunger forces its acceptance. This sounds good in theory, but in practice, at least where a show dog is concerned, it is hopeless. While the 'cure' is in progress the dog is getting thinner and thinner. If it does eat it will probably do so once and when satisfied will turn up its nose at its meals again until the pangs of hunger again become really acute. This is no way to condition a dog. It may be all right for a pet, if the owner is not temporarily concerned about its appearance, but the owner of a show dog wants it to look its best. To most people the sight of a thin and poor-looking dog is depressing and worrying.

If the dog is to gain weight it has to be coaxed to eat, and there are various ways of doing this. Mixing the ordinary food with either grated cheese or powdered malted mik often has magical results. Meat, grilled with a spot of butter, is hard to resist. Real luxuries such as chicken, game, or chopped baked liver generally tempt the most capricious appetites. A very light dusting of salt makes the meal more attractive.

Some picky feeders will eat quite a lot of food if it is handed to them, piece by piece, from the table, yet will ignore it if he is put on the floor for them in a dog dish. There are even some crafty characters who will eat what they think is the cat's food, yet refuse the same when fed to them direct. If there is something that the dog really likes, let him have it. Do not waste time trying to persuade him to eat other foods which you may feel would be more beneficial, but fill him up with something it apparently enjoys.

It is beneficial to show dogs if they will take a milk-and-cereal breakfast, and still eat a substantial main meal later in the day. If, however, the sloppy meal spoils the appetite for the meat, etc., it is best to drop it and to concentrate on persuading the dog to enjoy a good solid feed.

The same thing applies to the 'extras' people give to their dogs when they are trying to get them into better condition. There are all kinds of useful supplements—yeast tablets, seaweed powder, vitamin powders and tablets, cod-liver oil, compound tonics containing iron and minerals, condition powders, and so on—and the dog Press abounds with advertisements of them, the trade stands at dog shows are loaded with them, and chemists and corn-merchants stock them in variety. Some are invaluable, most are useful, but few are palatable, the exception being the yeast capsules which most dogs eat with relish. If the dog does not care for the taste of a powder or liquid, it is foolish to sprinkle it on the food, which is certain to be rejected. The food alone, if eaten, would have done the dog some good. If it is refused, the tonic preparation actually does harm, since it revolts the dog and causes it to refuse a nourishing meal. Only a greedy dog, the proverbial 'good doer', will gobble up a dish of food mixed with a strong-tasting medicine or powder. If such things must be given to other members of the kennel it is best to choose a tasteless variety, otherwise you defeat your end.

Offer fresh, good, nourishing food, and do all you can to persuade the dog to eat it. This is the best way of providing a dog with the essentials that will get it and keep it in show condition.

TWELVE

TRAINING THE CHIHUAHUA

THE Chihuahua is easy to teach, because it is amazingly
intelligent. It is a breed of dog which offers the lie to
anyone who believes that dogs cannot reason. Given the
sketchiest knowledge of dog psychology, it is perfectly possible
to watch a Chi working out a problem. There are no dull or
stupid Chihuahuas, but there are, occasionally, some owners
who lack the abilty to transmit to their dogs the things they
would like to have them do, and the fault lies in themselves,
not in their little animals.

House-training a puppy usually takes priority over everything else, and if approached in the right way should present
no difficulty. The length of time taken to get a puppy house-
broken is governed by the time of year and the age of the dog,
as well as by the patience and perseverance of the trainer.
Obviously it is not practicable to put a tiny Chi puppy out of
doors in very bad weather. Under such conditions it is much
better to teach the puppy to 'spend pennies' on newspaper.
Start by placing the paper near the door or french window,
then, as the weather improves, just outside. Gradually substitute a whole double sheet of newspaper for a small piece, and
do away with it altogether when the puppy learns to use the
same spot outside the house.

The younger the puppy the longer it will be before it is
completely reliable, day and night. A baby needs its nappies
changed at frequent intervals, but will eventually learn to ask
for its 'potty' less often as it gets older. It will be just the same
with the young dog. It is unfair to expect it to go for long
periods without making a mess, but as it begins to understand
what is wanted of it, and as it grows up and learns to control
bowels and bladder, so it will become clean.

164

One advantage of owning a dog as small as a Chihuahua is that if it does make a mistake on the carpet it is such a small one that little damage is done, and it is easily wiped away. Most of the newer liquid detergents are excellent for removing tell-tale puppy stains, but if noticed immediately there is nothing better than plain soda-water. A little should be poured on to the mark and wiped off with a clean cloth. For rapid 'first aid', paper tissues and towels—Kleenex, Polyrol, etc., soak up 'puppy pennies' very well, and should be kept on hand.

If the weather is reasonably good then the puppy can be put out in the garden, but it must be watched. It might stray through a hole in the fence, but in any case it is no use trying to train the puppy to be clean unless it is supervised when expected to relieve itself. It is important to make sure that it does its jobs before it returns indoors, otherwise, acting on its instincts, which tell it that the warm carpet is much more comfortable than the damp grass, the puppy will misbehave the moment it comes indoors.

To begin with, it is unlikely to understand what is wanted. It may do so if it is popped outside at the right moment—after a meal, after waking from a nap, or when it begins to run round the room sniffing at the floor. So pick a likely time to put it out, and even if it is boring and chilly, hang about for a few minutes so that with luck the puppy can be petted, praised, and congratulated before coming back into the house.

If an accident happens, take the puppy to the spot, grasp it firmly by the scruff of the neck and scold it. Then carry it to its newspaper, or out into the garden for a minute or two.

Chihuahuas are most sensitive little creatures. They thrive on love and long to be cradled in affection. Nothing makes them more wretched than to know they have fallen from grace. If someone is cross they will mope and pine, perhaps refuse food, and look utterly pathetic until a change in tone of voice or a caress tells them they are forgiven. Then the whole de-meanour changes, they become sprightly and happy again. It is scarcely ever necessary or even wise to smack a Chihuahua. Just the unsympathetic touch of the hand that grips them, the angry tone of voice, is sufficient punishment. The dog knows at once that it has displeased you, and begins to reason why.

Never attempt to house-train more than one puppy at a time. Many people do make this mistake, and then one hears a wail to the effect that Chihuahuas are hard to house-break. This is not true. They are naturally clean and fastidious. Once trained the bitches are scarcely ever dirty, and if a male should forget himself, it is generally only if a new bitch, or a bitch in season, has been around and taken his mind off his good manners. Many Chihuahuas, of both sexes, will suffer discomfort for fear of soiling the wrong place.

The trouble with two or more puppies is that it is difficult to keep a wary eye on more than one at a time. If the puppies are running about there is sure to be an accident sooner or later, and then it is impossible to identify the culprit. It would be cruel to scold the lot when only one has been naughty, so the offence has to be overlooked; the little criminal finds that crime pays, and will be smart enough to do it again.

As puppies cannot be expected to be clean for long periods, some arrangement must be made for the night hours, or if it is necessary to leave them unattended for any length of time during the day.

It is best to fix up some kind of small pen, with the floor space covered with newspaper, which can be easily rolled up and burned. This is much easier than dealing with the entire floor after a few puppies have been running about for two or three hours or more.

In general puppies will not soil their beds if they can help it, but accidents can happen, so it is as well to give them wood-wool, soft hay (see that it has no prickles in it), or a small piece of old blanket. Thus the bedding can be burned and renewed if it gets dirty. It is a mistake to give a puppy an elaborate cushion or mattress, and even large rugs or blankets are tiresome to wash, though such things are quite practicable for older dogs.

Contact with the puppy should soon show an observant and intelligent owner that it is beginning to understand what it has to do, and it becomes easy to know when the dog has a clear idea of right and wrong. Similarly constant association with a puppy should give one a kind of sixth sense, enabling the puppy's wants to be anticipated. In this way the owner should be able to decide when the dog can be reasonably expected to stay clean all night or for longer spells during day-time. Then the little dog can be trusted to be allowed to sleep in a bedroom or sitting-room without being confined to a pen. It will learn to ask to be let out, and will either run to the door or whine when it feels it is necessary.

While the house training is in progress it is usual to accus-tom the puppy to collar and lead. Walks will probably not begin for some time but it is much better to do these things gradually. Choose a very fine, light collar, preferably one made of soft leather. See that it fits properly; it must not be tight, and it should be possible to slip a couple of fingers inside when it is on. It must not, however, be loose enough to slip past the ears or so that the dog can get its paw caught up inside and do itself an injury. The collar can be put on the dog just before feeding-time. The puppy, instead of disliking it, will associate it with a pleasant occurrence, and its attention will be distracted by the arrival of the dish, so it is less likely to try to scratch or rub the collar in an attempt to remove it.

Soon the puppy will not notice the collar, and this is a good time to try attaching a light lead. Let this trail about after the dog for a bit, then pick up the loop end and try to attract the puppy towards you with a tit-bit, and encouraging words. Always pet it when it reaches you. Even if the puppy has been disobedient, perhaps hard to catch, you must never be cross with it when you finally get hold of it. In the puppy's mind anything disagreeable must happen only when it is a distance away from you. Coming to you and reaching you must be regarded as something enjoyable; it must feel sure that it will get stroking and loving once your hands are on it. This is the best way to own an obedient dog, one that comes running to you the moment it hears its name.

At first, when the puppy moves and the lead tightens, it may panic and struggle. Stand firm, talking to the little dog, calling it by name, gradually drawing it towards you, loving and petting it when it is within reach. If it comes to you willingly make a special fuss of it, play with it, love it, give it a little treat—a scrap of cheese, a malted milk tablet, a tiny piece of chicken or liver. Do this even if it has moved only a few steps towards you.

Five minutes or so night and morning are quite sufficient for a youngster, and if regularly adhered to this routine is much more successful than a longer period once or twice a week. It is surprising how soon there is some progress, and how jauntily the puppy will be trotting beside you.

A puppy should be accustomed to going about in car, omnibus, or train fairly early in life. As soon as it is used to a collar and lead it should go short journeys. It should not be expected to follow on a leash, but it is important to be able to restrain it so that it can be carried around safely and cannot jump out of your arms. A basket or a shopping bag are often most useful, cosy containers for a puppy, but do make sure it cannot leap out. If you want to take the dog in the car it is best transported in a little hamper or transparent carrying box, from which it can see what is going on around it, without its worrying the driver. Better still, get a second person to sit with the pup on his lap while you drive, or nurse it yourself and let someone else act as chauffeur.

Very few Chihuahuas suffer from car-sickness. Most of them love motoring, and even if a puppy suffers nausea for the first few trips it generally gets over it.

Everyone who has a pet Chihuahua enjoys taking it around with them. Because the dogs are so tiny it is perfectly possible to do so, and this appeals to people who hate leaving their dog at home, especially for as long as a holiday period, but who find that average-sized canines are not always welcome. Lots of Chihuahuas go to theatres, cinemas, into restaurants which ordinarily ban dogs, to church, and to all sorts of places. They arrive in a pocket or a handbag, and leave again just as mysteriously, so are never seen by those in charge. Even if they are spotted they are generally made the exception and welcomed.

If the puppy is destined to be your best friend, but nothing more, his education is more or less complete by now, but if he is to be a show dog there is much more to learn, all of it very important.

Start, at an early age, to lift the dog's lips so that the teeth can be inspected. This can be done frequently, when the dog is picked up, and there is no need to make a fuss about it. Stroke and pet the dog directly you have done it. The judge is going to ask to see the 'bite', that is, the way in which the teeth fit together in front, and will expect the dog to let you show this to him without struggling, snapping, and screaming. It may well do all three if you have not practised this at home.

Start lifting the puppy on to a table, but first be sure that it stands on something firm—a piece of carpet or a rubber mat will do. If it slips about it will become nervous and upset. Place the dog standing all square on its legs. To do this it may be necessary to push the forelegs back, or gently to pull the back legs outwards. It may just need one leg adjusted, but it must stand evenly. It must not lean backwards on its front legs, or have its hindquarters tucked underneath or splayed apart.

While you arrange the puppy, keep a firm hold on it so that it cannot jump off the table and hurt itself. Now and again tickle it under the chin or on the chest, and all the time the lesson is in progress talk, talk, talk. Tell the puppy it is good and clever; soothe it if it seems at all worried or frightened. Run a hand repeatedly down its back, and very carefully lift the tail, holding it upright in a sickle-shaped curve. Dogs do not like having their tails touched, and the puppy, unused to this, is sure to sit down or turn round to see what is going on. Carefully, slowly, gently place it in the standing position again, stroke the tail upwards, and tell the pup he is wonderful. You may secretly think he is being rather silly and even rather tiresome, but never let him know it. Just keep on doing it a few times then give the dog a tit-bit, pop him on the floor, and make a great fuss of him again. A little of this and the dog will behave nicely at his first show. You will not have a red face when the judge tells you to put your exhibit on the table for examination.

If the lead training has been going well the request to walk up and down the ring will not present a problem. The puppy should trot along, happy and gay, neither pulling forwards nor dragging backwards or sideways.

Another aspect of show training is one that has become very specialized in recent years. Obedience classes are held at most of the Championship and Open shows, and working trials are separate entities which draw enormous entries from the ranks of almost all breeds of dogs, for none is barred. If it is intelligent it can learn the exercises; and proficiency, not beauty, is the only passport required to enter these competitions. People who can spare the time should enjoy teaching their Chihuahuas the obedience tests laid down by the clubs specializing in training.

The elementary exercises include: walking to heel on a lead without pulling; sitting down—without a special command—whenever the handler stops; doing this all over again off the lead; staying at the 'Sit' and the 'Down' positions while the handler goes a distance away, or out of sight; staying sitting, and coming in when called; retrieving a small object, usually a dumb-bell, which is particularly easy for a dog to pick up in its mouth; and many more accomplishments which become harder as the classes become more advanced.

These lessons cannot be dismissed as tricks or stunts. They are all extremely useful whether the dog is a pet or a show animal. The elementary exercises make a companion dog very nice to have around, and safer to take out. They are easily taught with patience, perseverance, kindness, and endless encouragement to the dog.

Dog training of this kind was the monopoly of the Alsatian breed when it was first introduced into this country, and the obedience classes and trials were all confined to Alsatians. Owners of other intelligent dogs naturally became interested, and gradually the door was thrown wide open until all sorts of breeds proved themselves formidable contestants. Some very small dogs have won against strong competition, and one or two Chihuahuas have been seen working. So far, however, nobody has promoted the breed very seriously in the working-dog world in this country, but this is not because the Chihuahua cannot learn the exercises as well as any other kind of dog.

In the United States there have been some notable Chihuahuas which have become quite famous as workers, earning the much-sought-after titles of 'Utility Dog (U.D.)' and 'Companion Dog (C.D.)' which permits them to use these letters after their names. We use these titles in Britain, though our tests are not the same. But on either side of the Atlantic training a dog to competitive standards requires some ability and great patience on the part of the handler, and intelligence and response on the part of the dog. Given both there is absolutely no reason at all why a Chihuahua and the right owner should not go places and beat the other breeds.

Training, since the last war, has become tremendously popular in doggy circles, and in consequence clubs and societies to promote and encourage it have sprung up all over the country. There can be few areas which do not have regular training classes organized for their local dog owners, and it is at such meetings that the beginner can learn how to train. Apart from the learning made available at these gatherings, the whole atmosphere of a training class is good for a young dog. The presence of strangers, of other dogs of various breeds, the loud voices, occasional barking, all produce something of the conditions that prevail at a dog show and are invaluable for accustoming a shy or nervous puppy to such distractions.

Even if the owner of a pet Chihuahua is disinclined to go in for obedience class training there is constant delight in teaching a Chihuahua tricks. The little dog is quick to learn, and with its anxiety to please, sharp brain, and agility, plus the patience and love which the owner must bring to the lessons, there is no end to the fun and games to be enjoyed by the two of them. It is not surprising to read that there was once an entire professional troupe of performing Chihuahuas.

THIRTEEN

SHOWING THE CHIHUAHUA

PREPARING FOR THE SHOW

Dog showing is undertaken for several reasons because it is an absorbing, fascinating, and eminently satisfying pastime and hobby. Showing is almost essential for the breeder. It is difficult, if not impossible, to run a successful kennel at which the stud dogs are well patronized, and puppies and other surplus stock sold without difficulty at sensible prices, unless a reputation for producing winners is made and maintained.

Those people who have time on their hands—and even in these days when help of all kinds is hard to come by there are still plenty of people who are looking for a pleasant occupation —will enjoy showing dogs. There is no finer means of making friends, because everyone you meet has a share in the same interest. Travel enters into the picture too, for shows are held in all parts of the British Isles, and journeys to and from them enable one to cover much fresh ground.

Unfortunately the quarantine laws of this country make it impossible for us to exhibit our dogs at foreign shows, since they would be detained for six months on their return, but there are many fine overseas dog shows, and such can be made the focal points of a holiday trip, or as our experience increases we may even be honoured by an invitation to judge at one of these exhibitions. Such excitements all add to the fun. Persons who would, I am sure, describe themselves as 'ordinary' have even found themselves taking part in television and sound-radio broadcasts as a result of some success at a dog show. There is never a dull moment!

Even the journeys, in themselves, can be enjoyable, for rail parties are organized for most of the big shows, and compartments reserved for the exhibitors and their dogs. Although the carriage may contain anything from Great Danes to Chihuahuas, nobody is likely to complain about the presence of the dogs, and journeys are rapidly covered when there are so many people to talk to, and such lots to talk about. At the destination there are one or two kindred spirits anxious to share a taxi to the show hall or site, and plenty of friends to greet you when you get there.

Chihuahuas are so easy to transport by train, for they cuddle up in little carrying cases and are light and easy to handle, but even so it is often more convenient to travel to a show by road, and here again we often find one or more exhibitors combining to drive to a show together. It is nice to have congenial company, and if the cost of petrol can be shared it keeps the expenses down, and such trips usually work out cheaper than by going by rail.

Railway charges for dogs on leads are usually half the price of one's own adult ticket, whereas dogs small enough to travel in boxes or baskets carried by their owners can be transported free of charge. It is, therefore, much more economical to take Chihuahuas with you in their cases.

The dates and places where dog shows are to be held can be found in the columns of the weekly dog papers *Our Dogs* and *Dog World*, both published on Fridays. It is not always possible to buy these magazines from any newsagent or bookstall, and it is best to place a regular order for them, either direct with the publishers or with a local shop.

It is assumed that the potential exhibitor has already attended some dog shows without a dog of his own. There is far more to showing dogs than just turning up at a show with one, so visit a few local events and at least one big Championship show. Watch the dogs being judged in the Chihuahua ring, see how the exhibitors handle their dogs, and try to take particular notice of the principal winners and the people who show them. Without at least some elementary 'know-how' the novice handler and the dog are both handicapped, and the first dog show can be a hectic and bewildering affair.

Only very occasionally do we hear real Cinderella stories about completely new and unknown owners and dogs that have rocketed to fame at the first attempt. These happenings are rare indeed, and as a rule the beginner must expect to be at a disadvantage until he learns the secrets of the superior ringcraft and presentation which comes only with experience.

Even after visiting one or two shows, however, the shrewd observer will notice that some exhibits look more alert and behave better than others, also that a few seem to be spoiling their chances by doing the reverse, and this gives an idea of what the new dog-show enthusiast must try to do when his turn comes.

Have a look in the dog papers and see if there is a small show within reasonable distance of home. A small show is one that is described as a Members, Sanction, Limited, or Open show. A few dog societies hold Match meetings, which are usually variety competitions. These are not really shows, but useful gatherings for enabling a young dog to get accustomed to strangers and other exhibits.

Some advertisements will give full details of the classes provided for the various breeds. Others just mention the date, place, and judge or judges. A postcard to the Secretaries will bring schedules by return of post, and when they arrive try to choose a show that is putting on a class or classes for Chihuahuas. If there are no Chi classes at any of the shows you plan to attend, you will have to put your puppy in the Any Variety classes.

One or two, or at the most, three, classes are quite enough for a start. A puppy could be entered in Puppy, Maiden, Novice, or Junior classes at its first show, and the class definitions will be clearly stated on every schedule. The classification may include an 'Any Variety Toy' class, in which only the breeds classified by the Kennel Club in the Toy Group may compete, and such a class would also be quite suitable for the Chihuahua puppy's début.

If there are some Chi classes, however, your Chi will feel

more at home surrounded by its own kind; it is a great ordeal for a tiny puppy to find itself surrounded by enormous dogs of other breeds. Even a cocky, bold, aggressive puppy that seems chock-full of spirit at home can become intimidated and panic-stricken on its first appearance in a variety ring.

Fill up the entry form, copying the necessary particulars from the puppy's pedigree and Kennel Club registration certificate. Check that the class numbers are correctly filled in, and make sure that the puppy has been officially transferred to your name, if it is one that you have bought. Otherwise, if it wins a prize, the Kennel Club may disqualify it. Tot up the sum due in entry fees, and so on, and post it all off to the show secretary on or before the stated closing date. If sent late the entry will not be accepted. If in any doubt about the choice of classes, or the eligibility of the dog, ring up the secretary or a local exhibitor or club member, who will advise you.

The period between the date when entries close and the day of the show varies from a week to a month. Either way it often seems all too short, especially if preparation for the show has been neglected. Long before the entries are made the dog should be well ahead with its training to pose on table or floor, and it should be walking nicely on the lead. Study the chapter on training and spend plenty of time practising.

The dog should also be in first-class health and condition. It is no use waiting until the show date draws near to decide that the exhibit is too fat or too thin, or that the coat lacks lustre and is in poor shape. A smooth-haired Chihuahua, if properly fed and cared for, is in show condition all the year round. Its coat should shine and should require very little special attention. Long-coats moult once or twice a year, and do not look their best at such times; they take far longer to come back into full bloom and to grow new feathers and fringes.

Some smooth Chis, especially puppies during the teething stage, have a tendency to lose their hair and become bald, mainly on the chest, under the chin, on skull, ears and hocks, and sometimes on the feet. There are various oils and unguents reputed to correct this and to encourage the hair to grow again. The preparations range from such things as coconut oil, which can be bought over the counter at any chemist, to proprietary remedies, some procurable only on a prescription from a veterinary surgeon. If the dog's bare patches are at all extensive it would be best not to enter it for a show because it takes time for hair to grow again, so it is unlikely that the dog will look its best when the show date arrives. Better to postpone its début until it looks really well.

Ears and teeth must be inspected. If the ears look dirty inside, take a small piece of cotton-wool and wrap it round the end of an orange-stick. Be sure that the stick is blunt and well padded, and use the greatest care. Never push or probe, or injury may result. Dip the stick in olive oil, twirl it gently and withdraw, repeating with fresh cottonwool each time until the ear is clean. If the ear is smelly and there are signs of a discharge, or of really deep-seated wax or dirt, ask a Vet to attend to it without delay. Ears that become 'crisp' round the edges should be rubbed each day with oil or 'Vaseline'.

Teeth should not require much cleaning if the puppy is young. An older dog may need its teeth scaled, and although this is not difficult to do it is best to watch the Vet coping with the job at first, and afterwards to buy a scaler of the right type and try your own hand at it on some future occasion. The tartar comes off in big chunks, and then the teeth can be cleaned with a paste made of peroxide of hydrogen mixed with either powdered pumice or precipitated chalk. Dogs hate having their teeth cleaned, and it is always necessary to get somebody to hold them. Use an orange-stick and cottonwool, as required for the ears, dipped in the paste and rub it on each tooth separately. Do not be heavy-handed over this, because, like most other toy breeds, Chihuahua teeth become loose early in life. Their teeth are very small and are easily pushed out during cleaning. Because of their size they are rather fiddling to clean, especially if the dog objects and struggles, and if there is real difficulty it is best to let the Vet do it. As an expert he can probably manage it more easily than you can.

If the teeth are loose leave them alone. Some judges penalize a show dog for missing teeth, so it is better to have a few dirty teeth than large gaps. If the teeth are loose and very decayed, however, they can have a bad effect on the dog's health, apart from causing its breath to be most offensive, so the matter must be discussed with the Vet who may advise removing the teeth under an anaesthetic.

Young dogs enjoy chewing hard biscuits or big bones, but older dogs can loosen their teeth with such things.

Claws come next on the list. Some Chihuahuas, especially those having well knuckled up, tightly closed, and slightly rounded feet, scarcely ever require a pedicure, but the majority of Chi's have the elongated, slender hare foot which is flat, and the nails on such feet need regular trimming. Even dogs exercised on concrete, gravel, and paving-stones seem to be unable to wear down the claws.

At one time the wording of the breed standard suggested that very long, canary-like nails were desirable and that it was wrong to cut them. Chihuahuas never have short nails, even when trimmed, and when allowed to grow long they catch in clothing or in bedding, and often become badly torn when exercising on rough ground. If really neglected they grow into circles, the dog is almost unable to walk, the feet spread and turn out, and the shape is spoiled for ever. This dangerous growth happens most often to the dew-claws—extra 'toes' found on the front legs in all new-born puppies, sometimes left but more often removed shortly after birth. These claws grow into circles and the sharp end pierces the fleshy pad, causing sores. They must also be kept short.

Small puppies can have their nails pared with ordinary sharp, curved scissors. Older dogs, whose little nails though fine and slender are quite strong, need proper nail-clippers. Some chemists sell these, and so do many firms manufacturing dog appliances, especially those which take stalls at shows. Never attempt a job like this without some help, especially if you are doing it for the first time. Get someone to hold the dog firmly, and then cut each claw carefully, taking care not to snip them off too close to the quick, which will bleed and cause the dog pain. Chi's nails have extra long quicks.

Most dogs dislike having their toe-nails cut, and many will struggle and bite. Some people successfully file the nails instead of using scissors or clippers. The files used for human hands are not coarse enough, but suitable files called 'bastard' files can be bought at an ironmonger's, and at least one of the leading dog-requisite firms sells these. The dog can sometimes be persuaded to lie quietly on the lap as each nail is gently filed. If the dog winces or withdraws a foot it probably means that the nail is short enough. The pale pinkish or fawn-coloured nails are the easiest to trim, because they are semi-transparent and the quick is clearly visible. Black toe-nails are harder to cut, and only guesswork can tell one how far to go.

We are assuming that the dog will not be entered for the show unless it is in good condition, so we will not go further into that question, but will consider the coat. A little time devoted to its care is bound to pay off. Special dog-grooming gloves, which have a rough, bristly surface on one side and soft velvet on the other, are made. These are suitable for the smooth Chihuahuas. Brushes with short, fine bristles are also suitable. Glove or brush should be used daily for a few minutes, finishing with the velvet or with a silk handkerchief. Wire-backed gloves, whalebone or nylon-bristled brushes are too scratchy and make the skin scurfy. If scurf is present—and it often troubles the blacks or chocolates—the dog should be brushed regularly with one of the advertised preparations sold for the cure of dandruff and similar scalp conditions. It should also be shampooed weekly with a special medicated soap.

Long-haired Chihuahuas shed their coats at regular intervals, generally twice a year. At such times they look ragged and are not usually shown. They should be entered for a show only when coming into, or having just reached their best and most profuse coat. Even so, as with any long-haired dog, they may look perfect when entries close and start shedding immediately afterwards so that they do not look nice by the time the show is held. This, however, is a risk that must be taken, but it is considered a mistake to show a heavy-coated dog during its moult as it is always handicapped in the ring.

The longs require regular daily grooming, and while this is an *advantage* for the smooths, it is *essential* for the maintenance of a really healthy coat in a long-haired Chi. With the same type of brush recommended for the short-haired dogs, brush briskly, paying special attention to the featherings on ears, legs, tail, and brisket. A medium-fine steel comb will be needed to tease out any tangles.

Exhibits of either types of coat should have a bath a day or two before the show. The smooths, though greatly improved by a wash, can get by without one, but the longs never look their best unless they have had a dip. The washing makes the coat stand out, enhances the appearance of the featherings, and without this extra touch of glamour the dogs can look droopy and unattractive.

Chihuahuas are easy to bath and there is absolutely no excuse for presenting a dirty dog in the ring, yet even some experienced exhibitors have been criticized for doing this very thing. The dog can be washed in the kitchen sink or in the wash-basin. Use warm, but not hot, water. Wet the dog thoroughly, rub with a good cream shampoo and rinse with care, making sure no water goes into eyes or, if possible, ears. As an added precaution, dry the ears gently with orange-stick and cottonwool. By far the best way to dry a wet dog, smooth-haired or long, is with a clean chamois leather. Buy one and keep it for this purpose, and do not use it for anything else— above all, hide it so that none of the other members of the household can borrow it for windows or car. Have a large bowl of hot water on the table and stand the dog beside it on a towel. Get someone to keep an eye on it, in case it tries to jump down, while you wring out the chamois as tightly as you can. Wipe the dog thoroughly, rinse the leather, wring out as dry as possible and wipe again. Repeat a few times and you will be astonished to find the dog is bone-dry, a state achieved far more thoroughly and efficiently than with a towel. Let the dog sit in a warm place for half an hour or so before allowing it to go back into its bed, or outside the house. After being doused in warm water it must not be allowed to get a chill.

It is now spotlessly clean, and all it will require is a good grooming with a glove if it is smooth, or a brush and comb if it is long-haired, just before leaving for the show and on arrival there.

The dog is ready—what about the owner? There is still much more to be done, for all sorts of odds and ends will be needed for the show. A canvas 'zip' holdall is as useful an accessory as you can have, and it must be packed the day before the journey.

The dog will need a light leather or chain collar and lead, if he is travelling loose, and just a collar if he is to be transported in a little box or case, in which event he will need a small piece of blanket to lie on. A fine nylon slip lead will show off the dog's points best.

You will need two small dishes, one for milk or water, the other for a main meal which you will take with you. Choose something the dog likes best, for it may be distracted and excited by all the unusual happenings around it and be put off its food; something irresistible and tempting is recommended. This will probably be minced cooked meat or liver, chicken or rabbit, and it travels best in a plastic bag or container. Once packed it should be left in a cool larder or refrigerator until the last minute, together with a plastic bottle of milk sweetened with glucose, or some ready-made malted milk.

Take another plastic bottle of water. This is always available but very often the tap is a long way from the benches, and it saves trouble if one has one's own supply handy. Some show halls are overheated and stuffy, and the dogs get very thirsty.

Take a special tit-bit to use as an attraction in the ring. Dogs get obsessions about all manner of things. Some love chocolates and sweet biscuits, and most of them get excited over malted milk tablets; others will show well for scraps of liver or chicken. Not a few exhibitors use a hare's foot or a scrap of frog from a horse's hoof! A dog that is keen on a ball usually shows well, and will keep alert and on its toes if one is concealed in hand or pocket. Even squeakers of various kinds are used as last resorts. Never toss balls, toys, or tit-bits about the ring in case you annoy other exhibitors or upset their dogs.

The schedule of the show will state whether or not the dogs will be benched. If not, then a show carrier, in which the dog can stay quietly before and after the judging, and yet still be seen by the public, is a necessity. Special cases for this purpose are made in a variety of shapes, sizes, and materials. The most attractive are of clear perspex; some have transparent top and sides, and plywood ends or backs; some have wooden tops, backs, and sides, and transparent doors. There are also hampers, square or domed, with wire mesh fronts. The solid cases can be stuffy and airless, and the baskets are often draughty in cold weather. It is exceedingly important to make sure that any case used has ample ventilation. There should be holes or grilles at both ends to admit a current of air, and even then the atmosphere inside the box should be checked from time to time to make quite certain it is not uncomfortably warm. It becomes stuffy if two or three dogs are carried in the same case, and in general it is not wise to leave the dogs for more than a very short time if the weather is at all sultry. There have been tragedies when dogs shut in these cases inside motor cars have been suffocated.

Even if the show is benched it will probably be convenient to take the Chihuahua to the show in a travel case. It can remain in it, as long as it is visible to the public, or be put into the wire pen which the management will have provided at table height. Unless it is particularly cold the dog will probably prefer the extra space in the bench, and it is usual to hang some little curtains round the wire.

Exhibitors vie, one with another, in decorating the pens with attractive materials, the curtains usually being suspended with tapes or hooks, or clipped on the wire with coloured plastic clothes-pegs. The pegs are the least trouble but also the least satisfactory, since the lively little occupants are likely to start romping and swing on the curtains. The pegs are then not strong enough to hold the curtains in place. All toy dog pens at shows are not exactly the same size, but they are usually 24 ×24 ×24 in. Curtains planned to drape the back and sides of such pens may be a little on the large side when smaller benches are supplied, but this does not really matter and they can usually be arranged to fit.

On a tour of the toy dog section of the show one may see startling decorations in satin, brocade, richly embroidered fabrics, Mexican flags, chilly-looking plastic, even crinkled paper; but nylon, seersucker or waffle-weave materials look best and are the most practical. They do not crease, but emerge from the zip-bag looking crisp and fresh, and they are easily laundered and drip-dried between shows. Choose a colour that sets off the dog to the best advantage, and take, to match or tone, a coloured, cot-size blanket, which will cover the wooden base of the bench.

Many people are inclined to scoff at the curtains, dismissing them as unnecessary affectations. This is far from true because the wire cases, unadorned, are draughty and chilly. They provide far less comfortable shelter than the benches of different design put up for the bigger dogs, most of which are better equipped to stand up to discomforts, and the toy dog's hangings are really practical.

A row of ordinary dog-show benches can be a shabby sight, and there is no doubt that the nicely draped toy pens provide a striking background for the little aristocrats, and brighten things up for the visitors. Some exhibitors take a small bottle of disinfectant and a piece of cloth and wipe the pen before putting the dog inside.

By the time the curtains and blanket are rolled up in the show bag it is quite full. Do leave room, however, for a few things for yourself. A packed lunch, with a thermos flask of soup, tea, or coffee, or in hot summer weather an iced drink, will be a great comfort on the journey or at the show. Although refreshments of some kind are always available, the buffets get very crowded and are often situated in a distant part of the hall or grounds. The judging takes place at different times, and if the Chihuahuas are called into the ring as soon as the show opens it may be long past lunch-time, with most of the eats sold out, before the poor handler is able to give a thought to his own requirements. In such cases it is comforting to have food and drink handy.

If the show is to be held out of doors the dogs will be benched under cover, but it may be some distance between car park, tents, judging rings, cloakrooms, trade stands, secretary's office, and so on, which will all be outside, so a light raincoat is a 'must'. As a final thought slip in an extra blanket and an old newspaper, also a clean towel. Accidents can always happen, especially with puppies. And don't forget to take your Exhibitor's Pass, and the schedule with all the important information.

If you dislike standing about, take a light folding chair or stool because it is by no means certain that chairs will be provided. There are usually seats round the rings, though not always, but if exhibitors want to sit with their dogs at the benches they very often have to provide their own seats.

We seem to have thought of everything now, so all that remains is to set the alarm clock for an early start. Prepare to arrive at the show in plenty of time, even with a dog requiring as little preparation as a Chihuahua. Nothing is more harassing for the owner, or more off-putting for the exhibit, than a last-minute rush.

AT THE SHOW

The official veterinary surgeon will be on duty at the gate, and will examine the dog. If it is a male he will, as well as looking to make sure it is healthy, check that it is entire: that is, with both testicles descended. A dog with only one testicle is a monorchid; one with no testicles a cryptorchid. Neither is eligible for exhibition, under Kennel Club rules, and the Vet would not allow one to enter the show. (If you have any doubts as to the correctness of your dog in this respect, get a Vet's opinion on it before you waste money on entry fees.) The show Vet may go over the dog very quickly and give it a perfunctory examination, or he may decide to look at its throat, take its temperature, etc.

This does not take long, either way, and all being well you will soon be on your way to the benches. There are usually stewards or officials standing about who will direct you to the Toy section. If there is a number on your pass you can go straight to your bench; if not, buy a catalogue and look it up. Spread out the blanket, hang up the curtains, and then take the dog for a short run round on a lead. Try to find a quiet spot—

not so difficult at an outdoor show but more of a problem in a hall. The larger shows are usually able to provide exercising space, well sprinkled with sawdust, and if not it is best to take the puppy outside for a few minutes. If it can make itself comfortable it is sure to show better, and it has a long day before it.

Afterwards, return the dog to the bench and let it rest quietly. Do not make the mistake of walking it round and round the show or taking it on and off the bench for people to see. Puppies get tired easily with so many strange distractions, and if the judging takes place late in the day it may not give a good account of itself. This is where the portable seat is so useful. It is pleasant to be able to keep an eye on the dog, and it will probably settle better than if it is left alone. You may offer the puppy a drink of milk or water.

The catalogue may or may not give the order of judging and detail the ring numbers for the various breeds. If in doubt, ask one of the other exhibitors who may know, or go to the Secretary's office. The information is important, because if Chihuahuas are first in the ring you must be on hand and not wander away. If they are to be judged later, it is safe to go off for a short spell to see the rest of the show or to get some refreshment; but never leave the dog for more than a few minutes at a time, unless the owner of an adjacent pen volunteers to baby-sit until you come back.

Directly the steward calls out 'Chihuahuas in the ring,' or you see the other owners getting ready to leave their benches, take your exhibit to the ringside—and carry your chair with you because there may be some waiting about between classes.

When your class is called, enter the ring and collect your number from the steward. Keep a sharp eye open on what is going on, and do not be tempted to gossip with neighbours. There is a keen competition in progress and it is unwise to let one's attention be distracted.

The judge may begin by looking at the exhibits individually, or walk up and down, giving the class a quick once-over. Or he may ask the handlers to walk their dogs round the ring a few times. When this happens do not let your puppy lunge forward, or tug backwards, or sniff the dog in front. When the cavalcade stops, watch what the exhibitors are doing. Follow on, and when your turn comes either hand your dog to the judge or put it on the table, whichever procedure is being followed on the day. Answer the judge's questions, but do not attempt to converse with him. If in doubt about procedure, ask the ring *steward*.

The judge will want to see the dog's teeth; he may lift the lips himself, or ask you to do it, and he will want to know the age of your exhibit. Then walk up and down the ring, once, or twice, according to the judge's wishes. Then return to your place, beside the person whose dog was examined immediately before your own. Stand still and relax, and either hold the dog in your arms or leave it on the floor if it seems quite happy there. Do not keep fussing it or showing it tit-bits or toys when the judge is busy with the others in the class, otherwise it will become bored, and at the very moment when you want it to put up its ears and look alert it will appear slack and disinterested. But spring to attention as soon as the judge starts to look at the last entrant, get your dog standing nicely, and glance at the judge occasionally in case he is motioning you to move the dog again or to stand in a different position.

The judge will pick out the winners, placing the first four or five in order. The steward will hand out the coveted cards: red for First, blue for Second, yellow for Third, and Green for Reserve. Some shows give a white card for 'Very Highly Commended', and very occasionally 'Highly Commended' and 'Commended' to the next in order.

Leave the ring, unless you are in the next class, when you will be asked to stand on one side with other dogs already seen by the judge. The new dogs, those which were not entered in a previous class, stand separately and are examined in detail. If you are not in the next class, but in one a little later, do not leave the ringside, otherwise you may miss your turn. Some classes do not take nearly so long to judge as others, especially if most of the entries are 'old' dogs, already seen or placed, and not the new competitors.

Once your classes have been judged return to the bench, give the dog a meal and have something to eat and drink yourself. It may not be possible to leave until an hour which will have been stated in the schedule, perhaps 5 or 6 p.m. Only one show, the unique Cruft's Dog Show, insists on all exhibits staying until 8 p.m.

The rules are made so that the public, which generally streams into the show from tea-time onwards, can have a fair opportunity of seeing the dogs. If no rules were made, exhibitors would dash off home directly judging was completed, and people who paid to come in would see nothing but rows of empty benches. The money taken at the gate is often an important part of a show committee's revenue, and the more visitors there are to dog shows the better publicity it is for pedigree canines. In fact, quite a lot of business is done round the benches at shows, and Chihuahuas never fail to command a great deal of admiration. It is rare not to find a team of photographers and Press reporters round the Chi's, and publicity in daily and local newspapers often results, all of which is good for the breed.

An entire day at a dog show sounds rather an undertaking, but in fact it passes very quickly. It is possibly a little less interesting for the beginner, but very soon there are familiar faces, friends to talk to, and it does not take long to get snared in the mesh of the dog-show world, from which it is indeed hard to escape, so fascinating does it become.

The judging for the best exhibit in the show usually winds up the events of the day. All the Best of Breed winners parade, and it is always most interesting to watch. It is also tremendously exciting if a Chihuahua is one of the finalists. When it is all over the hall empties rapidly, people crowd out, jostling, chattering, tripping over leads and baskets. Some are clutching prize cards, and perhaps a silver trophy or two. Others have had a disappointing day but even they, together with most others present, are already making plans to go to another show in another place.

Success at one of the small shows usually tempts the exhibitor to try out his dog at one of the big Championship show events. There are twenty-one all-breed Championship shows held in Britain each year. Three of these are in Scotland, one in Northern Ireland, and one in Wales. Some breeds whose popularity merits the honour are also allowed to have one or more Championship shows, run by the breed societies.

Not all breeds have classes at all the shows. Chihuahuas have Champion show status at most of the shows.

Prizes won at Championship shows are not very much more valuable financially than at the Open fixtures, but such awards add greatly to the value and prestige of the winners. Exhibitors show, not for the money to be gained, since this rarely covers the expenses, but for the honour and glory. If a dog becomes a Champion its value can rise from, say, £100 or £150, to anything up to a staggering four-figure sum. In consequence, the top wins at Championship shows are very much sought after, and competition is tremendously strong. This should be borne in mind since many a novice show-goer has followed up a good win at a small show with the experience of being left out of the cards at the larger event, and has suffered great disappointment as a result. Never be downcast over a defeat. If you are confident that you have a good dog, keep on showing. If the first judge does not appreciate it the next one may do so. You are bound to have ups and downs; the dog which went straight to the top and stayed there has seldom been born. But be realistic. Appraise your exhibit and compare it with the competitors. If it does not nearly approach them in merit, waste no more money on its show career. By all means keep it—it will be no less lovable and companionable—but set about buying or breeding a better one for the ring.

It is because it is 'tough at the top' that we advise the newcomer to start in a modest manner at a few small shows. A little experience may make all the difference when the time does come—as it surely will to anybody who really goes about this show business in the right way and with the right spirit—to take on all comers at the leading Championship shows.

FOURTEEN

SELLING, EXPORTING, AND IMPORTING

B EFORE a beginner embarks on dog breeding, the fact
must be faced that it is not always easy to find a ready
market for the puppies; the best-known kennels usually
have a steady demand, but until a young kennel becomes
known it is hard to compete with their salesmanship. Showing
winning dogs is still the best advertising medium. A few wins
do far more good than advertisements in papers, and as
successes increase so a demand for stock is created.

This does not mean that advertising in the Press should be
ignored, for it, too, is of tremendous value. Regular advertisements should be used, together with the efforts to win recog-
nition in competitive circles, and should be worded to draw
attention to the kennel's achievements.

Some local daily or weekly newspapers have wide circula-
tions, and many people find these helpful when it comes to
disposing of puppies suitable for the pet market. For quality
stock the weekly dog publications bring the best results, since
their readers are almost entirely composed of people who are
primarily concerned with the showing and breeding of pedigree
dogs.

Stud dogs should be well advertised, and a small advertisement each week usually attracts more customers than an
occasional announcement, even one in a larger space.

If a buyer seeks to reserve a puppy, ask for a small deposit.
People are sometimes very casual. They will choose a dog,
arrange to collect it at a later date, and then go away and
change their minds or buy something different elsewhere. The
poor breeder keeps the dog for a considerable length of time
at his own risk and expense, and loses other opportunities of

selling it in the meanwhile, at a time when it was at its younger and most attractive stage.

Give the buyer a pedigree, Kennel Club registration certificate, and a signed transfer form when the puppy is handed over. Also make out a receipt, filling in full details of the transaction on a counterfoil for future reference, and give a diet sheet so that the puppy can progress without the possible setbacks caused by a sudden change of feeding.

If an enquiry for a dog is received in writing, offer the stock for sale 'subject to its being unsold when a reply is received', otherwise a client may call in response to a letter and be very annoyed if the dog described has gone.

Never send original pedigrees, or important photographs to strangers. They may get lost in the post, or the person may lose them or fail to return them. Send a copy of a pedigree, and either have a block made from the photo and some illustrated leaflets printed, or do not send a picture at all. If you do enclose anything you wish to have returned, include a stamped, addressed envelope.

The first enquiry from abroad is always a great excitement, but it is unwise to attach too much importance to such potential business since disappointments often result. A great many people overseas read the dog papers and study the advertisements, and then send out circular letters to all and sundry. The request is usually for copies of pedigrees, photographs of front, side, and back views, and a long list of specific details including an inclusive quotation for freight and documentation. The seller complies with the request, sending all the material by air mail. Sad to say, time and money are expended in vain, because all too often nothing more is heard, and the snapshots, etc., are not returned. The optimistic buyer has probably been holding back a dog in the hopes that an important export order is pending, and has missed a sale nearer home.

Against this, of course, there are genuine enquiries, and a large number of dogs are exported from Great Britain to all parts of the world, so it would be wrong to paint an entirely black picture.

Before arranging to export a dog, however, make sure that it will be going to a good home. Most overseas countries have their own kennel clubs, and the addresses of all those affiliated with and recognized by our own governing body can be found in the Kennel Club Stud Books. Write to the club concerned and ask for confidential information as to the suitability or otherwise of the home to which the dog would go. Unfortutately the attitude towards animals differs in various countries and in many places dogs are not, by our standards, well cared for. There have been instances where show dogs were reasonably well looked after when they were winning and useful for breeding, but on becoming too old were turned adrift and left to fend for themselves or die. Many non-Europeans are well-meaning but have no idea how to treat a dog, and for one kept with the care and devotion that is the lot of animals in our own country, to be precipitated into such hands must be terrible. Since there are still some enlightened people who will give a dog a good home, it is as well to make enquiries in well-informed quarters. If in doubt, do not export the dog.

When negotiations progress, however, and a favourable reply has been received, arrangements will be made to forward a remittance. It is easiest if an all-in quotation is made, one which includes the price of the dog, the estimated cost of freight, crate, Kennel Club export documents, delivery to airport or steamer, and so on. It is best to get an estimate for the transport costs from one of the firms which specialize in shipping dogs abroad. There are several of these concerns whose experience and knowledge can save the sender a lot of time and trouble and ensure a comfortable journey for the dog.

The estimate usually includes provision of a roomy crate or travelling kennel, food for the journey, port and Customs dues, tips to staff, the cost of travel by sea or air, and so on. In addition, there will be the veterinary surgeon's fee for examining the dog and issuing a certificate of health, the Kennel Club transfer and Export Pedigree Certificate, a collar and lead, and possibly one or two other minor items.

Dealing with strangers always involves some risk, and it is therefore wise to make sure that the purchase price and transit costs have all been paid in full before the dog is dispatched. If this has not been done it may well be difficult or impossible to collect them afterwards, as a few people have found to their cost.

It is, or should be, scarcely necessary to say that it is most important to send dogs that are typical and good value for the money. The vast majority of breeders are conscientious over their exports, going to great lengths to ensure satisfied clients at the other end. When there is any dissatisfaction it is often due to a conflict of opinions. One has only to realize how much tastes differ where dogs are concerned—how one judge can give a dog a prize and another ignore it—to realize that what *A* considers a handsome dog *B* may think is nothing outstanding: both could produce credible reasons for their opinions.

It is probably a good rule to refuse to sell inexpensive 'pet dog' specimens to clients overseas. Too many instances have been known where people have bought such dogs and, having received them, and in order to impress their friends, have spread it about that enormous sums of money have been paid for them. The cognoscenti know that these dogs are not worth anything like as much, and conclude that unscrupulous sellers have sent out dud dogs at exorbitant figures. Yet nothing could be further from the truth—the unfortunate sellers have sent out pet dogs at pet prices, but were unwise to send the dogs at all since they do not enhance the reputation of British breeders.

There is a good market for dogs as pets in our own islands, where the small distances make it easier to negotiate sales to mutual satisfaction. It is much better to refuse to sell to over-seas buyers the dogs that do not come up to show standard, but to place them in suitable homes in this country.

Charge a good price for a good dog and send it out with pride as a good ambassador for its breed and for the kennel from which it is exported.

Many buyers like to call at the kennels to select a dog themselves, but others may conclude a transaction over the telephone or through the post, and ask for the dog to be sent to them. Chihuahuas are frequently sent by train and seem to travel perfectly well, but it is usual to make careful arrange-ments to ensure that they are met at the other end, or at points in the journey where changes are necessary. Some of the firms which specialize in livestock export, also several individuals living in London, will collect dogs from any of the main London termini and take them over to the next station, putting them on a train in charge of the guard, and thus saving much delay. They charge a small fee for this most useful service.

It is not wise to send small dogs away in extremely cold weather, even when they are carefully packed. For all journeys a proper travelling box is an essential, well ventilated but not draughty, and painted a bright colour so that it is easily recognized on a crowded station or among a lot of other crates and parcels. A bed of deep hay or wood-wool is cosier than a blanket. Clear labels are important, one or two gummed on the top of the box and another tied to the handle or the fastening. The catch should be secure, but not locked, unless the key is tied to the box. Never lock a dog in a box and then send the key by post.

Before sending a Chihuahua away enquire about the best times for dispatch. For very long journeys it is often wise to rail the dog in the evening; travelling by night it does not miss any meals and reaches its destination early the next morning.

Air travel is highly recommended. The air companies manage to give all livestock the individual attention so often lacking on the railways, and go to endless trouble to make the travelling comfortable for the dog, and the formalities simple for the owner. The box is required to be nose, paw, teeth, and moisture-proof, and should be light but strong. Hampers, though light, are too draughty to be satisfactory because the freight compartments of many aircraft are very cold; boxes made of plywood or hardboard are best.

Journeys by sea should be arranged by experts. The professional livestock shipper knows exactly what has to be done, and the arrangements are so complicated that the novice may leave some important documents out, or fail to provide sufficient food for the trip, and there are other things which could be forgotten and which might lead to all sorts of difficulties.

The Chihuahua breed has been greatly strengthened by the imports from the U.S.A., and from time to time breeders feel inspired by the successes of the stock brought over to import a dog or bitch for themselves from the country that keeps Chihuahuas in such great numbers and offers a wide choice. Not unnaturally, however, they are deterred by not knowing just how to set about it.

Addresses of American breeders can be found in their dog magazines, and it is also a good idea to obtain a recommendation from one of the people who have already completed satisfactory transactions with a kennel on the other side. From time to time well-known American judges and handlers visit our principal Championship shows, and they are always good enough to suggest kennels likely to have good stock for sale.

Be prepared to pay a top price for a top dog, and remember that it costs just as much to import a poor dog as a good one; the expenses are the same and only the cost of the dog itself varies.

Most people send Chihuahuas to this country by air, and from the U.S.A. it costs from about £30 to fly a Chihuahua to Britain; the exact figure depending on the point of departure and the weight and size of dog and box.

Every dog imported into this country must undergo a compulsory period of six months' detention in quarantine. Before the dog can be admitted to this country an import licence must be obtained from the Ministry of Agriculture and Fisheries. They will supply a list of approved quarantine kennels and of their appointed carrying agents. The importer is liable for the cost of board throughout the six months' period of detention, and the costs, which tend to escalate, vary from kennel to kennel. Veterinary surgeons' fees are extra.

There are good, bad, and indifferent quarantine kennels and it is important to find one with suitable accommodation for toy dogs, preferably where previous Chihuahua imports have been satisfactorily housed. The kennels should always be inspected before the dog arrives, and the type of kennel buildings noted, also the number of available runs and the general appearance of the establishment and the standard of cleanliness.

The kennels fix their own visiting hours, but generally owners may visit their dogs on most weekdays.

The six months seem an interminable period, and although the 'prisoners' usually settle down and do well, the time must drag. It is very exciting when the day of release arrives and the new acquisition comes home at last.

FIFTEEN

AILMENTS

GENERAL

CHIHUAHUAS are not delicate dogs. They do not suffer from illnesses more than other canines, and are healthier than many other breeds. Careful feeding and exercising, attention to hygiene, an indoor atmosphere in winter of about 60°F., and plenty of love are the necessities, without which trouble is certain.

With most beginners it is a problem to know when to call the Vet. Very naturally they do not want to incur bills unnecessarily, and many veterinary surgeons are not pleased if they are summoned for trivialities, especially during the night hours or at short notice. At the same time they resent the case where the dog has been ill for some time before they are asked to attend to it, since so many indispositions can be arrested in the early stages and are difficult or impossible to cure when of long standing. The best advice is: 'When in doubt, get the Vet,' for it is better to be sure than sorry. This is especially true of whelping, since delay in getting assistance when complications are present may well result in dead puppies and even a dead bitch.

Every dog breeder should keep a doggy first-aid chest or medicine cupboard. The following is a list of what it should contain:

Two or three eye-droppers or fountain-pen fillers.
Cottonwool.
Curved surgical scissors.
Clinical thermometer.
Friar's Balsam or tincture of steel.

Optrex eye lotion.
Ointment for bare patches.
Dettol.
Worm medicine (small quantities only as some brands lose
potency when kept for any length of time).
Vaseline.
Syrup of Figs.
Milk of Magnesia.
Brands' Essence of beef or chicken.
Jar of honey.
Tin of Bengers' Food.
T.C.P.
Garlic Capsules

In various illnesses the Vet will prescribe different things,
and obviously one cannot be prepared for every eventuality,
but the above equipment provides the essentials for most
emergencies.

AILMENTS

ABRASIONS. Bathe the sore carefully, dry with sterile cottonwool, and apply an antiseptic ointment.

ACID MILK. This condition occurs occasionally in nursing
bitches, and makes itself known when the puppies cry, wail,
and cease sucking.
Get some blue litmus paper from the chemist. Squeeze a
drop of milk from one of the bitch's teats on to the paper, and
it will turn bright pink if the milk is very acid, mauveish if it is
normal. Dosing the bitch with bicarbonate of soda or milk of
magnesia may help to reduce the condition, but the puppies
often fade out even when removed from the dam and artificially
fed.

ALOPECIA. A peculiar type of baldness sometimes afflicts
Chihuahuas of all ages, though it is perhaps most common
among puppies of three and a half to five months of age. The
signs are usually most noticeable on top of the head, under the
chin, and on fore and hind legs. Coconut oil is said to give

results in certain cases, but the Vet is generally the best person to prescribe since there are proprietary lotions and ointments which are most effective, and will cause the hair to grow rapidly. This particular type of baldness is not accompanied by irritation, redness, or soreness as are other skin disorders.

ANAL GLANDS. Chihuahuas do not suffer much from congested glands, but occasionally older dogs, or dogs which have been allowed to remain constipated for a while, may drag themselves along the ground in a sitting position, try to lick the sore places which can become inflamed and even discharge. The Vet will show you how to empty the glands by gentle squeezing, and will give you a small tube of penicillin ointment with instructions to apply it through the tiny nozzle right into the little openings. Very obstinate or recurrent cases can be successfully operated upon.

APPETITE, MORBID. Dogs of all breeds occasionally develop the repellent habit of eating excreta of all kinds. The cause of this is not completely known, though it is thought it may be brought about by some vitamin or mineral deficiency. It is as well to try some tonic or supplement, also to treat a pile of excreta liberally with cayenne pepper—sometimes a very effective cure.

BAD BREATH. Many toy dogs, and Chihuahuas are no exception, suffer from halitosis. The fact that the teeth decay comparatively early has a lot to do with this, also the fact that many dogs suffer from digestive upsets through unwise feeding. Teeth scaled and kept clean do not smell, and very badly decayed teeth should be extracted. They can be pushed out with the finger when very loose, without causing the dog distress, but if firmly fixed it is work for a Vet, who will give an anaesthetic. Attention to diet and keeping the bowels moving will help when teeth are not to blame.

BALANITIS. This is the name of the slight yellow discharge which many stud dogs have on the prepuce. It is frequently

licked and is not obvious all the time, and though it is unsightly it is not serious or harmful. If treatment is thought
advisable the sheath can be syringed daily with a tepid
solution of an antiseptic of the bland type used as a gargle.

BILIOUSNESS. Many dogs vomit froth and bile, and this
often means nothing to worry about, certainly not when it
just happens once. Persistent vomiting is a serious symptom,
however. The dog should be kept warm, water should be removed, and nothing given by mouth unless the Vet orders teaspoonfuls of raw white of egg and soda-water. The Vet may
wish to give a saline injection, and should be consulted.

BITES. Chihuahuas are not fighters and although they
occasionally get involved in arguments there is seldom a blood
bath. Bites from larger dogs are perhaps the greatest risk. A
dog bite is inclined to become septic since the sharp canine
teeth make deep punctures. The wound must be kept open to
drain, and should be fomented if it closes, otherwise it may
result in a serious abscess. Penicillin ointment squeezed into
the wounds is most usually prescribed.

BLADDER IRREGULARITIES. Bladder disorders are quickly discernible. The dog or bitch urinates all the time, or tries to
urinate, and produces a few drops or nothing at all. It looks
unhappy and loses weight. Give barley water to drink, and
call the Vet.

BOWELS. A carefully fed dog should pass firm, dark brown
motions. Sloppy motions, yellow, grey, or tinged with blood
are danger signs. Bitches pass loose, black material after whelping, and this is normal. It disappears after a day or two. Some
dogs suffer from constipation. There is incessant straining,
obvious discomfort and distress. A teaspoonful of olive oil on
the food each day usually removes the trouble.

If a laxative is required, a half-teaspoonful of Syrup of Figs
or a teaspoonful of Milk of Magnesia are very good. Such
things as Castor oil are too drastic for toy dogs, and though

they purge they leave the animal constipated afterwards.

If diarrhoea persists for more than a day, or if it is tinged with blood, call the Vet immediately. A haemorrhage from the rectum is a sign of very acute enteritis and the Vet should be urgently summoned, as the dog can die in a matter of hours unless it receives expert treatment.

BRONCHITIS. This is not very common, and when it does occur the patient will usually be under the care of a Vet. Rubbing the chest with Vapour Rub, giving an inhalant at intervals, and keeping the dog warm and comfortable all help.

CHOKING. A distressing and dangerous emergency, it can be caused by the dog swallowing a small piece of bone, or a large chunk of meat, or, in the case of a puppy, a foreign body with which it has been playing. With the first finger, try to push the obstruction down the throat, and if this does not work rush the dog to the Vet.

CHOREA. This is a side-effect following one of the virus diseases of the distemper-hard-pad type. The dog develops a decided twitch: sometimes of a fore or hind leg, sometimes it nods the head. Any nervous symptom of this kind is serious, since if it becomes very bad and if it is accompanied by convulsions it may necessitate the dog's being destroyed. In mild cases sedatives help, and sometimes the dog will outgrow the trouble. If the twitch remains it is generally an insuperable handicap in the show ring.

CONJUNCTIVITIS. Any discharge of the eyes may be a symptom of one of the serious dog diseases, and the subject should always be isolated. This is a wise precaution even though it may be due only to a cold wind, dust, or slight infection. Bathe with Optrex or a solution made by dissolving half a teaspoonful of boracid acid in half a pint of warm water.

Eyes that water but are not inflamed can be helped by regular bathing with strained cold tea.

CONSTIPATION. See Bowels, and Laxatives.

CONVULSIONS. There is nothing more distressing than a dog in a fit. It twitches, looks wild-eyed, and falls to the ground, struggling and thrashing the legs. Pick it up gently and put it on a soft blanket until it recovers consciousness. Never try to give anything by mouth until the dog is completely round. If it is a young puppy, dose it for worms. If an older dog, give a mild sedative such as a small dose of bromide or phenobarbitone, both of which will be prescribed by your Vet. In an uninoculated dog keep a careful watch for other symptoms which may develop since fits are sometimes associated with distemper and hard-pad diseases.

COUGHS. Dogs rarely get coughs as such. If a dog coughs it is usually a symptom of hepatitis. Send for the Vet at once, and keep it well away from the other dogs.

CUTS. See Abrasions.

DANDRUFF. Many dogs with the type of coat owned by the smooth-haired Chihuahuas, and even some of the long-hairs, suffer from dandruff. It can be treated by regular shampooing with one of the much-advertised preparations sold for human heads. It looks very unsightly, especially on the black and dark chocolate coats, and such dogs should be bathed with good-quality shampoos, avoiding some of the synthetic, soapless types which dry the skin.

DIARRHOEA. See Bowels.

DISLOCATIONS. Chihuahuas are occasionally subject to dislocated stifle, patella, and hip joints. Much research is at present taking place into the causes of hip-displasia. Any such condition is one which a Vet should examine.

DISTEMPER. The old-fashioned distemper has largely disappeared and been replaced by a different virus which causes hard-pad disease. Both are serious diseases accompanied by a high mortality, and both are preventible now that excellent inoculations may be given from the age of nine weeks upwards, which give almost one hundred per cent protection.

Because so many dog owners take advantage of this price-less protection for their dogs, the disease is becoming increas-ingly rare. The symptoms are loss of appetite, lassitude, diarrhoea, and a yellowish discharge from the eyes. The dog looks miserable and the temperature is high. As the injections are prophylactic and therapeutic, the veterinary surgeon should be called as soon as possible, as the injections are very helpful in the early stages and much less so when the illness has become established. The Vet will prescribe treatment and diet, and the dog must be isolated, kept warm, and provided with newspapers upon which to pass water and excreta. Chihuahuas become very fastidious when house-trained and will often refuse to relieve themselves indoors. In such cases it is neces-sary to ask the Vet if the dog may be permitted out of doors if covered with a jacket.

DOSES. It should always be remembered that Chihuahuas are tiny little dogs. Very few proprietary medicines, even when they prescribe for toy breeds, give quantities small enough for a Chi. When in doubt, measure the quantity on the small side.

DYSENTERY. See Bowels.

EAR-ACHE. It is mostly the dogs with pendant ears which suffer the most from canker, but even the prick-eared breeds can get this, especially if water enters the ears during bathing or when out in the rain, and is not carefully dried off. The dog shakes its head, rubs its head along the floor, and scratches the ear. Ask the Vet for some lotion and pour this into the ear as directed. Later, clean the ear most carefully and gently with an orange-stick well padded with soft cottonwool.

EARS. Dryness of the ears themselves is common in adult Chihuahuas. The edges feel crisp and look scalloped and un-even. Daily application of some kind of oil will dispose of the trouble, which is prevalent in summer-time.

Soft ears are always a hazard in any prick-eared breed. Although ears usually stand up by the time teething is completed, and often much earlier, there are always a few Chihuahuas which put their ears up late, and some which never put them up at all. Treatment can begin, if the ears look doubtful, at about five months. The ears should be covered with transparent plastic sticky tape, wound carefully round, and pressed flat until the ear is held erect. An alternative material is plastic adhesive surgical plaster. If this can be kept on for ten days or more and repeated as necessary, it is usually very effective. Be sure, however, to see that the ears do not sweat and become sore, nor that the plaster is too tight. Another method is to smear double strength collodion (obtainable at any chemist) over the flap of the ear, repeating as each layer dries until the ear is very thickly coated and stiff enough to stay erect. This can be removed with surgical spirit, but wears off in time of its own accord.

ECZEMA. I have never heard of a Chi suffering from eczema, but the condition is common enough in other breeds, so perhaps there is a first time for everything. Treatment consists of carefully cleaning the sore with scraps of cottonwool dipped in T.C.P. and water solution, mixed with a little Stergene. A soothing antiseptic ointment, or a paste made of flowers of sulphur, olive oil, with a little paraffin or kerosene, should be rubbed in daily. Attention to the diet helps; cut out starch and feed on raw meat or carefully boned, cooked fish. Mix some finely chopped parsley, or other comparable green vegetable, finely grated raw carrot, or the chopped leaves of the rampion (wild garlic). A heaped teaspoonful or two is sufficient. In very obstinate cases, the Vet may suggest injections of arsenic or cortisone, which are usually very effective.

EMETICS. If a dog is believed to have swallowed poison it can be given an emetic to promote vomiting, and thus get rid of the obnoxious matter. Common salt, about as much as will cover a sixpence, in a tablespoon of warm water, given as a drench, usually works. Also, a tiny piece of plain washing soda given as a pill can usually be relied on to make a dog sick.

ENTERITIS. A 'killer' complaint where Chihuahuas are concerned and to be regarded with the utmost concern. Symptoms are loose, bloodstained faeces, or the passing of what appears to be pure blood from the rectum. The animal may or may not vomit. Give nothing by mouth, except possibly a little white of egg well stirred with a fork (but not beaten until frothy), and rush the dog, kept warm with blankets and a hot water bottle on the journey, to the Vet. Very prompt treatment, usually in the form of coagulents and salines, is essential and an hour's delay can be fatal.

FRACTURES. Chihuahuas have fine but strong bones, and accidents are uncommon. Should a Chihuahua be dropped from a height, allowed to spring out of the arms, or even jump from a couch or table to the floor, fractures can occur. A flat piece of wood, a pencil, a paper-knife, even a stiff knitting-needle can be used as first-aid splints. Wind some soft material round the 'splint' and bind it carefully to the limb with a soft bandage. Take the dog to a Vet.

GASTRITIS. Frequent vomiting, thirst, and diarrhoea are the symptoms. Keep dog warm and quiet, offer pieces of ice to lick, and, if the Vet advises it, give small teaspoonfuls of egg white well stirred, but not well beaten, with a fork. Small doses of bismuth may be prescribed. When the sickness stops, the return to even liquid nourishment must be exceedingly gradual.

GUMS. Bleeding gums suggest that the teeth are in a state of chronic decay, and it is generally best to ask a Vet to remove them, as the health of the dog will suffer if they remain to poison the system.

HARD-PAD. See Distemper.

HEPATITIS. A disease with variable symptoms. Temperature can be very high or very low. The dog looks ill and miserable. Sometimes it vomits and it may have diarrhoea. Veterinary attention is essential. In advanced stages one or both eyes turn turquoise blue. When diagnosis has been difficult, a blue eye is an almost certain sign that the dog is suffering from hepatitis.

Hepatitis is usually less infectious than such diseases as distemper or hard-pad. Sometimes it only affects one or two occupants in a large kennel. Those affected are generally the younger dogs.

HERNIA. Many puppies have small umbilical hernias and frequently these cause no trouble. A large hernia should have veterinary attention, and a simple operation will dispose of it.

HYDROCEPHALUS. Water on the brain has been observed in young Chihuahuas, usually in unweaned puppies. The skull appears swollen and the puppy wobbles its head from side to side. It is unsteady on its legs and often walks in circles. Sometimes it whines and cries. It usually develops convulsions and dies, and there is very little that can be done for it.

HYDROPHOBIA. Also known as rabies. It is to prevent this disease, easily communicated to man and to other animals, that the quarantine laws of this country are in force. Even in countries where rabies is common it is exceedingly rare among Chihuahuas, since as a rule these cherished little creatures are not permitted to run loose in the sort of places where contact with a rabid animal might be made. Although quite a large number of Chihuahuas have been imported into Great Britain, as far as can be ascertained from the records none has ever developed rabies while in quarantine. Rabies takes as much as six months (the period of detention) to develop.

HYSTERIA. Hysteria can occur in dogs of all ages. When it is endemic in a kennel it is usually a sign of some sort of digestive disturbance caused by the type of food being consumed. In uninoculated dogs it can be a symptom of the nervous complications of distemper. If one puppy shows signs of hysteria it need not occasion overmuch alarm, especially if the rest of the young stock are unaffected. It may have gobbled its meal and given itself acute indigestion. Dose with milk of magnesia, keep it quiet, and in a dark kennel for the rest of the day. Call the Vet if attacks persist.

It is easily identifiable for the dog starts barking on a shrill, high-pitched note, refuses to be quiet, and rushes about in circles. It looks wild-eyed, terrified, and may bite if cornered.

IMPOTENCE. Chihuahuas are ordinarily virile little stud dogs. Impotence, when it exists, is usually caused by overwork at stud, or following a severe illness. There are various treatments which can be tried by the Vet, but unfortunately these are not very often successful.

JAUNDICE. Usually leptospiral or caused by a chill. The dog is excessively thirsty, vomits a colourless fluid, and passes greyish-coloured motions. The whites of the eyes, and the skin, look yellow. The dog is always extremely ill and urgent professional attention is essential if it is to recover.

KIDNEYS. Various kidney disorders are not uncommon among dogs, and especially as they get old. Symptoms are scanty urine, frequent unsuccessful efforts to urinate, and sometimes a temperature. The dog arches its back and looks miserable. Sometimes blood is observed in the urine. There is excessive thirst. This should not be treated by a layman. Call your Vet.

LAXATIVES. Healthy dogs should not require medicine. Constipation is best corrected by all-bran mixed with the food, or by a teaspoonful of olive oil or liquid paraffin. See also bowels.

MENINGITIS. This is an inflammation of the brain, and usually occurs in young puppies or in dogs of any age which have been suffering from distemper or hard-pad disease. The dog has fits, during which it loses consciousness, staggers in circles, struggles on the floor, is incontinent, and froths at the mouth. When it regains consciousness it is dazed, unsteady on its legs, and will cry and whine. The fits tend to become more and more frequent and severe in character, and at such a stage the veterinary surgeon will usually advise putting the dog to sleep as it is suffering acutely and its chances of complete recovery are negligible.

NAILS. The slim, rather long nails of the Chihuahua are inclined to catch and tear. Prevention is better than cure, and if they are kept trimmed, and the dog has some exercise on roads or pavements or in a cemented run, they should not give trouble. A bad sore should be bathed with boracic lotion, plastered with an antiseptic ointment, and kept covered with a clean bandage until it heals.

OBESITY. Almost all the toy breeds tend to grow rather fat, especially those kept in towns and living in flats. Obesity shortens life and is a handicap to a stud dog or a brood bitch. Exercise should be increased, tit-bits, extras, saucers of milk, and the like strictly forbidden. The dog should be fed once daily on a small meal of chopped raw meat, the quantity being graded according to the size of the dog. Keep the bowels open.

These remarks do not apply to puppies, which should always be plump and well covered, and will usually fine down as they grow older.

PARTURIENT ECLAMPSIA. This occurs mostly in nervous or excitable bitches, after whelping. It can happen at any time, and to any bitch, but usually begins when the puppies are about two or three weeks old. The bitch's eyelids may twitch, she shivers and shakes, and may have convulsions. A veterinary surgeon should be sent for immediately, and he will administer large doses of calcium. It may be necessary to remove the puppies and rear them by hand. Prompt diagnosis will normally bring a satisfactory conclusion, but eclampsia can prove fatal.

PURGATIVES. See Laxatives, also Bowels.

PYMETRIA. This is a chronic inflammation of the womb, which can fill with pus. The bitch is very ill, has a high temperature, may vomit, and there is a discharge from the uterus. The veterinary surgeon should be called. He may attempt to treat the condition or advise an immediate hysterectomy operation.

RABIES. See Hydrophobia.

RHEUMATISM. Elderly dogs are generally affected with this, but Chihuahuas are not very subject to it. The dog appears stiff in its movements, and cries out in pain when touched. The bowels should be kept open, and aspirin can be given when pain is acute. Warmth and freedom from damp is essential.

RICKETS. Chihuahua puppies are easy little dogs to rear, and management must be sadly at fault if they get rickets, which is a condition caused by malnutrition. If it occurs it is usually before the puppies are five months old. The joints of the legs enlarge and the legs are misshapen and weak. Apart from poor feeding, rickets can be caused by worms, lack of daylight and liberty. The remedies are nourishing food, cod-liver oil and malt with Vitamin D supplement, warm, dry bedding, and gentle exercise in the fresh air and sunshine, preferably on gravel and not on cold or wet concrete or in long grass.

SHOCK. Shock can be caused by a fall or an accident, or by contact with a live electric wire. The dog may be semiconscious, the breathing shallow and feeble, and the limbs cold. Place the dog in a box on a hot-water bottle, cover with blankets and hurry to the Vet.

STINGS. Wasp and bee stings can cause a dog great discomfort, and if the dog is stung on the lip or tongue it can be most dangerous. Ordinarily, the sting should be removed with tweezers and the spot rubbed with half a cut, raw onion, or dabbed with T.C.P. If the dog suffers great discomfort or appears to be suffering from shock, the Vet should be advised, and will probably suggest an anti-histamine injection.

TEETH. Chihuahua puppies often grow two rows of teeth, the second set coming through the gums before the milk teeth have been discarded. In such cases the gums are sore and inflamed, the puppy is disinclined to eat. A Vet should be consulted as to whether or not the baby teeth should be removed under an anaesthetic. This is usually done only as a last resort, since Chihuahuas in common with some other Toy breeds, are not always good subjects for anaesthesia and fatalities have not been unknown even when undergoing such a relatively simple operation. The trouble is that unless the surplus baby teeth come out, they may push the permanent teeth out of alignment. The teeth should always be kept as clean as possible and free from tartar. Directions for this can be found in Chapter Thirteen.

TEMPERATURE. The dog in health usually has a temperature of 101·2°F. A very small deviation is no cause for anxiety, especially in puppies or in nervous or excitable dogs. An incident such as a car drive can send the temperature up a degree.

But a sudden rise or drop in temperature, especially if it is accompanied by the smallest sign of malaise, is a danger-sign and the cause should be sought. A half-minute thermometer should have the end greased and inserted just inside the rectum. It should be held there a little longer than the half-minute, and the mercury should be shaken well down before insertion. If the reading is as much as 102°F. or below 100°F., keep the dog warm and send for the Vet.

TONSILLITIS. The dog usually runs a temperature, the throat is red and inflamed, and the animal is listless and disinclined to eat. This is generally regarded as a possibly contagious condition and the Vet should see the patient and advise treatment.

VOMITING. Many dogs vomit white froth and grass which they have eaten, and this is harmless. Vomiting of bile, colourless slime, or food, especially if persistent, is a cause for great concern and may mean that the dog is suffering from enteritis or gastritis, among other things. Withhold water, give ice to lick occasionally, and unless the Vet advises it, do not give any kind of food or drink other than, perhaps, small teaspoonfuls of white of egg with glucose.

WORMS. Chihuahua puppies suffer from round worms, as do puppies of most other breeds. But as worms do not vary so very much in size whatever the host, they can do more harm to a tiny toy dog than to a larger one. Puppies showing signs of worms should be dosed: if under six weeks of age, only with the advice of the Vet. Over six weeks, use a reliable vermifuge, follow the directions carefully, and repeat after a week or ten days. Adult Chihuahuas occasionally suffer from round or tape worms, but as so many toy dogs are kept under more hygienic conditions than many larger breeds in kennels, they may never be affected. Most worm medicines have dosage graded according to the weight of the dog. Never guess at this; use the scales.

ADDENDUM

In the last few years some intensive research has been undertaken by Mrs Eileen Goodchild, a Chihuahua breeder whose kennel prefix is 'Talaloc'. She has come up with a mass of revealing information which throws a new slant on the whole puzzling mystery.

Mrs Goodchild believes that the vital clue comes from Malta. Known as Maltese Pocket Dogs, a tiny Chihuahua-type breed has been bred on the island for centuries. Many have the molera, and mention is made in the *Holinshed Chronicles* of Tudor times, in which the writer said 'the smaller they are, the better they are liked, especially if they have a hole in the foreparts of their heads', referring to them as Maltese Pocket Dogs.

Authorities working at the British Museum say that the little dogs were taken to Malta from North Africa by Carthaginians around 700 B.C. By Roman times, Strabo was writing in 55 B.C. about 'Malta, whence come the little dogs . . .'. A contemporary potter depicted two tiny dogs with huge, erect ears and round skulls. From time to time over the centuries individual specimens were imported into England and it seems almost certain that it was one of these that is shown in Edward Landseer's painting *Diogenes*. Where the Carthaginians settled they left little smooth-coated, prick-eared toy dogs, and these can be found on Gibraltar, in the Balearic Islands and in Portugal where they are known as Toy Podencos. They could have been taken to the latter country from North Africa or from Malta. After all, some of the Portuguese fishermen speak Maltese! Dogs very like long-coated Chihuahuas seem to have started on a small island off the coast of Dubrovnik, in the Adriatic, depicted on vases dated the third century B.C.

By A.D. 1600 there were dogs of this type to be found in Spain, France, the Netherlands, and Germany.

The Papillon breed began to emerge in Belgium and a small spitz-type dog, some of which were almost certainly taken to Mexico by the Spaniards, which may explain why the famous

Caranza, one of the first imports from Mexico to the U.S.A.,
was a long-coat.

I am exceedingly grateful to Mrs Goodchild for allowing
me to use this precis of her fascinating manuscript, and would
like to record the thanks of all lovers of the Chihuahua who will
realise only too well the time she has spent on this exhaustive
investigation.

APPENDIX A

The Kennel Club Breed registration figures from 1953, the year when Chihuahuas were granted separate register and were removed from the section 'Any Other Variety'.

	Smooth-Coat	Long-Coat
1953	111	—
1954	145	—
1955	242	—
1956	369	—
1957	530	—
1958	768	—
1959	1022	—
1960	1586	—
1961	1978	—
1962	2513	—
1963	2810	—
1964	2691	569
1965	2701	720
1966	2595	790
1967	2436	1043
1968	2502	1223
1969	2714	1435
1970	2701	1514
1971	2330	1801
1972	2494	2017
1973	2279	1938
1974	2225	2008
1975	1724	1954

The Kennel Club changed its registration system in 1976, thus preventing the continuation of the above method of listing annual registration figures.

APPENDIX B

British Chihuahua Club.
Chihuahua Club of Scotland.
Chihuahua Club of South Wales.
The Long-coat Chihuahua Club.
Midland Chihuahua Club.
Scottish and Northern Counties Chihuahua Club.
Smooth-coat Chihuahua Club.
Ulster Chihuahua Club.
West Country Chihuahua Club.

As the names and addresses of breed club secretaries change frequently they have not been included here. Any reader wishing to contact a club is advised to write to the Kennel Club, 1–4 Clarges Street, London, W1Y 8AB, who will supply these details.

APPENDIX C

APPENDIX C

BRITISH CHAMPIONS

From March 6, 1954, when Challenge Certificates were first offered for Chihuahua's until December 31, 1977.

SMOOTH-COATS

Name	Sex	Date of Birth	Colour	Sire	Dam	Breeder	Owner
Ch. Rozavel Diaz	D	17.3.53	Red	Salender's Darro Pharche	Rozavel La Oro Sena de Ora	Mrs T. Gray	Breeder
Ch. Bowerhinton Isabela	B	6.9.52	Reddish-brown and white	Denger's Don Carlos	Denger's Doña Maria	Mrs Horner	Mrs M. Fearfield
Ch. Brownridge Jofos Paloma	B	22.3.53	Cream	Bowerhinton Chico of Belamie	Jofos Millinita	Mrs J. Forster	Mrs J. Rawson
Ch. Denger's Don Armando	D	17.2.53	Black and tan	Pepito IX	Denger's Doña Carmencita	Mrs G. Horner	Mrs D. Wells
Am. Ch. and Ch. Kelsbro Dugger's Spice	B	19.12.53	Chocolate and tan	Dugger's Colonel Meron	Sweet Celinda Sue	Mrs C. Dugger	Mrs K. Stuart
Ch. Maria Carmello of Wytchend	B	17.1.55	Golden red	Ch. Rozavel Diaz	Mixcoac	Mrs A. Ellis-Hughes	Mrs F. C. Raine
Ch. Rozavel Gringo	D	19.5.54	Cream	Ch. Rozavel Diaz	Rozavel La Oro Memoria de Ora	Mrs T. Gray	Mrs M. Rider
Ch. Adella of Bendorwyn	B	8.2.54	Pale fawn	Belamie Zequi	Jofos Lucia of Bendorwyn	Mrs D. W. Benvie	Breeder
Ch. Cisco Kid of Winterlea	D	17.11.54	Red and white	Scott's Si Si Boy	Bigo's Zoranna of Winterlea	Mrs M. Mooney	Breeder
Ch. Jose Alfarez of Wytchend	D	17.1.53	Red	Ch. Rozavel Diaz	Mixcoac	Mrs A. Ellis-Hughes	Mr A. A. Martin

				Salender's Darro Pharche	Rozavel Irra Pettina	Mrs T. Gray	Breeder
Ch. Rozavel Francisco	D	4.10.54	Gold				
I.K.C. Ch. and Ch. Seggieden Jupiter	D	16.3.54	White	Am. Ch. Allen's Snowball	Pearson's Angela La Ora	Lady M. Drummond-Hay	Breeder
Ch. Rozavel Mantilla	B	19.5.54	Fawn and white	Ch. Rozavel Diaz	Rozavel La Oro Memoria de Ora	Mrs T. Gray	Breeder
Ch. Rozavel Shaw's Violet	B	11.12.53	Blue, white, and tan	Kibbe's Little Cinco	Little Darling	Mrs M. Shaw	Mrs T. Gray
Ch. Bowerhinton Ollala	B	13.6.56	Cream	Ch. Rozavel Francisco	Bowerhinton Carmencita	Mrs M. Fearfield	Breeder
Ch. Don Silver of Wytchend	D	19.4.56	Red fawn	Dalhabboch Grosart's Corky	Donna Rita of Bendorwyn	Mrs A. Ellis-Hughes	Mr T. Hutchinson and Mr D. Cady
Ch. Rowley Emrill Lolita	B	17.5.57	Red	Emrill Son-Ko's Red Rocket	Jofos Driada	Mrs M. Huxham	Mrs Rider
Ch. Dalhabboch Rio Tinto King	D	6.3.56	Cream	Seko King of Dalhabboch	Veronica-Vi Dalhabboch	Miss D. Russell-Allen	Breeder
Ch. Rozavel Uvalda Jemima	B	25.1.58	Tricolour	Ch. Rozavel Humo	Uvalda Jofos Moomin	Mrs M. Payne	Mrs T. Gray
I.K.C. Ch. and Ch. Seggieden Tiny Mite	D	18.4.57	Cream	I.K.C. Ch. and Ch. Seggieden Jupiter	Faye of Bendorwyn	Lady M. Drummond-Hay	Breeder
Ch. Brownridge Native Gold	D	21.3.58	Black and tan	Brandman's Modelo's Memory	Ch. Brownridge Jofos Paloma	Mrs J. Rawson	Mrs Twining
Ch. Rozavel Bienvenida	B	31.10.58	Fawn	Ch. Rozavel Diaz	Ch. Rozavel Platina	Mrs T. Gray	Breeder
Ch. Kaitonia's Meronella Venderesse	B	13.10.56	Brown	Emrill Son-Ko's Red Rocket	Nellistar Arrieta	Mrs H. Morgan	Mrs K. Stuart

Name	Sex	Date of Birth	Colour	Sire	Dam	Breeder	Owner
Ch. Rozavel Humo	D	16.8.56	Blue fawn	Ch. Rozavel Francisco	Rozavel Shaw's Constance	Mrs T. Gray	Breeder
Ch. Rozavel Platina	B	15.10.57	Fawn and white—	Ch. Rozavel Humo	Rozavel Jofos Onlyone	Mrs T. Gray	Breeder
Ch. Kaitonia's Lulubelle	B	2.8.58	Blue and tan	Kaitonia's El Pedro	Kaitonia's Twinkletoes	Mrs Gowing	Mrs K. Stuart
Ch. Ellicia of Bendorwyn	B	23.5.55	Black and white	Primo of Belamie	Jofos Lucia of Bendorwyn	Mrs D. W. Benvie	Breeder
Ch. Pedro of Yevot	D	7.5.58	Fawn	Emrill Buck's Peppie	Jofos Christina	Miss M. Tovy	Breeder
Ch. Chitina Majestic Sprite	D	19.9.59	Black and tan	Mabelle Pepito	Mabelle Conchita	Mrs Turner	Mrs Garlick
Ch. Winterlea Snow Queen	B	2.9.58	White	I.K.C. Ch. and Ch. Seggieden Jupiter	Bigos Zorranna of Winterlea	Mrs M. Mooney	Breeder
Ch. Seggieden Little Heracles	D	28.2.59	Red	Ch. Cisco Kid of Winterlea	Seggieden Cassiopaea	Lady M. Drummond-Hay	Mrs M. Mooney
Ch. Rowley Silver Cloud	D	5.2.60	Cream, gold markings	Seggieden Zeus	Ch. Rowley Emrill Lolita	Mrs M. Rider	Breeder
Ch. Jofos Victoria of Sillwood	B	19.4.59	Fawn and white	Montezuma Travato of Wytchend	Evana Perdita	Mrs J. Forster	Mrs R. Wakefield
Ch. Simchalas Bartholomew	D	23.9.59	Fawn and black	Simchalas Gay Kim	Simchalas Evana Orchide	Mrs L. A. Busson	Breeder
Ch. Lippens Koko of Yevot	B	20.6.60	Chocolate and tan	Ch. Pedro of Yovet	Lippens Hsiago Solano	Mrs P. Blake	Miss M. Tovey

Ch. Heathtop Titania	B	31.1.60	Cream	Ch. Pedro of Yevot	Pentrebach Perky Pet	Mrs M. Edwards	Breeder
Ch. Rozavel Aguardiente	D	30.7.63	Red, white trimmings	S.A. Ch. Rozavel Mexican Idol	Ch. Rozavel Trace of Silver	Mrs T. Gray	Breeder
Ch. Dalhabboch Sweet Honesty	B	1.10.60	Pale fawn	Luce's Little King Blue of Dalhabboch	Ch. Dalhabboch Sweet Primrose	Miss M. D. Russell-Allen	Breeder
Ch. Rozavel Amorosa	B	18.7.60	Golden red	Ch. Rozavel Humo	Rozavel Karlena's Bambi	Mrs T. Gray	Mrs G. Kesper
Ch. Eugenie of Yevot	B	7.8.63	Chocolate	Gaviola of Yevot	Cosita	Mrs S. Blissett	Miss M. Tovey
Ch. Jofos Jim Dandy	D	5.5.62	Black and tan	Jofos Pim	Jofos Robeena	Mrs M. Watts	Mrs J. Forster
Ch. Rozavel Chief Scout	D	30.3.64	Blue fawn	Ch. Rozavel Wolf Cub	Rozavel Star Sapphire	Mrs T. Gray	Breeder
Ch. Kaitonia's Don Armando	D	16.9.63	Silver sand	Ch. Kaitonia's Little Jo	Kaitonia's Rosabelle	Mrs K. Stuart	Breeder
Ch. Jolengra Dandini	D	3.10.63	Black, tan and white	Greveny Herodero	Jolengra Alhaja	Mr J. Shipley	Breeder
Ch. Valdama Honeysuckle	B	10.5.62	Fawn and white	Valdama's Figaro	Valdama Snowdrop	Mrs V. F. J. Ashton	Breeder
Ch. Weycome Antonio	D	20.12.60	Fawn and white	Lippens Cracker Bang	Lippens Treacle	Mr G. R. Down	Breeder
Ch. Rozavel Hasta la Vista	B	12.5.61	Red, white trim	Rozavel Big Bad Wolf	Rozavel Huasteca	Mrs T. Gray	Breeder
Ch. Nita of Glenjoy	B	1.10.59	Brown brindle	Dalhabboch Yonder He Goes	Pepita of Glenjoy	Mr J. F. Turner and Miss P. D. Massey	Breeders

Name	Sex	Date of Birth	Colour	Sire	Dam	Breeder	Owner
Ch. Kaitonia's Wee Jo Jo Zuma	D	19.9.60	Golden, black mask	Kaitonia's Don Perro	Kaitonia's Little Gem	Mrs K. Stuart	Breeder
Ch. Evana Peppermint of Edgebourne	B	6.7.61	Black, tan and white	Jofos Pim	Jofos Tarahumara	Mrs B. W. Evans	Lt.-Com and Mrs Egerton-Williams
Ch. Rozavel Trace of Silver	B	27.1.62	White, red markings	St. Erme Sorreldene Brandts Brandy	Ch. Rozavel Platina	Mrs T. Gray	Breeder
Ch. Kaitonia's Little Jo	D	26.3.62	Cream	Ch. Kaitonia's Wee Jo Jo Zuma	Kaitonia's Dona Anita	Mrs K. Stuart	Breeder
Ch. Snowdrop of Glenjoy	B	9.12.62	Fawn	Hacienda Gomez of Glenjoy	Talaloc Tasmina	Mrs V. Jones	Mr J. F. Turner and Miss P. D. Massey
Ch. Rozavel Youngelve Pixie Poo	B	25.10.60	Pure White	Rozavel El Padre	Youngelve Petinkie	Mrs E. Young	Mrs T. Gray
Ch. Kaitonia's Tony Jo	D	22.3.61	Golden Fawn	Kaitonia's Rano Kaoki	Ch. Kaitonia's Meronella Venderesse	Mrs K. Stuart	Breeder
Ch. Rozavel Large as Life	D	30.4.61	Blue Fawn	Rozavel Big Bad Wolf	Ch. Rozavel Bienvenida	Mrs T. Gray	Breeder
Irish Ch. and Ch. Seggieden Mighty Dime	D	4.8.61	White and Cream	Ch. Seggieden Tiny Mite	Seggieden Brynkerth Gretchen	Lady M. Drummond-Hay	Breeder
Ch. Rowley Josephine	B	23.4.64	Pale Fawn	Ch. Rowley Perito of Sektuny	Rowley Ruby of Daleavon	Mr A. W. Green	Mrs M. Rider

Name	Sex	Date	Colour	Sire	Dam	Owner	Breeder
Ch. Kaitonia's Golden Girl	B	9.8.60	Golden	Ch. Seggieden Tiny Mite	Fulani Paberlina	Mrs K. Stuart	Breeder
Ch. Kaitonia's King Bee	D	7.10.64	Fawn	Ch. Kaitonia's Little Jo	Kaitonia's Sabina	Mrs K. Stuart	Breeder
Ch. Rowley Ruby of Daleavon	B	14.7.61	Fawn	Jofos Pim	Evana Sari	Mrs Anderson	Mrs M. Rider
Ch. Rozavel Blue Flagship	D	11.1.65	Blue	Rozavel Blue Flag	Rozora Santa Monica	Mrs H. Pitt	Mrs T. Gray
Ch. Candifloss of Wytchend	B	19.7.65	Fawn and white	Hsaigo My Boy Lollipop	Julieta of Wytchend	Mrs A. Ellis-Hughes	Breeder
Ch. Rowley Copyrite	D	12.6.65	Cream	Ch. Rowley Perito of Sektuny	Ch. Rowley Ruby of Daleavon	Mrs M. Rider	Breeder
Ch. Rowley Clarissa	B	12.6.65	Cream	Ch. Rowley Perito of Sektuny	Ch. Rowley Ruby of Daleavon	Mrs M. Rider	Breeder
Ch. Rozavel Cadbury	D	1.3.66	Chocolate and tan	Rozavel Trader Vic	Rozavel Aliciente	Mrs T. Gray	Breeder
Ch. Winterlea Twinkle of Mingulay	B	22.12.65	Gold and white	Winterlea Rozavel Blue Flash	Dusk of Mingulay	Mrs H. Stevenson	Mrs M. Mooney
Ch. Kaitonia's Dona Veleta	B	14.8.62	Fawn Sable	Ch. Kaitonia's Wee Jo-Jo Zuma	Kaitonia's Minitura	Mrs K. Stuart	Breeder
Ch. Lilycroft Trotter	D	30.9.62	Red and white	Lilycroft Tiny Tim	Alonquin Trigoletta	Mrs J. Gagen	Breeder
Ch. Lilycroft Son of Fortune	D	29.11.64	Red	Lilycroft Good Fortune	Alonquin Camella	Mrs J. Gagen	Breeder
Ch. Sternroc Babycham	B	28.11.64	Cream	Ch. Seggieden Mighty Dime	Sternroc Seggieden Pimpernel	Mrs P. Cross-Stern	Breeder

Name	Sex	Date of Birth	Colour	Sire	Dam	Breeder	Owner
Ch. Dalhabboch Alfy	D	8.11.65	Black and tan	Donamarie's My Friend Flicka	Andrea of Buddletown	Miss M. Russell-Allen	Breeder
Ch. Strondour Valdama Sweet Memory	B	15.4.65	White	Valdama Figaro	Valdama Snowdrop	Mrs V. J. Ashton	Mrs. W. Walker
Ch. Josalisa Anstorie Silver Star	D	22.9.63	Cream	Anstorie Hsaigo Magnus	Anstorie Fortinmark White Angel	Mrs A. Martin	Mr J. Lockey
Ch. Rozavel Chief Scout	D	30.3.64	Blue fawn	Ch. Rozavel Wolf Cub	Rozavel Star Sapphire	Mrs T. Gray	Breeder
Ch. Kaitonia's King Bee	D	7.10.64	Fawn	Ch. Kaitonia's Little Jo	Kaitonia's Sabina	Miss K. Stuart	Breeder
Ch. Candifloss of Wytchend	B	19.7.65	Gold and white	Hsaigo My Boy Lollipop	Julieta of Wytchend	Mrs A. Ellis-Hughes	Breeder
Ch. Lilycroft Son of Fortune	D	28.11.64	Red	Lilycroft Good Fortune	Algonquin Carmella	Mrs J. Gagen	Breeder
Ch. Lilycroft Trotter	D	30.9.62	Red	Lilycroft Tiny Tim	Algonquin Nicoletta	Mrs J. Gagen	Breeder
Ch. Rowley Copyrite	D	12.6.65	Cream	Ch. Rowley Perito of Sektuny	Rowley Ruby of Daleavon	Mrs M. Rider	Breeder
Ch. Rozavel Blue Flagship	D	11.1.65	Blue	Rozavel Blue Flag	Rozora Santamonica	Mrs H. Pitt	Mrs T. Gray
Ch. Cluneen Red Velvet	B	16.3.65	Red	Talaloc Tambo	Mount Albion Twinkletoes	Mrs E. M. Banks	Breeder
Ch. Hayclose Howpretty	B	7.7.66	Red and white	Hayclose Huskie	Brettleon Chikeeta	Mrs M. A. B. Davies	Mr J. Stott

Name	Sex	Date	Colour	Sire	Dam	Breeder	Owner
Ch. Jofos Kitty's Little Joe	D	15.12.66	Red, fawn and white	Am. Ch. Culberson's Muggins II	Payne Daisy Mae	Mrs K. Culberson	Mrs. J. Forster
Ch. Larkwhistle Vanilla	B	5.3.66	Cream	Ch. Rowley Perito of Sektuny	Rozavel Perinola	Miss E. J. Boyt	Owner
Ch. Lilycroft Ballyduff Timothy	D	18.6.65	Black and tan	Ch. Emmrill Fudge	Lilycroft Kattrine	Mrs B. Docking	Mrs J. Steinmetz
Ch. Lilycroft Penny Lane	B	1.10.66	Red	Lilycroft Honey Boy	Lilycroft Sheena	Mrs J. Gagen	Breeder
Ch. Rowley Lansdahlia Candytuft	B	.3.66	Cream	Ch. Rowley Perito of Sektuny	Lansdahlia Sallyann	Mrs S. Lansdale	Mrs M. Rider
Ch. Rozavel Peterkin	D	7.7.66	Blue fawn	Rozavel Blue Flag	Rozora Marie Elena	Mrs H. Pitt	Miss M. Braun
Ch. St Erme Pussycat	B	23.12.65	Red and white	Rozavel Prarie-Wolf	Tejuana Tillylilly	Mrs N. K. Hallam	Mrs St Erme Cardew
Ch. Winterlea Blue Blue Tu	B	25.6.65	Dark blue fawn	Winterlea Rozavel Blue Flash	Winterlea Orozco Texas Rose	Mrs M. Mooney	Mrs M. Moorhouse
Ch. Truxillo Miss Cadbury	B	7.7.67	Chocolate and tan	Ch. Rozavel Chief Scout	Truxillo Sovereign	Mr and Mrs G. Motherwell	Breeders
Ch. Rozavel Brass Button	B	23.5.68	Red	Pedmore Pearl Button	Rozavel Abinkie	Mrs T. Gray	Breeder
Ch. Salsam Don Carlos	D	26.4.66	Fawn	Kemple's Little Strutter	Kemple's Perrilla	Mr and Mrs S. Carlyon	Breeders
Ch. Rowley Uvalda Winston	D	17.7.66	Black and cream	Ch. Rowley Perito of Sektuny	Uvalda Lady	Mrs F. M. Payne	Mrs M. Rider

Name	Sex	Date of Birth	Colour	Sire	Dam	Breeder	Owner
Ch. Rowley Prime Minister	D	4.1.68	Fawn	Rowley Uvalda Winston	Rowley Fairytail	Mrs M. Rider	Breeder
Ch. Queenselms Celia	B	30.3.67	Cream	Seggieden Pooka	Queenselms Titania	Miss D. Gaffikin	Breeder
Ch. Kittalah Connie's Starr	B	13.12.65	Gold and white	Greveny Herodero	Kittalah Baralicia Dusty	Mrs G. Hayes	Breeder
Ch. Stoberry Delcarchi Melinda	B	2.11.66	Blue fawn	Ch. Rozavel Chief Scout	Delcarchi Golden Oriole	Mr J. Parker	Mrs V. Roberts
Ch. Rozavel Silvershadow	B	29.4.68	Blue fawn	Ch. Rozavel Large as Life	Rozavel Skylark	Miss E. J. Boyt	Mrs T. Gray
Ch. Rozavel Pewter Model	D	7.1.68	Blue and tan	Ch. Rozavel Chief Scout	Rozavel Perinola	Miss E. J. Boyt	Mrs T. Gray
Ch. Rosaree Crusader of Brynkerth	D	18.4.66	Black and tan	Brynkerth Leonardo Lampazos	Brynkerth Glow	Mrs E. Lloyd	Mrs E. H. Banks
Ch. Oljon Bineite Honey Boy	D	29.12.66	Gold	Pedmore Saturday Night	Montezumas Bonnie April	Miss M. Betts	Mrs O. L. Harris
Ch. Maidenslea Nephthys	B	21.1.66	Red	Maidenslea Revaldo of Yevot	Maidenslea Mary Poppins	Mrs J. Rees	Mrs J. Meldrum
Ch. Edgebourne Cock a Hoop	D	30.6.68	Fawn and white	Edgebourne Escudo	Seggieden Wee Lizzie	Mrs V. Preece	Lt Commander and Mrs Egerton-Williams
Ch. Johara Jezebel-Me-Tu	B	20.12.65	Fawn	Johara Samson	Johara Romeo's Juliet	Mrs V. Riley	Breeder

Name	Sex	Date	Colour	Sire	Dam	Owner	Breeder
Ch. Ardick Mystic Ash	D	9.5.67	Light sable	Ardick Witch Doctor	Ardick Zsa Zsa of Genjoy	Mr R. Dick	Breeder
Ch. Maidenslea Antonio	D	5.11.67	Light red	Ch. Rozavel Chief Scout	Valdama Tallulah	Mrs D. Hughes	Mrs J. Rees
Ch. Kingsmere Merry Mascot	D	21.11.68	Red	Ch. Rozavel Chief Scout	Kingsmere Geogiana of Dum Dum	Mrs J. Kings	Breeder
Ch. Maerlake Tansy	B	1.1.69	Blue fawn	Maerlake Red Pepper	Maerlake Misty Violet	Mrs C. Robinson	Breeder
Ch. Totland Hamilton of Hamaja	D	25.10.67	Cream	Carlo of Dapplemere	Totland Topaz	Mrs M. Greening	Miss P. Wood and Mrs M. Greening
Ch. Myavon Penny Blue	B	14.9.68	Blue fawn	Ch. Rowley Uvalda Winston	Rowley Miss Muffet	Mrs M. Motherwell	Mrs C. J. Kennard
Ch. Lilycroft Trotabout	D	3.4.69	Red	Ch. Lilycroft Trotter	Ch. Lilycroft Penny Lane	Mrs J. Gagen	Breeder
Ch. Hobart Boulton de Boutique	D	15.2.65	Cream	Seggieden Mighty Guinea	Seggieden Winkle	Mrs M. Hall	Breeder
Ch. Molimor Anyako Astronaut	D	22.9.69	Red	Ch. Rozavel Chief Scout	Ortega Prima Dona	Mrs H. Mitchell	Mrs M. Moorhouse
Ch. Molimor Talent Scout	D	15.1.68	Blue fawn	Ch. Rozavel Chief Scout	Rozavel Marbellup Carabella	Mrs T. Gray	Mrs M. Moorhouse
Ch. Rowley Sweetie Pie	B	17.6.69	Red	Ch. Rozavel Chief Scout	Ch. Rowley Josephine	Mrs M. Rider	Breeder
Ch. Truxillo Rowley Algernon	D	8.5.68	Black and cream	Ch. Rowley Uvalda Winston	Ch. Rowley Ruby of Daleavon	Mrs M. Rider	Mr and Mrs G. Motherwell

Name	Sex	Date of Birth	Colour	Sire	Dam	Breeder	Owner
Ch. Clanden Mulgawood Peppercorn	B	15.1.70	Black and tan	Wingreen Poppets Delight	Mulgawood Mixed Spice	Mrs J. Watson	Mr and Mrs D. F. Goodwin
Ch. Lanelea Mexican Cream	B	1.4.70	Cream	Lanelea Rockafella	Totland Tadorna	Mr R. A. Pearson	Breeder
Ch. Apoco Ballybroke Billy Bunter	D	1.7.70	Light sable	Ardick Witch Doctor	Ballybroke Sowatt Foxtrot	Mr and Mrs Foote	Mr W. F. Stevenson
Ch. Mulgawood Lady Fern	B	6.10.70	Gold and white	Ch. Jofos Kitty's Little Joe	Wynworth Mulgawood Lady Tirzah	Mrs J. N. Watson	Breeder
Ch. Rowley Coronet	B	16.11.69	Red	Ch. Rowley Courtier	Ch. Rowley Kismet	Mrs M. Rider	Breeder
Ch. Nixtrix Whizzby	D	17.12.70	Red and white	Ch. Kingsmere Merry Mascot	Nixtrix Gee Whizz	Mrs E. F. McNicholl	Breeder
Ch. Molimor Zillah	B	22.8.70	Red	Ch. Molimor Rozavel Talent Scout	Molimor Zenita of Glenjoy	Mrs M. Moorhouse	Breeder
Ch. Salsam Contessa	B	28.11.68	Cream	Kemple's Little Strutter	Kemple's Perrilla	Mr and Mrs S. Carlyon	Mrs S. M. A. Lawson
Ch. Knockenjig Little Lulu	B	27.2.69	Red	Strondour Durability	Knockenjig Berinshill Amber	Mrs I. R. Peters	Breeder
Ch. Larkwhistle Macaroon	D	20.12.70	Cream	Pedmore Pearl Button	Rozavel Perinola	Miss E. J. Boyt	Mrs J. Bruton
Ch. Goldsborough King Midas	D	3.2.71	Red	Ch. Kingsmere Merry Mascot	Clewcarn Violetta Mia	Mr J. Leonards	Mrs E. I. Foster
Ch. Maidenslea Aristo	D	18.12.70	Fawn	Ch. Maidenslea Antonito	Maidenslea Khmut	Mrs J. Rees	Mr M. Oliver

Name	Sex	Date	Colour	Sire	Dam	Owner	Breeder
Ch. Oljon Carbon Copy	D	13.3.71	Black and tan	Truxillo Copy Prince	Pedmore Night Ride	Mrs N. V. Shaw	Mrs O. Harris
Ch. Mikoli Starlight	B	15.6.72	Fawn	Ch. Maidenslea Aristo	Adoram Iona	Mr M. Oliver	Breeder
Ch. Goldsborough Tiny White Lady	B	10.7.70	White	Int. Ch. Seggieden Mighty Dime	Clewcarn Violetta Mia	Mr J. Leonards	Mrs E. I. Foster
Ch. Carlinders News Boy	D	10.8.70	Sable	Maidenslea Revaldo of Yevot	Adoram Iona	Mr L. A. Oliver	Mr M. Oliver
Ch. Fairydown Border Chief	D	21.4.71	Blue and fawn	Ch. Rozavel Chief Scout	Mulgawood Moon Gold	Mrs G. Waanders	Mrs J. C. Forster
Ch. Innesville Golden Wonder of Apoco	D	5.12.72	Pale gold	Ch. Apoco Ballybroke Billy Bunter	Innesville Tiny Tina	Mrs M. Innes	W. F. Stevenson
Ch. Molimor Bronzel	D	3.4.71	Gold, brown and white	Molimor Jofos Memphis	Molimor Floraspa Bronzetta	Mrs M. Moorhouse	Breeder
Ch. Molimor Grageo Talstar	D	1.1.73	Blue and fawn	Ch. Molimor Rozavel Talent Scout	Grageo Sallyann	Mrs G. Thompson	Mrs M. Moorhouse
Ch. Molimor Melvino	D	9.11.71	Fawn	Ch. Molimor Anyako Astronaut	Leyju Molimor Zerbinetta	Mrs S. Lee	Mrs M. Moorhouse
Ch. Rumawill Sun Dancer	D	9.12.71	Gold with white trim	Ch. Oljon Bineite Money Boy	Oljon Ballerina	Miss R. Dinham	Breeder

Name	Sex	Date of Birth	Colour	Sire	Dam	Breeder	Owner
Ch. Leyju Amor Miranda	B	20.12.72	Cream	Ch. Molimor Anyako Astronaut	Leyju Molimor Zerbinetta	Mrs S. E. Lee	Breeder
Ch. Mereliz Donna Rosetta	B	13.5.72	Fawn	Ch. Rozavel Chief Scout	Roseridge Tiny Opal	Mrs E. Reeve	Breeder
Ch. Molimor Kettleden Angeline	B	14.7.73	Fawn and black mask	Ch. Apoco Ballybroke Billy Bunter	Strongdour Rachel	Mrs M. Y. Reid	Mrs M. Moorhouse
Ch. Molimor Talentina	B	28.12.72	Blue and fawn	Ch. Molimor Rozavel Talent Scout	Molimor Grageo Salome	Mrs M. Moorhouse	Breeder
Ch. Playhill Chipkin	B	13.12.71	Red, gold and dark mask	Barbrinden Copykin	Playhill Chippy's Colleen	Mrs S. M. Crossle	Breeder
Ch. Totland Tia Francesca	B	16.8.69	Red, sable and white	Totland Fox Cub Zapangu	Totland Tebsin Cokernut Ice	Miss P. E. Wood	Breeder
Ch. Ballybroke Jasper of Fernq	D	4.9.71	White and fawn	Ch. Apoco Ballybroke Billy Bunter	Ballybroke Knockenjig Bunty	Mrs J. and Mr G. B. Foote	Breeder
Ch. Maerlake Mastermind	D	11.12.73	Red, black mask	Karajon's Dandini	Maerlake Mignonette	Mrs Robinson	Breeder
Ch. Marchez Saucy Sam	D	2.11.73	Red, black mask	Maer Lake Prancer	Saucy Susie of Sanchez	Mrs M. Y. Williams	Breeder

Name	Sex	Date	Colour	Sire	Dam	Owner	Breeder
Ch. Royal Rocket of Winterlea	D	28.11.73	Red and white	Ch. Winterlea Star Shine	Stillponds September	Mrs P. Buffaline	Mrs M. Mooney
Ch. Anaquito of Veucia	D	13.9.75	Blue and fawn	Dalelang Teekbec Blue Banbee	Dalelang Teekbec Blue Banbee	Mrs D. E. Davey	Mrs V. Robson
Ch. Oaxaca Dandy Brown	D	24.6.75	Tricolour	Ch. Apoco Ballybrook Billy Bunter	Ch. Verande's Silver Lining	Mr and Mrs J. J. Brincat-Smith	Breeder
Ch. Rozavel Scouts Uniform	D	1.4.73	Blue and Fawn	Ch. Rozavel Chief Scout	Rozavel Chocolate Truffles	Mrs T. Gray	Breeder
Ch. Unalie Icarus	D	23.9.74	Red	Ch. Rozavel Chief Scout	Unalie Brecha	Mr and Mrs C. W. Parkin and Sons	Breeder
Ch. Verande's Angelo	D	28.3.75	Cream	Ch. Molimor Melvino	Janmall Pretty Peach	Mrs V. M. Parker	Breeder
Ch. Winterlea Blonde Viking	D	30.3.74	Cream	Molimor Astroman	Winterlea Zoranna	Mrs M. Mooney	Mrs T. Lapeous
Ch. Belmuriz Bodicia	B	24.5.74	Red and White	Clanden Caranza	Bellegarde Bambelle	Mrs E. C. Murray	Breeder
Ch. Golden Nina of Honeyditches	B	23.5.74	Gold, black mask	Karajon's Dandini	Maerlake Ebony	Mrs R. Sharp	Mrs E. MacDonald
Ch. Leyju Amor Giselle	B	9.11.71	Blue and Fawn	Ch. Molimor Anyako Astronaut	Leyju Molimor Zerbinetta	Mrs S. Lee	Breeder
Ch. Pretty Jenny of Winterlea	B	28.11.73	Red and White	Ch. Winterlea Star Shine	Stillponds September	Mrs D. Buffaline	Mrs M. Mooney

Name	Sex	Date of Birth	Colour	Sire	Dam	Breeder	Owner
Ch. Yaverland Fribby of Innesville	B	17.12.72	Red	Yaverland Mousehound	Yaverland Mitkin	Mrs E. Bateman	Mrs M. Innes
Ch. Cliffelyn Christmas Hymn of Prindor	D	1.8.73	Light fawn	Simchalas Christmas Gift	Cliffelyn Wandering Star	Miss G. D. Ratcliffe and Mrs C. L. McCarthy	Mrs Berman
Ch. Constanthope Vital Spark of Fernq	D	12.5.75	White	Fernq Lord Jim	Fernq Coral	Mrs B. Wapier	Mrs M. Davidson
Ch. Nixtrix Whizzkidd	D	24.10.75	Red	Ch. Nixtrix Whizzby	Goldsborough Lady of Meurville	Mrs E. M. Nicholl	Breeder
Ch. Molimor Astrodelia	B	8.12.75	Red, black mask	Ch. Anyako Astronaut	Chipperlake Timara	Mrs D. Timberlake	Mrs M. Moorhouse
Ch. Verande's Silver Lining	B	4.7.73	Black and tan	Yaverland Mousehound	Antonia Vee	Mrs V. M. Parker	Mr and Mrs J. J. Brincat-Smith
Ch. Affalon Hi Gizeh	D	21.7.76	Cream	Affalon Hi Simon	Affalon Gaea Woo Wee	Mrs A. Baker and Mrs R. Hogg	Breeder

LONG-COATS

Name	Sex	Date of Birth	Colour	Sire	Dam	Breeder	Owner
Ch. Cholderton Little Scampy of Teeny Wee	D	24.2.57	White and fawn	Meron of Teeny Wee	Lacher's White Fluff	Mrs K. Lacher	Mrs M. Bedford

Ch. Nellistar Schaefer's Taffy Boy	D	23-3-54	Red,fawn, and white	Am. Ch. Schaefer's Captain Boy Blue II	Lindsay's Little Sister	Mrs D. Lindsay Schaefer	Mrs C. M. Erskine
Ch. Rowley Perito of Sektuny	D	15.9.58	Deep cream	Ch. Rozavel Francisco	Pixie of Sektuny	Mrs E. D. Pearce	Mrs M. Rider
Ch. Rowley Umberto	D	19.6.59	Red	Ch. Rozavel Humo	Ch. Rowley Emrill Lolita	Mrs M. Rider	Breeder
Am. Ch. and Ch. Aztec Son-Ko's Ita Star-Dust	B	28.7.59	Honey	Carter's Little Koko Boy	Champagne Lady of Son-Ko	Mrs D. E. Baesel	Col. and Mrs V. d'Oyly Harmar
Ch. Rozavel Mermaid	B	2.5.63	Red sable	Ch. Rozavel Wolf Cub	Rozavel Marineria	Mrs T. Gray	Breeder
Ch. Lansdahlia Talaloc Twinkle	B	4.12.62	Red	Ch. Rowley Perito of Sektuny	Talaloc Taranga	Mrs E. Goodchild	Mrs A. P. Lansdale
Ch. Rozavel Alfonso Zapangu	D	1.8.64	Sable	Ch. Rozavel Wolf Cub	Geanau Babe-Bell	Mr B. Mitchell	Mrs T. Gray
Ch. Duniver Angel's Ace	D	21.3.61	Cream	Carlitos of Yevot	Duniver Angelita of Glenjoy	Mrs M. C. R. Burt	Breeder
Ch. Emrill Fudge	D	12.12.61	Dark red and fawn	Ch. Rowley Umberto	Emrill Candy	Mrs M. Huxham	Breeder
Ch. Pequeno Miney	B	11.11.61	Golden sable	Am. Ch. Bradshaw Pequeno Belleza	Pequeno Bradshaw's Tomasa	Mrs O. Frei-Denver	Breeder
Ch. Winterlea Lone Wolf	D	14.5.63	Red	Ch. Rozavel Wolf Cub	Winterlea Orozco Texas Rose	Mrs M. Mooney	Breeder
Ch. Rozavel Wolf Cub	D	30.4.61	Red sable	Rozavel Big Bad Wolf	Ch. Rozavel Bienvenida	Mrs T. Gray	Breeder

Name	Sex	Date of Birth	Colour	Sire	Dam	Breeder	Owner
Ch. Deodar Winterlea Wolf Whistle	D	12.7.64	Fawn	Ch. Winterlea Lone Wolf	Winterlea Carann Dona Gigi	Mrs M. Mooney	Mrs Borthwick
Ch. Rowley Courtier	D	3.3.63	Red	Ch. Rowley Perito of Sektuny	Rowley Zarah	Mrs M. Rider	Breeder
Ch. Rowley Kismet	B	14.10.63	Cream	Ch. Rowley Perito of Sektuny	Rowley Queen of the May	Mrs M. Rider	Breeder
Ch. Kaitonia's Canberra Bilabong	D	8.7.65	Red	Marbellup Mr Pepys	Rediviva Sylvia Minx	Mrs D. Colburn-Hart	Mrs K. Stuart
Ch. Chitina's Cuddles	B	2.3.64	Light red	Chitina's Dinky Gem	Chitina's Du-Bonet	Mrs D. S. Garlick	Breeder
Ch. Deodar Honey Dew	B	13.12.62	Red	Ch. Rowley Perito of Sektuny	Deodar Ginger Quill	Mrs S. Borthwick	Breeder
Ch. Winterlea Seckar Samantha	B	27.10.64	Sable	Ch. Winterlea Lone Wolf	Mickleton Mantilla	Mrs A. Teasdale	Mrs M. Mooney
Ch. Pequeno Maria	B	13.5.64	Black, fawn and cream	Ch. Rowley Perito of Sektuny	Ch. Pequeno Miney	Mrs O. Frei-Denver	Breeder
Ch. Pequeno Little Caesar	D	8.2.65	White	Serrano of Yevot	Montoya Roma	Mr and Mrs F. Griffiths	Mrs O. Frei-Denver
Ch. Ballybroke Ryanlea Wee Babycham	D	5.3.63	Red and white	Anstorie Sirius	Caranza of Drumwalt	Mrs A. Murray	Mr G. B. and Mrs J. Foote
Ch. Rozavel Fine Feathers	B	4.8.64	Blue and fawn	Ch. Rozavel Humo	Rozavel My Fur Lady	Mrs T. Gray	Breeder

Name	Sex	Date	Colour	Sire	Dam	Owner	Breeder
Ch. Hayclose Harrison	B	22.12.63	Light red	Ch. Duniver Angel's Ace	Parabar Rosaleta	Mr J. Stott	Breeder
Irish Ch. and Ch. Dorrow Small Fry	D	9.3.64	White	St Erme Samarium Robingochddu	Jokarlyns Charmaine	Mrs Steels	Mrs D. Hollows
Ch. Dekobras Danny Boy	D	27.8.65	Red	Dekobras Midnight Dan	Dekobras Caxbridge Deana	Mrs J. Steinmetz	Breeder
Ch. Venico Memento	D	30.11.65	Light red	Ch. Deodar Winterlea Wolf Whistle	Venico Deodar Pussy Willow	Mrs E. F. M. Nicoll	Breeder
Ch. Wingreen Aphrodite	B	19.11.64	White	Wingreen Poppet's Delight	Cream Cracker of Elsdyle	Mrs P. A. Jennings	Breeder
Ch. Taydors Gitana	B	1.5.66	Black and cream	Ch. Duniver Angel's Ace	Taydors Dorrow Trudy-Pru	Mr and Mrs W. Taylor	Breeders
Ch. Rozavel Astra	B	29.9.65	Blue and fawn	Ch. Rozavel Chief Scout	Rozavel Good as Gold	Mrs T. Gray	Breeder
Ch. Ranji's Carmenchita	B	16.4.66	Black and tan	Ch. Emmrill Fudge	Simchalas Maggie May	Mr E. Helm	Mrs M. V. Kempson
Ch. Montezuma Mr Chips	D	17.10.65	Apricot	Pancho of Dapplemore	Montezuma Rediviva Sunshine	Mrs A. G. Horton-Hall	Breeder
Ch. Emmrill Meringue of Aes	B	5.9.66	Light red	Ch. Emmrill Fudge	Xepherine of Aes	Mrs O. Harbottle	Mrs M. Huxham
Ch. Aztec Star Wolf Goddess	B	14.11.67	Red and white pied	Aztec Star Brave Wolf	Aztec Star Cocoa Goddess	Col. and Mrs V. D'Oyly Harmar	Breeders
Ch. Chitina's Nixtrix Prince Charming	D	16.6.67	Red	Chitina's Peregrine	Nixtrix Windmill Za Za Zoe	Mrs E. F. M. Nicoll	Mrs Garlick

Name	Sex	Date of Birth	Colour	Sire	Dam	Breeder	Owner
Ch. Kaitonia's Canberra Kavrakatta	B	8.7.65		Mickleton Marbellup Mr Pepys	Rediviva Sylvia Minx	Mrs D. Colburn Hart	Mrs K. Stuart
Ch. Kimanchi's Honey Bee	D	1.3.66	Light red	Ch. Rowley Umberto	Kimanchi's Golden Tansy	Misses E. Pantin and I. M. Friars	Breeders
Ch. Lilycroft Forever	D	1.10.66	Red	Lilycroft Honey Boy	Lilycroft Sheena	Mrs J. Gagen	Breeder
Ch. Nixtrix Puffa Puffa Bear	B	28.7.68	Gold	Chitina's Peregrine	Nixtrix Windmill Za Za Zoe	Mrs E. F. M. Nicholl	Breeder
Ch. Rozavel Tarina Song	B	3.6.67	Red sable	Ch. Rozavel Pirate Flag	Tarina Melody	Mr and Mrs Grevett	Breeders
Ch. Kingsmere Abraxas Michael Angelo	D	6.10.67	Light red	Rozavel Palomino	Abraxas Rozavel Gracia	Miss V. Drummond-Dick	Mrs King and Miss V. Drummond-Dick
Ch. Venico Widogi Mr Whippy	D	3.6.67	Cream	Ch. Montezuma Mr Chips	Crestview Good Companion	Mrs J. Fraser	Mrs E. I. Foster
Ch. Winterlea Roving Minstrel	D	8.11.66	Fawn sable	Ch. Winterlea Lone Wolf	Winterlea Carann Dona Gigi	Mrs M. Mooney	Breeder
Ch. Nixtrix Boo Boo Bear	D	28.7.68	Red	Chitina's Peregrine	Nixtrix Windmill Za Za Zoe	Mrs E. F. M. Nicholl	Breeder
Ch. Rozavel Pirate Flag	D	21.1.66	Black	Rozavel Blue Flag	Ch. Rozavel Platina	Mrs T. Gray	Breeder
Ch. Kimanchi's Golden Eagle	D	30.12.68	Red	Kimanchi's Crest-O-Wave	Kimanchi's Shot Taffeta	Misses E. Pantin and I. M. Friars	Breeders

Ch. Rowley Crown Jewel	B	22.11.68	Red	Ch. Rowley Courtier	Rowley Bridget	Mrs M. Rider	Breeder
Ch. Danchis Peach Blossom	B	18.9.67	Light red	Chitina's Peregrine	Kemples Bridget	Miss J. E. L. Hawkins	Breeder
Ch. Rowley Majic Circle	D	7.7.67	Cream	Ch. Rowley Umberto	Ch. Lansdahlia Talaloc Twinkle	Mrs S. Lansdale	Breeder
Ch. Rowley Petticoat Line	B	7.7.67	Cream	Ch. Rowley Umberto	Ch. Lansdahlia Talaloc Twinkle	Mrs S. Lansdale	Mrs M. Rider
Ch. Rozavel Tarina Do-Re-Mi	B	6.10.68	Red	Ch. Rozavel Chief Scout	Tarina Honeybun	Mr and Mrs Grevett	Mrs T. Gray
Ch. Taydors Galoping Major	D	25.5.67	Black and tan	Duniver Colonel Bogey	Taydors Arosa	Mr and Mrs W. G. Taylor	Breeders
Ch. Winterlea Knockenjig Royal Star	D	13.7.69	Gold	Cont. and Int. Ch. Winterlea Delcarchi Dolphin	Knockenjig Lindina Jaunty Judy	Mrs J. R. Peters	Mrs M. Mooney
Ch. Johara Peregrine	D	18.5.67	Pale gold	Johara Velena Tinto Star	Johara Red Squirrel	Mrs V. Riley	Breeder
Ch. Johara Ponsonby	D	18.2.69	Fawn	Johara Paddington	Johara Red Squirrel	Mrs V. Riley	Breeder
Ch. Truxillo Prince Consort	D	2.3.68	Light red	Ch. Rowley Courtier	Truxillo Rowley Sovereign	Mr and Mrs G. Motherwell	Breeders
Ch. Rozavel Sea Scout	D	16.11.67	Black and tan	Ch. Rozavel Chief Scout	Ch. Rozavel Mermaid	Mrs T. Gray	Mrs Bruton
Ch. Rozavel Blue Feathers	D	4.2.69	Blue	Ch. Rozavel Large as Life	Rozavel Black Limelight	Mrs T. Gray	Breeder

Name	Sex	Date of Birth	Colour	Sire	Dam	Breeder	Owner
Ch. Knockenjig Roving Gypsy	D	27.2.70	Sable	Ch. Venico Memento	Knockenjig Lindina Jaunty Judi	Mrs J. R. Peters	Breeder
Ch. Chitina's Beautinas Chocolate Drop	B	7.11.68	Red	Chitina's Peregrine	Beautinas Glamour Puss Jill	Mrs G. M. Latham	Mrs D. S. Garlick
Ch. Chitina's Little Cuddles	B	31.12.68	Gold and white	Chitina's Peregrine	Ch. Chitina's Cuddles	Mrs D. S. Garlick	Breeder
Ch. Larkwhistle Quill	D	13.4.71	Blue and fawn	Ch. Rozavel Blue Feathers	Larkwhistle Theresa	Miss E. J. Boyt	Miss D. Clark
Ch. Raygistaan Rumbunny	B	26.5.66	Red	Ch. Rozavel Wolf Cub	Raygistaan Deodar Honey Bunch	Mrs E. King	Breeder
Ch. Raygistaan Fieldhill Sparkle	B	14.10.67	Gold and white	Ch. Venico Memento	Deodar Gay Donmar	Mrs B. Wilson	Mrs E. King
Ch. Rozavel Real Wolf	D	22.4.68	Fawn	Ch. Rozavel Wolf Cub	Dorrow Miss Pinky	Mrs Ponsford	Mrs T. Gray
Ch. Taydors Sergeant Blackie	D	15.11.70	Black and tan	Ch. Taydors Galoping Major	Taydors Pollyanna	J. R. Speak	Mr and Mrs W. G. Taylor
Ch. Kimanchi's Modern Trend	D	24.12.71	Light red	Ch. Kimanchi's Golden Eagle	Kimanchi's Black Cherry	Misses I. M. Friars and E. Pantin	Breeders
Ch. Chitina's Peregrina	B	31.12.68	Gold	Chitina's Peregrine	Ch. Chitina's Cuddles	Mrs D. S. Garlick	Breeder

Name	Sex	Date	Colour	Sire (Pequeno Didly)	Dam (Pequeno Witchytoo)	Owner	Breeder
Ch. Pequeno Sockitoem Tammy	B	24.4.70	Chocolate, tan and white	Pequeno Didly	Pequeno Witchytoo	Mrs O. Frei-Denver	Breeder
Ch. Kinos Zappelle	D	17.5.70	Fawn	Dresden Rockafella	Stanzaker Flamenco	Mrs P. M. Atkinson	Mrs E. Foster
Ch. Widogi Playboy	D	5.2.71	Red	Ch. Molimor Anyako Astronaut	Widogi Miss Otis	Mrs J. Fraser	Breeder
Ch. Limmerlease Suki-Sue	B	26.5.71	Cream	Delfji Fancy Fare	Limmerlease Wild Silk	Mrs L. H. Cleeve	Messrs Bond and Farmer
Ch. Redyak Honeyball	D	25.6.69	Light gold	Chitina's Peregrine	Dorrow Snowflake	Mrs Yates	Mrs B. G. Currie and Mr A. Wight
Ch. Rowley Royal Gem	B	6.10.71	Red	Ch. Rowley Majic Circle	Ch. Rowley Crown Jewel	Mrs M. Rider	Breeder
Ch. Whisky Galore of Billtip	D	4.9.71	Dark red	Gamelands Caramel Fudge	Gamelands Gin Fizz	Miss M. Williams	Mr W. H. Tipton
Ch. Rozavel Larkwhistle Nutkin	B	13.4.70	Sable	Ch. Rozavel Blue Feathers	Larkwhistle Therasa	Miss E. J. Boyt	Mrs T. Gray
Ch. Nixtrix Beau Brummel	D	29.10.70	Red and white	Ch. Rowley Majic Circle	Ch. Nixtrix Puffa Puffa Bear	Mrs E. F. M. Nicholl	Breeder
Ch. Winterlea Starshine	D	24.1.72	Gold and white	Ch. Winterlea Knockenjig Royal Star	Stillponds Bright-n-Gay	Mrs M. Mooney	Breeder
Ch. Raygistaan Toytrain	D	12.3.72	Pale golden	Raygistaan Golden Train	Zaleti Piacoxicola	Mrs E. King	Breeder
Ch. Walkenried Tiny Kemish	D	3.9.72	Dark gold	Yaverland Summamorn of Walkenried	Kingsmere Johara Fascination	Mrs W. J. Scott	Breeder

Name	Sex	Date of Birth	Colour	Sire	Dam	Breeder	Owner
Ch. Argedin Dona Pandora of Ballybroke	B	24.2.71	White with red marking	Ch. Ballybroke Ryanlea Wee Babycham	Delcharchi Nora of Argedin	Mr I & Mrs J. Brown	Mr G. B. & Mrs J. Foote
Ch. Delchardi Aquamarine	B	4.12.71	Red	Ch. Truxillo Prince Consort	Delcharchi Pussy Willow	J. P. Parker	P. Clements
Ch. Twinley Golden Melody	B	26.12.71	Red sable with white trim	Tarina Cobbler	Twinley Aztecs Star Garnet Goddess	Mrs A. Block	Breeder
Ch. Chitina's Champers	D	6.10.72	Champagne and cream	Ir. Ch. Chitina's Pietro	Chitina's Peregrinella	Mrs D. S. Garlick	Breeder
Ch. Midnight Man of Apoco	D	14.4.73	Black and tan	Ch. Apoco Ballybroke Billy Bunter	Joygor Wonder Mitz	Mrs MacLeod	W. F. Stevenson
Ch. Chitina's Beautinas Perrijill Pearl	B	15.12.69	Gold, white, cream and black point	Chitina's Peregrine	Beautinas Gamour Pushjill	Mrs G. M. Latham	Mrs D. S. Garlick
Ch. Dachida's Angelique	B	2.7.74	Red sable	Dachida's Star Quality	Dachida's Bobby Dazzler	Mrs C. A. Davies	Breeder
Ch. Rozavel Songbird	B	23.4.72	Blue sable	Ch. Rozavel Blue Feathers	Ch. Rozavel Tarina Do-Re-Mi	Mrs T. Gray	Messrs B. A. Bond & G. W. Farmer

Name	Sex	Date	Colour	Sire	Dam	Owner	Breeder
Ch. Sunpark Cadbury Bouquet of Rozavel	B	31.9.71	Chocolate, pale shading on face	Rozavel Real Wolf	Lilycroft Lucky Jane	Mrs V. Cooper	Mrs T. Gray
Ch. Truxillo Melody	B	12.12.71	Silver fawn	Rowley Steffan	Truxillo Rowley Sovereign	Mr and Mrs G. Motherwell	Breeder
Ch. Widogi Smartipants	B	28.7.73	Red	Ch. Widogi Playboy	Widogi Glamourpants	Mrs J. Fraser	Breeder
Ch. Apoco Deodar Anyako Hill Billy	D	2.2.76	Fawn sable	Ch. Apoco Ballybroke Billy Bunter	Apoco Knockenjig Amanda	Mrs H.E. Mitchell	Mr W. F. and Mrs S. Stevenson
Ch. Apoco Innesville His Lordship	D	8.8.73	Fawn	Ch. Ballybroke Billy Bunter	Innesville Pepsi	Mr W. F. and Mrs S. Stevenson	Mrs J. and Mrs K. Bruton
Ch. Billtip Royal Scot	D	13.9.73	Fawn	Gamelands Mini Man	Deodar Dolly Mixture	Mr W. H. Tipton	Breeder
Ch. Deodar Don Cortez	D	27.4.73	Red	Deodar Littledene Tim	Deodar Sweet Talk	Mrs S. Borthwick	Breeder
Ch. Eclatant Smart Bonny	D	11.2.72	White with red marking	Eclatant Sonny Boy	Eclatant Smart Bess	Mrs M. Sheeny	Mrs J. M. Candelent
Ch. Billtip Highland Dancer	B	23.2.73	Sable	Whisky Galore of Billtip	Knockinjig Lady Bird	W. H. Tipton	Breeder
Ch. Cheveraz Moonstone	B	28.5.74	Peach and fawn	Ch. Widogi Playboy	Cluneen Vida Mia	Mrs N. M. Armstrong	Breeder
Ch. Deodar Passion Flower of Lindina	B	14.6.74	Golden	Ch. Deodar Don Cortez	Deodar Cactus Flower	Mrs S. Borthwick	Mr W. F. and Mrs S. Stevenson

Name	Sex	Date of Birth	Colour	Sire	Dam	Breeder	Owner
Ch. Plushrue Rose	B	26.6.73	Blue and fawn	Fancy Fare	Limmerlease Wild Silk	Mrs M. Turner	Messrs. B. A. Bond and G. W. Farmer
Ch. Rinardus Supergirl	B	19.8.73	Fawn and white	Ch. Winterlea Knockenjig Royalstar	Strongdour Ruth	Mrs J. R. Reynolds	Breeder
Ch. Apoco Deodar Music Man	D	26.11.75	Black and tan	Ch. Midnight Man of Apoco	Apoco Winterlea Little Suzette	Mr W. F. and Mrs S. Stevenson	Breeder
Ch. Ballybroke Polar Bear	D	28.9.74	White with red patches over eyes and ears	Fernq Lord Jim	Argedin Dona Pandora of Ballybroke	Mr G. B. and Mrs J. Foote	Breeder
Ch. Molimor Adastro	D	9.3.76	Golden sable	Ch. Molimor Anyako Astronault	Rialo Firegold	Mrs M. Moorhouse	Breeder
Ch. Deodar Flamenco	B	26.6.74	Red sable with white flashes	Ch. Deodar Don Cortez	Deodar Innesville Castinette	Mrs S. Borthwick	Mr W. F. and Mrs S. Stevenson
Ch. Deodar Moon Flower	B	14.6.74	Cream	Ch. Deodar Don Cortez	Deodar Cactus Flower	Mrs S. Borthwick	Mrs P. G. Carpenter

Ch. Prizing Magic Touch	B	21.9.75	Fawn sable	Prizing Circle of of Magic	Prizing Pandora	Mrs Phillips	Mrs N. Brind
Ch. Esef Graceful Gina	B	28.3.75	Red	Yaverland Summaplay	Yaverland Princess Grace	Miss E. Evans	Breeder
Ch. Widogi Russett Velvet	B	13.10.74	Red	Tarina Crackerjack	Widogi Pin up Girl	Mrs J. Fraser	Breeder

BIBLIOGRAPHY

MILO G. DENLINGER: *The Complete Chihuahua*. (3rd. edn., 1956.) Denlinger, Virginia, U.S.A.

HILARY HARMER: *Chihuahuas*. (1966) W. & G. Foyle Ltd., London.

RUSSELL E. KAUFFMAN: *The Chihuahua*. (1952.) Judy Publishing Co., Chicago, U.S.A.

M. RIDDLE: *This Is The Chihuahua*. (1960). T.F.H., New Jersey, U.S.A.

TRESSA E. THURMER: *Pet Chihuahua*. (1957.) All-Pets, Wisconsin, U.S.A.

CHARLES H. WALL: *This And That About Chihuahuas*. (1950). Buddy Publ. Co., Toronto, Canada.

INDEX

Bowerhinton Ollala, Ch., 82
Bowerhinton Rosita, 73
Brandman, Mrs Thelma, 64
Brandman's Chatito II, 67
Brandman's Modelo, 64, 67, 76, 78, 80
Brandman's Modelo's Memory, 67
Brazilian Brown Joy, Ch., 44
Breath, bad, 197
Breed registrations, 209
Breed standards:
　American, 106–7
　British, 96, 105–6
　Continental, 108–10
Brewster-Sewell, Mrs, 73, 74
British Chihuahua Club, 57, 74, 75, 82, 209
Bronchitis, 199
Bronze Idol of Rowley, 61
Brood bitch, 134–43
Brown, J., 67
Brownridge Jofos Paloma, 78, 79
Brownridge Kennels, 64

CADY, D., 82
Caesarian birth, 141
Car riding, training for, 168
Caranza, 43
Carlotta, Empress, 15
Casselli, Rosina, 30
Challenge Certificates, 47
Chatito II, 66
Chicata, 61, 72, 73, 74
Chichen Itza, 25
Chichimec Indians, 22
Chihuahua:
　adult, feeding the, 156–63
　ailments of the, 195–208
　as gundog, 16
　asthma and, 29
　at dog shows, 71 et seq.
　breed standards, 105–10
　choosing a, 85–94

first British registration of, 62
founding of British stock, 59 et seq.
given championship status, 75
housing the, 111–22
how to choose a, 84 et seq.
in art, 24 et seq.
in Great Britain, 48 et seq.
in the U.S.A., 41 et seq.
long-haired, 68–70
management of the, 117–21
Mexican mythology and the, 28
origins of, accounts of, 19 et seq.
points for judging the, 95–110
showing the, 172–87
size of the, 14
stud dogs, 122–33
television of, 15
Chihuahua Club of America, 42, 44
Chihuahuenos, 31, 32, 33
Chocolate Chips, 66
Choking, how to treat, 199
Cholderton Little Scampy of Teeny Wee, Ch., 59, 69, 82
Cholula, 76
Cholula pyramids, 21
Chorea, 199
Chow Chow, 27
Christen, Dr Walther, 26
Cisco Kid of Winterlea, 79, 80
Classes, show, 174
Claws, 177
Coat, 105
Colima, 25, 26
Collar and lead, training with, 167–8
Colour of coat, 100, 105
Columbus, Christopher, 23
Conchita of Manorgreen, 55
Conjunctivitis, 199
Constipation, 198
Consuelo of Winterlea, 80
Convulsions, 200
Corbett, T., 72, 73, 77, 80

Mabelle Carlita, 82
Macalister, Miss J., 54, 55, 57
McColl, Mrs, 62
McHale, Mrs, 79
McLean, Mrs, 42
Maltese Pocket Dogs, 209
Mansfield, Jayne, 14
Maria Carmello of Wytchend, 80
Mating, 123–6
Maxmilian, Emperor, 15
Mayan Indians, 17
Meals, size of, 161–3
Mealtimes, 118
Meat, 158–9
Medici, 24
Medicine doses, 201
Medida, 65
Meningitis, 205
Meron Kennel, 43
Metropolitan and Essex Canine
    Society, 72
Mexican Art, Exhibition of, 26
Mexican Kennel Club, 31, 33
Mexico, history of, 20 et seq.
Mi Pedro Juan of Belamie, Amer.
    Ch., 56, 60
Milk, 148, 160–1
Milk, acid, 196
Mitchell, Leslie, 56
Mitla, ruins of, 22
Mixcoac, 62, 77, 79, 80
Modelo, 66
Modelo's Memory, 66
Molera, 101
Moorhouse, Mrs M., 83
Montezuma, 28
Montgomerie, Viva, 48, 49, 50
Mooney, Mrs, 74, 76, 79
Morbid appetite, 197
Mourman, A., 43
Mouth, 105
Movement, 102
Mundey, Major, 31, 32, 33, 34, 35,
    59, 67

Mundey, Miss, 77
Mundo Canino, 33, 34
Munsun Chickenitza, 79
Munsun Nacon, 73
Murray, A., 76
Musgrave, Lady, 50
Muzzle, 100

Nails, 177–8, 205
Neck, 100, 105
Nellistar Schaefer's Taffy Boy, Ch.,
    59, 69, 81
Nigretto, 63

Obedience, training, 170–1
Obesity, 206
Olijon Teeny Roddy, 83
Our Dogs, 173

Pablo of Winterlea, 80
Paignton Championship Show,
    74–5
Palace Bambi, 57, 62, 72
Palacecourt Queen Zamira, 62, 77
Palenque, ruins of, 22
Papillons, 68, 70, 209
Parturient Eclampsia, 206
Patti, Adelina, 13
Pearson's Angela La Ora, 67
Peaster, Mrs Bertha, 43
Pedigrees, 189
Pepito IX, 62, 77, 79
Peppie, 65
Perla Pequena of Belamie, 74
Perrins, Leslie, 83
Philadelphia Kennel Club, 42
Popular Dogs, 31
Powell, Mrs, 53, 54, 55, 56, 63, 71
Primo of Belamie, 74
Prizes, show, 187
Puppies:
    appearance of, 154–5
    at birth, 141–2

choosing for breeding, 89–94
choosing pet, 85–9
exercising, 147
feeding, 148–55
hand-reared, 150
house-training a, 164–7
weaning, 142, 144–51
worming, 145–6
'Puppy arrangements,' 131–2
Purgatives, 198, 205
Pymetria, 206

QUARANTINE kennels, 193
Quetzalcoatl Mundey, 67

RABIES, 204
Railway travel, 173
Rawson, Mrs Jean, 64, 67, 76, 78
Records, stud, 132–3
Red Rocket, 65
Rheumatism, 206
Rickets, 207
Rider, Mrs M., 61, 74, 148–50
Robinson, Mrs Pearl, 61
Robson, Mrs Phyllis, 57
Royal Anthropological Institute of
    Great Britain and Ireland, 26
Rozavel Bienvenida, Ch., 82, 83
Rozavel Char-Els Cissie Maria, Ch.,
    66
Rozavel Chief Scout, 18
Rozavel Shaw's Constance, 66
Rozavel Diaz, 61, 64, 76, 77, 78
Rozavel Francisco, Ch., 64
Rozavel Gringo, 70, 78, 80, 81
Rozavel Humo, 66
Rozavel Irra Pettina, 64
Rozavel Jofos Onlyone, 80, 81
Rozavel Juarez, 64
Rozavel Karlena's Bambi, 66
Rozavel Kennels, 13
Rozavel La Oro Memoria de Ora,
    64

Rozavel La Oro Sena da Ora, 63,
    76, 80
Rozavel Mantilla, 79, 80
Rozavel Miguel, 64, 80
Rozavel Shaw's Violet, 66
Rozavel Uvalda Jemima, Ch., 14,
    82
Rozavel Virginia's Pumpkin, 66
Russell-Allen, Miss, 67, 79

SAHAGUN, Bernardino de, 25
Salender's Darro Pharche, 63
Sanders, H. G., 71
Saunders, Jas., 72, 79
Sea journeys, 192
Secker, Mrs, 56
Seggieden Jupiter, Int. Ch., 67
Seggieden Mighty Dime, Int. Ch.,
    83
Seggieden Tiny Mite, Int. Ch., 67,
    83
Seko King, 67
Selling dogs, 188–9
Shaw, Mrs, 74
Shiffner, Mrs, 80
Shock, treatment for, 207
Shoulders, 96
Shows:
    conduct at, 183–7
    entries for, 175
    equipment for, 180–3
    going to the, 180–2
    preparing for, 172–9
    the judges at, 185
    training puppies for, 169–71
Smith, Mrs Betty, 74, 80
Smith, Croxton, 53, 54
Smith, Mrs Croxton, 53
Sorta Solo, 62
Southworth, Mrs John, 52
Spanish expedition to Mexico, 23
Sporting and Dramatic News, The, 53
Stewart, Charles, 41, 43